Dr Johnson
Interviews and Recollections

DR JOHNSON

Interviews and Recollections

Edited by

Norman Page

Professor of Modern English Literature
University of Nottingham

MACMILLAN
PRESS

First published 1987

Published by
THE MACMILLAN PRESS LTD
Houndmills, Basingstoke, Hampshire RG21 2XS
and London
Companies and representatives
throughout the world

Typeset by Wessex Typesetters
(Division of The Eastern Press Ltd)
Frome, Somerset

Printed in Hong Kong

British Library Cataloguing in Publication Data
Dr Johnson: interviews and recollections.
1. Johnson, Samuel, *1709–1784* –
Biography   2. Authors, English –
18th century – Biography
I. Page, Norman
828′.609   PR3533
ISBN 0–333–39913–7

To E. E. Kirby
Johnsonian and mentor

Contents

vii

Acknowledgement

The editor and publishers wish to thank Oxford University Press for permission to reprint the extracts from *Thraliana: The Diary of Mrs Hester Lynch Thrale 1776–1809*, edited by Katharine C. Balderston (2nd edn, 1951) vol. 1.

Introduction

'He has distanced all his competitors so decidedly that it is not worth while to place them.' Thus Macaulay on Boswell; and, pursuing the metaphor on the back of a famous eighteenth-century racehorse, he added, 'Eclipse is first, and the rest nowhere.' Macaulay's aphorism is calculated to save the student of Johnson a good deal of trouble, but it is very far from the truth. To be sure, Boswell is by far the greatest of Johnson's biographers, and his portrait is unrivalled in its amplitude and its richness of detail; not only did he prepare himself more doggedly than did anyone else for the massive task, but he devised a superbly effective interviewing and notetaking technique, often in defiance of social decorum: 'Boswell's conversation consists entirely in asking questions, & it is extremely offensive', wrote Thomas Campbell,[1] and others were disconcerted or displeased when he sat aside from the company to make a written record of what was taking place. It is, however, grossly misleading to suggest that attention to Johnson's numerous other biographers and memoirists is 'not worth while'. This volume brings together some of their evidence, and in more ways than one it supplements the picture given by Boswell.

There are, for instance, episodes in Johnson's life, even in his later years, that Boswell leaves unmentioned or narrates in only the sketchiest terms, usually because he was not directly involved. Perhaps more importantly, his hero-worship of Johnson, touching and admirable though it is, makes it refreshing to turn to the more astringent records in which, with greater frankness or even downright hostility, others have shown different sides of Johnson's nature and behaviour. When all due allowances have been made for the conscious and unconscious distortions of envy and wounded egotism, not all of these unBoswellian accounts can be dismissed: to cite another example from Campbell, it seems at least as likely as not that Johnson actually delivered his views on the respective attractions of two of life's sensual delights (see p. 86), even though Boswell never presents him as speaking in this vein. It also remains true, of course, that at certain times some of Johnson's other friends – Fanny Burney, for instance – rivalled Boswell in their love and admiration.

'No literary character ever excited so much attention,' said Arthur Murphy. The Romantic cult of authorial personality was just round the corner, yet not even Byron is shown to us through the eyes of others as intimately as is Johnson. Unlike some later literary celebrities, it was primarily as an intellectual, and a man of exceptional and exemplary wisdom and piety, that Johnson became famous: as early as 1764, *The Companion to the Playhouse*, a who's who of contemporary dramatists, concluded its article on Johnson by declaring that 'Benevolence, Charity and Piety are the most striking Features in his Character, and while his Writings point out to us what a good Man *ought to be*, his own Conduct sets us an Example of what he *is*'.

Not that all responses were as reverential as this: Johnson's great fame brought forth, predictably, a swarm of slanderers and sceptics. There is a considerable anti-Johnsonian literature or sub-literature, and touches of envy and malice are not absent from some of the selections in this volume. Even Johnson's friend David Garrick could not resist the temptation to depict the great man in an all too humanly ludicrous light, though it is fair to add that he was merely giving as good as he had received:

> In the latter part of his life Garrick permitted people to tell him what others said of him, and often suffered himself to be annoyed by petty warfare. Every rough remark of Johnson's was sure to reach his ears, or his eyes, through the public press. 'Garrick,' said Dr Johnson, 'begins to complain of the fatigue of the stage. Sir, a man that bawls turnips all day for his bread does no less.' Garrick had just cause to retaliate. His story of Dr Johnson's reciting and writing Irene, with Mrs Johnson . . . waiting for him to come to bed; 'Sacred to love, to pleasure, and Irene;' and tucking in the bed-clothes by mistake, as he was writing by the bed-side, was wonderfully ludicrous. Yet I am convinced they had the greatest regard for each other.[2]

The emphasis on 'Conduct' as well as 'Writings' in the *Companion to the Playhouse* is significant: there is no other major English writer, not even (for all his protestations to the contrary) Oscar Wilde, whose life is to the modern reader arguably of greater interest and importance than his published works. By 'life' is meant, very largely, conversation: as Mrs Piozzi said, 'his life, at least since my acquaintance with him, consisted in little else than talking, when he was not absolutely employed in some serious piece of work'.[3] There have been other brilliant talkers, and Johnson was the equal of any of them in the promptness, unexpectedness and felicity of his retorts; but he was not merely 'brilliant', speaking as he did from long-meditated experience of life and suffering as well as the accumulated stores of extraordinarily wide reading placed at his instant disposal by an incomparable memory. As well as being piercingly witty – Oscar Wilde, Sydney Smith and others could be that – he was profoundly wise. And if this sounds a little portentous, it must be added that there was no subject, however trivial, on which, once it was broached, he did not have something to say that was eminently sensible as well as memorably phrased. Furthermore (as is not usually the case), not only did he sustain his record-breaking performance over many years but, by extraordinary good fortune, so much of it has been transmitted to us: the maxim that the spoken word, once sent forth, never returns, does not apply in Johnson's case.

Mrs Piozzi said that he was 'a mighty converser', and it might be added that talk was meat and drink to him had not eating and drinking also been of great importance in his life. His own explanation of the pleasures of conversation is a simple one: 'I wonder so many people have written who might have let it alone. But that people should endeavour to excel in conversation, I do not wonder, because their praise is instantly reverberated.'[4] There is surely a little more to the matter than love of applause, however, though there was certainly an element of the performer in Johnson's conversational displays: repeatedly, one senses also the *creative* delight of the speaker as a particularly happy analogy or antithesis strikes his intensely active and agile mind. Johnson was not always eager or even willing to perform, though. He was well known for his reluctance to initiate a conversation, and was famously compared in this respect to the ghost of Hamlet's father (a comparison that, curiously enough, is also to be found in Boswell's account of their first meeting). Sometimes Johnson's hearers, who had come expecting so much, went away with a distinct sense of disappointment, as when he dined at Trinity College, Cambridge, as the guest of Richard Watson (who, in the engaging manner of the times, was successively Professor of Chemistry and Regius Professor of Divinity):

> After having spent the morning in seeing all that was worthy of notice, the sage dined at his conductor's table, which was surrounded by various persons, all anxious to see so remarkable a character, but the moment was not favourable; he had been wearied by his previous exertions, and would not talk. After the party had dispersed, he said, 'I was tired, and would not take the trouble, or I could have set them right upon several subjects, Sir; for instance, the gentleman who said he could not imagine how any pleasure could be derived from hunting – the reason is, because man feels his own vacuity less in action than when at rest.'[5]

That last sentence, reflecting Johnson's unceasing efforts to probe the sources of human action – first to understand why things are as they are, then to 'set people right' upon the matter – is highly characteristic. When the expected performance was not forthcoming, some resorted to provocation, not without success. Boswell resorted to this technique frequently and fruitfully, as on 12 April 1776:

I introduced Aristotle's doctrine in his *Art of Poetry*, of 'the . . . purging of the passions', as the purpose of tragedy. 'But how are the passions to be purged by terror and pity?' (said I, with an assumed air of ignorance, to incite him to talk, for which it was often necessary to employ some address).

And Johnson duly, and cogently, replies.

Sir Walter Raleigh has commented that 'Everything that Johnson said in conversation during the later part of his life was liable to be recorded for posterity',[6] and the question of the authenticity of these records, and the relative reliability of different transcribers or informants, inevitably arises. Not everyone was prepared, like Boswell, to make on-the-spot notes of Johnson's conversation, though some (like Mrs Thrale) certainly wrote it down quite promptly. Some of the accounts were not written until a generation or two after the spoken words had died on the air, though they may have been based on memoranda. Many of his sayings exist in several versions, which may reflect the imperfections of human memory or some more calculated process of censorship or 'improvement' – or may simply mean that, like most people who talk abundantly, Johnson sometimes repeated himself but not necessarily verbatim.

When a single informant gives two significantly different versions of the same utterance, we may suspect that a wilful disregard of accuracy may be in question. In her notebook, *Thraliana*, Mrs Thrale writes:

Ah Sir says a Coxcomb one Day at our Table while Pepys and Johnson were talking about Literature – I have lost all my Greek – Ay Sir replies Johnson and I on the same day lost all my Estates in Yorkshire.

When she comes to compile her *Anecdotes* after Johnson's death, the passage becomes:

A young fellow, less confident of his own abilities, lamenting one day that he had lost all his Greek – 'I believe it happened at the same time, Sir (said Johnson), that I lost all my large estate in Yorkshire.'

The transformation of Johnson's forthrightness, even rudeness, to archness seems likely to be a move away from, rather than towards, the truth. R. W. Chapman has shown by a comparison of Boswell's notebook with the published *Life* that Boswell does the same in some observable instances (and presumably in many others where evidence is lacking). Whereas, for example, his memoranda record Johnson saying of Sheridan 'He is like a man attempting to stride the English Channel', and, again, 'It is setting up a candle at Whitechapel to give light at Westminster', the *Life* neatly conflates the two separate epigrams into

'Sir, it is burning a farthing candle at Dover to shew light at Calais.'
Chapman defends this process while at the same time conceding that for
Boswell it seems to have been standard practice:

> The Notebook shows that Boswell was not content merely to
> transcribe his memoranda. He was not afraid to be an artist, and to let
> his knowledge and genius 'Johnsonise' what was necessarily raw
> material. It has hardly been realised how great a licence he permitted
> himself in this, the most important, part of his task.[7]

It might be objected that if artistry means distorting the truth, then a
biography is better off without it, and that it is no part of a biographer's
legitimate task to intrude his own 'knowledge and genius' into what are
offered as transcripts of conversation. The defence would presumably be
that since Johnson *did* often talk in the manner of the published version,
even if not strictly historically true it represents a higher, poetical truth
as conveying the essence of the Johnsonian manner.

Sometimes the nature of the transcriber's axe-grinding is all too
obvious. One of the many contemporary collections of Johnson's sayings
is *Dr Johnson's Table Talk: or, Conversations of the late Samuel Johnson, LL.D.
on a Variety of Useful and Entertaining Subjects*, published in London in 1785,
reprinted several times, and variously ascribed to the editorial hand of
Stephen Jones and D. E. McDonnell. Despite the prim title, the editor is
plainly concerned to stress the rudeness, abruptness and belligerence of
Johnson's manner, no doubt because the display of bad manners on the
part of respected public figures has always been a highly enjoyable
spectator sport. One anecdote runs as follows:

> Being one day at Mr Thrale's table, when there, as well as upon all
> other occasions, he never drank any fermented liquors – a gentleman
> next him was persuading him to drink a glass of wine – 'Come, Doctor,
> it will give you spirits.' 'Sir, I am in sufficient spirits already.' 'Aye, but
> in *Vino Veritas*, you know.' 'Well, Sir, and what does that make for you,
> except you happen to be a liar when you are sober?'

We find what appears to be another account of the same exchange in
Campbell's diary (see p. 86), identifying the 'gentleman next him' as
Boswell:

> Boswell arguing in favour of a chearful glass adduced the maxim *in vino
> veritas* – well, says Johnson, & what then unless a man has lived a lye. –
> B. then urged that it made a man forget all his cares – That to be sure.
> Says Johnson, might be of use if a man sat by such a person as *you*.

Both wording and tone are here markedly different. However, Campbell heard at the Thrales' table not the retort itself but Boswell's account of it; for Johnson was not present, though Boswell and Campbell were, at the dinner on 1 April 1775. When we turn to Boswell's *Life* we find yet another version, under the date 15 April 1772:

> Desirous of calling Johnson forth to talk, and exercise his wit, though I should myself be the object of it, I resolutely ventured to undertake the defence of convivial indulgence in wine, though he was not to-night in the most genial humour. After urging the common plausible topicks, I at last had recourse to the maxim, *in vino veritas*; a man who is well warmed with wine will speak truth. Johnson: 'Why, Sir, that may be an argument for drinking, if you suppose men in general to be liars. But, Sir, I would not keep company with a fellow, who lyes as long as he is sober, and whom you must make drunk before you can get a word of truth out of him.'

What took place is now fairly clear. Responding to Boswell's coaxing, Johnson in 1772 delivered his verdict, characteristically subjecting received opinions to fresh scrutiny, and Boswell presumably made a note of it; three years later, Boswell retailed it to Campbell and others, as he had no doubt done and would do again on other occasions; Campbell set it down (or as much of it as he could recall) in his diary; the compiler of the 1785 collection obtained it from some unknown but probably oral source, conceivably at several removes from the original; and Boswell in due course included in the *Life* a version that is notably fuller than the others and must be assumed to be the nearest we are likely to get to what Johnson actually said.

In the last quarter of the eighteenth century, collecting Johnson's dicta in little volumes became a minor industry, and it goes without saying that the hacks who performed this task must have had them at second or third hand, or even from a greater distance. Another typical collection, published in 1791, is titled *The Witticisms, Anecdotes, Jests, and Sayings, of Dr Samuel Johnson, during the whole course of his life, Collected from Boswell, Piozzi, Hawkins, Baretti, Beauclerk, Sir Joshua Reynolds, and other gentlemen in the habits of intimacy with the Doctor* – a title that speaks for itself, as does the pseudonym of its editor, J. Merry. In the process of transmission, what looks like a lamentable enfeeblement of the Johnsonian original could take place – the opposite of Chapman's notion of Boswell 'Johnsonising' his rough notes, like an eighteenth-century landscaper 'improving' the natural scene. In one collection, assembled 'by a person of fashion and sense, lately deceased' and published in 1776, there appears a version of a saying later made famous in a different and finer form by Boswell:

When doctor Johnson was last in Scotland, amongst other

curiosities shewn him, he was taken to a very antient and high castle, which was reckoned to command the most extensive view of any in the country. 'Well, Sir,' says his guide, 'what do you think of this prospect?' 'It is the finest in all Scotland,' says the doctor, 'for I can here see *the road to England*.'

Boswell's familiar version is more magisterially and mock-heroically witty, and one would like to believe that it is closer to what Johnson said; but to describe the version quoted above as an 'enfeeblement' of the original may conceivably be no more than a sentimental fallacy, though Boswell's closeness to the source and his methods of recording give us confidence in his results.

One effect of Johnson's great fame as a talker was that the sayings of others were sometimes attributed to him, as if he enjoyed a monopoly of wit and epigram. Cradock provides an example:

When stories were told of [Thomas] Gray by those who knew him, they were thought so unlike, that several were imputed to Dr Johnson; nay, were even printed amongst the Johnsoniana, which, Boswell says, the Doctor was much offended at. I can give one strong instance. Dr Johnson is made to reply to some impudent man: 'that in that face the north-west wind would have the worst of it'. Now the truth was this: some friends of mine ... went ... to Pembroke Hall, in Cambridge, where Gray then resided: one of them was rather a favourite of Gray; but to another he had taken a particular dislike. Standing by the fire in the hall, the offensive gentleman, who was then curate at Newmarket, thus addressed the celebrated poet: 'Mr Gray, I have just rode from Newmarket, and never was so cut in my life; the north-west wind was full in my face.' Gray, turning to the Rev. Mr Sparrow, said: 'I think in that face the north-west wind would have the worst of it.' This I had from Mr Sparrow.[8]

The misattribution acknowledges and applauds the distinctively Johnsonian style. After the inevitable step from the authentic to the apocryphal, the next giant step is to the outrageously fictitious or parodic, as in a 1787 send-up of popular collections of Johnsoniana, the scurrilous, scabrous and scatological *More Last Words of Dr Johnson, Consisting of Important and Valuable Anecdotes ...* , allegedly by 'Francis, Barber' (a transparent allusion to Johnson's negro servant). An early paragraph conveys the flavour:

Dr Johnson was certainly the greatest man of his time, Mr Bright, the Essex butcher, excepted. But he was not more great than virtuous; for, though his whole talk was insult and traduction, it does not appear that he ever robbed a church, or, like his friend Baretti, was tried for his life. So far indeed from wishing to rob a church, he could not withhold his bitterest indignation if any man was profane enough to exert his diuretic faculty against a church-wall.

Such oblique tributes are a long way from Boswell's notebook; but the foregoing comments will have served to suggest (what is tolerably obvious) that *any* account of Johnson's conversation must be approached with some degree of scepticism.

For all the distortions, however, both major and minor, deliberate or unconscious, prompted by admiration or malice, his range and power as a talker come across from a distance of two centuries more fully and richly than do anyone else's: as John Bailey said, 'we know him as we know no other man whose face we never saw, whose voice we never heard'.[9] The combination of knowledge and eloquence, authority and wit, above all the sense of a formidable mind brought to bear upon any subject, the least or the greatest, that swims into its vast orbit, are incomparable. Whether we are seeking meditations upon death or are anxious to know whether the ladies in a seraglio should wear wool or linen, we can turn to Johnson for wise and compelling pronouncements couched in that memorable speech which, according to W. H. Auden, constitutes poetry.

I have dwelt on Johnson as talker because that is, after all, his main claim to greatness; but the selections that follow also embrace other aspects of his life and personality, though his conversational *tours de force* are never absent for long from the accounts of eye- and ear-witnesses. The brief opening section offers a few vignettes of Johnson's scantily-documented early years, from childhood, through the brief bitter months at Oxford, marriage, and the prolonged struggles that lasted well into middle age and ended with the heroic labours on the *Dictionary*, fame, and the pension that for the first time provided a measure of financial security. Part II presents Johnson as he walked and talked, ate and drank, as seen from the viewpoint of more than a dozen different observers, and in some cases from different perspectives of time. Part III concentrates on the golden years at Streatham, when Johnson, cosseted and lionised, was in the plenitude of his conversational powers in the dining- and drawing-room of the Thrales' sumptuous home. Part IV includes some glimpses of Johnson, the provincial who became a great Londoner, on his travels in England and elsewhere. Finally, a perhaps surprisingly long section is devoted to the slow process of Johnson's physical decline and dying. The 'peculiar significance' (in A. O. J. Cockshut's phrase)[10] that many biographers have found in the death-bed and what leads up to it is much in evidence in the Johnsonian records: of his last weeks and days we have a much fuller picture than for most authors of his own or any other period.

In preparing and annotating this selection, I have drawn heavily and gratefully on the grand resources of Johnson scholarship, especially on George Birkbeck Hill's monumental edition of *Boswell's Life of Johnson* (in the revised and enlarged edition by L. F. Powell, 6 volumes, Oxford, 1934), on Hill's *Johnsonian Miscellanies* (Oxford, 1897) and on that extraordinary and perhaps unique labour of love, A. L. Reade's *Johnsonian Gleanings* (10 volumes, 1909–12). As usual, the *Dictionary of National Biography* (*DNB*) has been indispensable. On Johnson's early biographers, Robert E. Kelley and O. M. Brack Jr's *Samuel Johnson's Early Biographers* (Iowa City, 1971) has been useful; Brack and Kelley's *The Early Biographies of Samuel Johnson* (Iowa City, 1974) reprints fourteen of the pre-Boswell biographies. Among modern biographies, James L. Clifford's *Young Sam Johnson* (New York, 1955) and John Wain's *Samuel Johnson* (2nd edn, 1980) have been particularly helpful. Throughout, the place of publication is London unless otherwise stated.

Since anyone interested in Johnson is likely to have access to Boswell's *Life*, and will perhaps already know it well, I have included no selections from that work; but my notes exercise no such self-denial, and Boswellian parallels or divergences are cited where appropriate. Selections are included from Boswell's *Journal* of the Scottish tour, which is probably much less familiar than the *Life*. Where more than one account of the same episode or conversation appears, either from the pens of different writers or by the same writer at different dates, this is intended to suggest some of the variations that exist in the raw material for a biography.

A minor nomenclatorial problem is posed by two ladies, both major contributors to this selection, who changed their names in mid-career. My solution has been to call Mrs Thrale by that name when she was keeping a record of Johnson's visits to the home she shared as the wife of Henry Thrale, but to refer to her as Mrs Piozzi when, after her second marriage, she compiled her *Anecdotes*; and to use 'Fanny Burney' to denote the young girl whose impressions of Johnson went into her early diaries, but to designate the long-married woman who wrote about him much later in life as Madame d'Arblay. I hope that this practice, which seems logical and not discourteous to those concerned, will not cause confusion.

NOTES

1. *Dr Campbell's Diary of a Visit to England in 1775*, ed. James L. Clifford (Cambridge, 1947) p. 79.

2. Joseph Cradock, *Literary and Miscellaneous Memoirs* (1826) IV, 244.

3. Mrs H. L. Piozzi, *Anecdotes of the Late Samuel Johnson*, ed. S. C. Roberts (Cambridge, 1925) p. 18.

4. ?Stephen Jones, *Dr Johnson's Table Talk* (1785) p. 51.

5. *Johnsonian Miscellanies*, II, p. 405.

6. Walter Raleigh, *Six Essays on Johnson* (Oxford, 1910) p. 50.

7. *Boswell's Notebook 1776–1777*, ed. R. W. C[hapman] (Oxford, 1925) pp. xvi–xvii.

8. Cradock, *Memoirs*, IV, 225–6.

9. John Bailey, *Dr Johnson and his Circle* (1947) p. 5.

10. A. O. J. Cockshut, *Truth to Life: The Art of Biography in the Nineteenth Century* (1974) p. 41.

A Johnson Chronology

1709	Samuel Johnson born in Lichfield, Staffordshire, on 18 September, the son of Michael Johnson (born 1656), bookseller, and his wife Sarah (born 1669), who had married in 1706.
1712	Birth of Johnson's brother Nathaniel (died 1737). After attending a dame school, Johnson proceeds to Lichfield Grammar School; later he attends a school in Stourbridge, then returns home.
1728	Enters Pembroke College, Oxford, but leaves without a degree early in his second year and returns to Lichfield.
1731	Death of Johnson's father. Johnson teaches for a time at a school in Market Bosworth but in 1734 returns to Lichfield.
1735	Marries Mrs Elizabeth Porter (born 1689), a widow. Publishes an abridgement and translation of Lobo's *Voyage to Abyssinia*. Opens a small private boarding school at Edial, near Lichfield, but the venture is a failure.
1737	Goes to London but is unsuccessful in getting his tragedy *Irene* produced.
1738	Contributes to the *Gentleman's Magazine* and during the next few years becomes a frequent contributor. Publishes his poem *London*.
1742	Prepares a catalogue of the library of Edward Harley, Earl of Oxford.
1744	Publishes *Life of Richard Savage*.
1747	Issues a plan of a dictionary, addressed to Lord Chesterfield, and works on the dictionary during the next few years.
1749	Publishes *The Vanity of Human Wishes*. *Irene* is produced at Drury Lane without success. Forms a club that meets weekly at the King's Head, Ivy Lane.
1750–2	Publishes the *Rambler*, a twice-weekly series of essays written almost single-handed.
1752	Death of Johnson's wife.
1755	Receives an MA degree from the University of Oxford. Publication of the *Dictionary*.
1758–60	Publishes the *Idler*, a weekly series of essays.
1759	Death of Johnson's mother. Publishes *Rasselas*.
1762	Receives a pension of £300 a year from the King.

1763   Meets James Boswell. Soon afterwards, the Literary Club is founded and meets weekly (to 1783) at the Turk's Head, Gerrard Street.

1764   Meets the Thrales and soon becomes a frequent visitor to Streatham Park, sometimes for long periods.

1765   Publishes his edition of Shakespeare.

1767   Meets George III.

1773   Visits Scotland with Boswell.

1774   Visits Wales with the Thrales.

1775   Visits Paris with the Thrales. Publishes *A Journey to the Western Isles of Scotland*. Receives the degree of Doctor of Civil Laws from Oxford.

1779–81 Publishes *Lives of the Poets*.

1781   Death of Henry Thrale.

1783   Suffers a stroke. Forms a club at the Essex Head, Essex Street.

1784   (June) Mrs Thrale remarries; Johnson visits Oxford for the last time. (Nov) Visits Lichfield for the last time. (13 Dec) Dies. (20 Dec) Is buried in Westminster Abbey.

Part I

The Years of Obscurity

Early Days*

WILLIAM SHAW

Lichfield in Staffordshire is now very well known to be the place of Johnson's birth; a circumstance which may probably be recollected by posterity, when this ancient city, like others which have been made immortal by giving birth to great men, is forgotten.

It appears from the parish register, that Johnson was born in the month of September, 1709. His father kept a shop near the market-place, and chiefly dealt in books, stationery-ware, and book-binding; articles which, especially in a country situation, where literature is but rarely an amusement, and never a business, could not be very profitable. It was from this circumstance that Johnson was enabled to say, as he often did, that he could bind a book very well.

Old Mr Johnson, therefore, whose story being thus blended with that of his son, becomes an object of some attention, might be reputable, but could not be rich. He was a man of reserved manners, but of acknowledged shrewdness. From habits of steadiness and punctuality he acquired great personal respectability. The oldest people in the place would often tell the Doctor, who heard them with a sensible satisfaction, that his father continued to the last such a favourite among the boys, that he was perhaps the only one in town who never received any injury from their petulance and mischief. And it was said by himself, whose regards were incapable of betraying him into the flattery even of a parent, that *he was no careless observer of the passages of the times in which he lived*.[1] His intellectual abilities unimproved and called forth by no interest or emergency, were notwithstanding perhaps but moderate, as it does not follow that because the son made a figure, the father should be a prodigy. But that he preserved himself by his industry and attention in a state of honesty and independence, that he had prudence enough by no schemes or speculations of any kind to injure his credit with his neighbours, and that whatever disappointments and crosses occurred in his intercourse with the world, he discovered the same innate fund of satisfaction and cheerfulness which marked the most prosperous circumstances of his life, are particulars well known, and it is all we do know with certainty about him.

* *Memoirs of the Life and Writings of the Late Dr Samuel Johnson*, ed. Arthur Sherbo (1974) pp. 6–9. Originally published in 1785.

Even in the town of Lichfield, however, where so little is to be made by
the practice, we find him letting out part of his house in lodgings. These
at the time of Johnson's birth were occupied by a Mr Swynfen,[2] who had
a very pretty country house on an estate of his own a few miles distant
from Lichfield, where he practised physic, and where for that reason he
provided himself with occasional accommodation. He was a man of
considerable reputation in his profession as a physician, but was still
more eminent for the liberality of his mind and the goodness of his heart.
This gentleman, having stood godfather for the child, interested himself
not a little in whatever related to his subsequent tuition. Though perhaps not affluent, he was in easy circumstances, and being of a friendly
and susceptible nature, took an early liking to young Johnson, the first
openings of whose genius he superintended himself with much
satisfaction and confidence. These, though neither sparkling nor
premature, as Johnson was always rather solid and saturnine, than
volatile or forward, were yet so entirely original and spontaneous, as to
afford sufficient indications that his talents were not unhappily turned
for literature and science.

He imbibed the elements of erudition at the free grammar school of
Lichfield. A Mr Hunter[3] had then the direction of the school. To this
gentleman's elegant and correct method of teaching, the Doctor has
often acknowledged the highest obligations. It was a circumstance he
always mentioned with pleasure, that the place of his education had
produced a Wollaston, a Newton, a Willis, a Garrick, and a
Hawkesworth.[4] The two last particularly, whose names are not
unknown to fame, though a few years younger, were both his
schoolfellows, who then contracted that regard for his character, and
confidence in his talents and worth, which afterwards disposed them so
readily to list among his pupils and friends. For juvenile attachments
often continue to operate through life, and are generally the last to which
susceptible minds become insensible.

Thus situated, Johnson entered on the initials of learning, with an
eagerness equally persevering and insatiable. His exterior was always
sluggish, and he never did anything which had the least appearance of
gracefulness, taste, dexterity or dispatch. Even in the act of devouring
the sublimest passages of ancient literature, one who knew him not
would have thought him asleep with the book in his hand. But though his
diligence discovered no ardour, his perseverance was so singular and
exemplary that all attempts to divert him from the task assigned, or
which he assigned himself, were uniformly without effect. The rapacity
with which he commenced his primary pursuit, and grasped at every
object of classical intelligence, is obvious from the stubbornness of a
peculiar habit which he then contracted. To his dying day, he never
thought, recollected or studied, whether in his closet, in the street, alone,
or in company, without putting his huge unwieldy body, in the same

rolling, awkward posture in which he used while conning his grammar or construing his lesson, to sit on the form at school.

He is said, when a mere schoolboy, to have read indefatigably, and probably picked up no despicable acquaintance with books by occasionally attending his father's shop. Here he was, not infrequently, so absorbed by his predilection for the classical lore of antiquity, as entirely to neglect the business he had in trust. Being often chid for disobliging some of the best of his father's customers and friends in this manner, he replied with great shrewdness *that to supersede the pleasures of reading by the attentions of traffic was a task he never could master.*

It was, undoubtedly, by lounging here that he heard many of those biographical and literary anecdotes which he has since detailed, with so much elegance and vivacity, in his *Lives of the Poets*. To such a mind as Johnson's, thus early smitten with the love of science and philosophy, everything connected with men of genius and letters, we may well believe, would be eagerly devoured, and tenaciously retained. And it is remarkable, in what an exuberant vein of manly sensibility, those particulars, which he says *were told him* when a boy, occasionally break from him.

We are not informed at whose expense he was sent to college. His godfather, Dr Swynfen, was likely enough to be consulted on this occasion. And the gentlemen in the neighbourhood, prompted by his example and zeal, and sensible of the father's inability and the son's genius, probably agreed among themselves on some mode of thus finishing an education, from which they predicted much public utility. He was entered, however, of Pembroke College, Oxford, on 31 October 1728. Here he studied several terms,[5] and might have continued longer, nor left the university, as he certainly did, without any degree, but that he could not afford either to continue, or to pay for those honours, to which his proficiency as a scholar must have otherwise entitled him.

His conduct, during no long residence in that illustrious seminary, is but little known, or at least has been marked by no celebrity. He is said to have treated some of the tutors with disrespect, their lectures with negligence, and the rules of the college with rudeness and contumely. But this story, besides being supported by no authority, does not suit the tenor of the Doctor's behaviour, who at the same time that he despised the rules or ceremonies of fashion, in his deportment among the idle, the whimsical, the gay or the affectedly polite, regarded with reverence every form or regulation which had instruction or utility for its object.[6]

In such a situation Johnson could not be idle. It was here that he contemplated the wisdom of antiquity, and stored his capacious memory with whatever is valuable on record. He was formed by nature for a sedentary and recluse life. His strongest habits were those of indolence and austerity. All his subsequent exertions originated not in his own choice, but in stern necessity. Labour appeared to him impracticable whenever it was possible to be idle. He had not yet commenced as an author, nor thought of the profession. His performances then could be only such college exercises as he could not avoid. Some of these were much admired and are still remembered. He particularly translated Pope's Messiah into elegant Latin verse, which afterwards appeared in a volume of poems, published by one Husband.[7]

It is supposed that he remained between two and three years at college, which he left for the place of an usher to a free school at Market Bosworth in Leicestershire. This laborious capacity he sustained much longer than was expected by any who knew him. All his leisure time was employed assiduously in the pursuit of intellectual acquisition and amusement; and who can say what might have been the consequence of his continuing for life in such a situation.

NOTES

The Revd William Shaw (1749–1831), Gaelic scholar; his publications include *Analysis of the Galic Language* (1774) and *Galic and English Dictionary* (1780). He supported Johnson in the Ossian controversy, and when he was attacked Johnson came to his support in a pamphlet published in 1782 under Shaw's name but partly from Johnson's pen. As Professor Sherbo points out, his short *Memoirs* are inaccurate and unsympathetic: 'Shaw resented Johnson's successes and his own failures' (p. viii). But he recounts anecdotes of Johnson that are not found elsewhere, and, as James L. Clifford notes in the preface to his *Young Samuel Johnson*, transmits some important information concerning Johnson's early years, obtained from Mrs Desmoulins. Kelley and Brack (*Early Biographers*, p. 36) describe Shaw's book as 'the first critical biography of Johnson' and 'a commendable biography' while at the same time conceding his carelessness over dates and the tendency to 'self-aggrandisement' evident in his account of his own relationship with Johnson.

1. Adapted from a sentence in Johnson's life of Thomas Sprat (in the *Lives of the Poets*), referring to Johnson's father.

2. Dr Samuel Swynfen (sometimes spelt Swinfen) (1679–1734), father of Johnson's lifelong friend and protégée Mrs Desmoulins.

3. John or Joseph Hunter (?1674–1741), headmaster of Lichfield Grammar School, which Johnson entered at the age of seven. For the first two years he was taught by the undermaster, Humphrey Hawkins (?1667–1741); then he passed into the hands of Hunter, who told the boys that he flogged them in order to save them from the gallows. Boswell reports Johnson as recalling that Hunter was 'very severe, and wrong-headedly severe', but also as admitting that he owed a great deal to his teaching of Latin.

4. William Wollaston (1660–1724), moral philosopher; Thomas Newton (1704–82), Bishop of Bristol; perhaps Sir John Willis, eminent judge; David Garrick (1717–79), the most famous actor of his day; John Hawkesworth (?1715–73), author (see p. 83). The last two were friends of Johnson but not 'schoolfellows'.

5. To be precise, from 31 October 1728 to 12 December 1729.
6. See, however, pp. 10–12.
7. John Husbands, *A Miscellany of Poems by Several Hands* (Oxford, 1731).

First Lessons*

HESTER LYNCH PIOZZI

Dr Johnson first learned to read of his mother and her old maid Catharine, in whose lap he well remembered sitting while she explained to him the story of St George and the Dragon. I know not whether this is the proper place to add that such was his tenderness, and such his gratitude, that he took a journey to Lichfield 57 years afterwards to support and comfort her in her last illness; he had enquired for his nurse, and she was dead. The recollection of such reading as had delighted him in his infancy, made him always persist in fancying that it was the only reading which could please an infant; and he used to condemn me for putting Newbery's[1] books into their hands as too trifling to engage their attention. 'Babies do not want [said he] to hear about babies; they like to be told of giants and castles, and of somewhat which can stretch and stimulate their little minds.' When in answer I would urge the numerous editions and quick sale of Tommy Prudent or Goody Two Shoes: 'Remember always [said he] that the parents *buy* the books, and that the children never read them.' Mrs Barbauld,[2] however, had his best praise, and deserved it; no man was more struck than Mr Johnson with voluntary descent from possible splendour to painful duty.

At eight years old he went to school, for his health would not permit him to be sent sooner; and at the age of ten years his mind was disturbed by scruples of infidelity, which preyed upon his spirits, and made him very uneasy; the more so, as he revealed his uneasiness to no one, being naturally (as he said) 'of a sullen temper and reserved disposition'. He searched, however, diligently but fruitlessly, for evidences of the truth of revelation; and at length recollecting a book he had once seen in his father's shop, entitled *De Veritate Religionis, Etc.*, he began to think himself highly culpable for neglecting such a means of information, and took himself severely to task for this sin, adding many acts of voluntary, and to others unknown, penance. The first opportunity which offered (of

* *Anecdotes of Samuel Johnson*, ed. S. C. Roberts (Cambridge, 1932) pp. 13–15, 20–2.

course), he seized the book with avidity; but on examination, finding himself not scholar enough to peruse its contents, set his heart at rest; and, not thinking to enquire whether there were any English books written on the subject, followed his usual amusements, and considered his conscience as lightened of a crime. He redoubled his diligence to learn the language that contained the information he most wished for; but from the pain which guilt had given him he now began to deduce the soul's immortality, which was the point at which belief first stopped; and from that moment resolving to be a Christian, became one of the most zealous and pious ones our nation ever produced. . . .

Of parental authority, indeed, few people thought with a lower degree of estimation. . . . 'Poor people's children, dear Lady [said he], never respect them: I did not respect my own mother, though I loved her: and one day, when in anger she called me a puppy, I asked her if she knew what they called a puppy's mother.' We were talking of a young fellow who used to come often to the house; he was about fifteen years old, or less, if I remember right, and had a manner at once sullen and sheepish. 'That lad [says Mr Johnson] looks like the son of a schoolmaster; which is one of the very worst conditions of childhood: such a boy has no father, or worse than none; he never can reflect on his parent but the reflection brings to his mind some idea of pain inflicted, or of sorrow suffered.'

I will relate one thing more that Dr Johnson said about babyhood before I quit the subject; it was this: 'That little people should be encouraged always to tell whatever they hear particularly striking, to some brother, sister, or servant, immediately before the impression is erased by the intervention of newer occurrences. He perfectly remembered the first time he ever heard of Heaven and Hell [he said], because when his mother had made out such a description of both places as she thought likely to seize the attention of her infant auditor, who was then in bed with her, she got up, and dressing him before the usual time, sent him directly to call a favourite workman in the house, to whom she knew he would communicate the conversation while it was yet impressed upon his mind. The event was what she wished, and it was to that method chiefly that he owed his uncommon felicity of remembering distant occurrences, and long past conversations.'

NOTES

On Mrs Piozzi, see p. 82.
1. John Newbery (1713–67), London bookseller who originated the publication of children's books.
2. Anna Letitia Barbauld, née Aikin (1743–1825), published in 1773 a popular collection of poems and (with her brother) a volume of essays showing the influence of Johnson, who remarked that she was the best of his imitators, 'for

she has imitated the sentiment as well as the diction'. The reference here is presumably to her *Hymns in Prose for Children*.

Schooldays*

EDMUND HECTOR

Johnson and I were, early in life, schoolfellows at Lichfield, and for many years in the same class. As his uncommon abilities for learning far exceeded us, we endeavoured by every boyish piece of flattery to gain his assistance, and three of us, by turns, used to call on him in a morning, on one of whose backs, supported by the other two, he rode triumphantly to school. He never associated with us in any of our diversions, except in the winter when the ice was firm, to be drawn along by a boy barefooted. His ambition to excel was great, though his application to books, as far as it appeared, was very trifling. I could not oblige him more than by sauntering away every vacation that occurred, in the fields, during which time he was more engaged in talking to himself than to his companion. Verses or themes he would dictate to his favourites, but he would never be at the trouble of writing them. His dislike to business was so great, that he would procrastinate his exercises to the last hour. I have known him after a long vacation, in which we were rather severely tasked, return to school an hour earlier in the morning, and begin one of his exercises, in which he purposely left some faults, in order to gain time to finish the rest.

I never knew him corrected at school, unless it was for talking and diverting other boys from their business, by which, perhaps, he might hope to keep his ascendancy. He was uncommonly inquisitive, and his memory so tenacious, that whatever he read or heard he never forgot. I remember rehearsing to him eighteen verses, which after a little pause he repeated verbatim, except one epithet, which improved the line.

NOTE

Hawkins quotes the extract from 'a paper now before me, written by a person yet living'. Its author is identified by Boswell as 'Mr Hector Surgeon at Birmingham

* Sir John Hawkins, *The Life of Samuel Johnson, LL.D.* (2nd edn, 1787) pp. 7–8.

who was at school with [Johnson] & used to buy tarts with him of Dame Reid'
(*Notebook*, p. 4). Edmund Hector (1708–94) was a source of information for
Boswell. Johnson visited him in Birmingham in 1776 and 1781, and wrote letters
to him.

Oxford*

VARIOUS SOURCES

(1)   When he came to Oxford he had for Tutor Mr Jorden,[1] a fellow of
Pembroke, a very worthy man but a heavy man & he did not profit much
by his instruction. Indeed he did not attend him much. The first day
after he came to college, he attended him and then stayed away four. On
the sixth Mr Jorden asked him why he had not attended. Said Mr
Johnson, 'I have been sliding upon the ice in Christ Church meadow',
and this I said with all the *nonchalance* as I am now talking to you (Oxford,
20 March 1776). I had no notion that I was wrong or irreverent to my
Tutor. Why said I that was great fortitude of mind. – No, Sir, stark
insensibility.

(2)   He much regretted that his *first* tutor was dead; for whom he
seemed to retain the greatest regard. He said, 'I once had been a whole
morning sliding in Christ Church meadow, and missed his lecture in
logic. After dinner, he sent for me to his room. I expected a sharp rebuke
for my idleness, and went with a beating heart. When we were seated, he
told me he had sent for me to drink a glass of wine with him, and to tell
me, he was *not* angry with me for missing his lecture. This was, in fact, a
most severe reprimand. Some more of the boys were then sent for, and we
spent a very pleasant afternoon.'

(3)   The pleasure he took in vexing the tutors and fellows has been often
mentioned. But I have heard him say, what ought to be recorded to the
honour of the present venerable Master of that College, the Reverend
William Adams, D.D.,[2] who was then very young, and one of the junior

* (1) *Boswell's Notebook, 1776–1777*, ed. R. W. Chapman (1925) p. 7; the entry
is based on Johnson's own account communicated to Boswell when they were at
Oxford together in 1776. (2) Thomas Warton's account (reprinted in G. B. Hill's
edition of Boswell's *Life*, i, 272), based on information given to him by Johnson
when they were in Oxford together in 1754. (3) Excerpt from a letter from
Thomas Percy to Boswell, 5 March 1787, in Hill, i, 74. (4) Hawkins's *Life*, pp. 9,
12–13. All the above are included in *Johnsonian Gleanings*, v, 8–9, 17–18.

fellows, that the mild but judicious expostulations of this worthy man, whose virtue awed him, and whose learning he revered, made him really ashamed of himself, 'though I fear [said he] I was too proud to own it'.

I have heard from some of his contemporaries that he was generally seen lounging at the College gate, with a circle of young students round him, whom he was entertaining with wit, and keeping from their studies, if not spiriting them up to rebellion against the College discipline, which in his maturer years he so much extolled.

(4)   The college tutor at that time was a man named Jordan, whom Johnson, though he loved him for the goodness of his nature, so condemned for the meanness of his abilities, that he would oftener risk the payment of a small fine than attend his lectures; nor was he studious to conceal the reason of absence. Upon occasion of one such imposition, he said to Jordan, 'Sir, you have sconced me two-pence for non-attendance at a lecture not worth a penny.'

It was the practice in his time, for a servitor, by order of the master, to go round to the rooms of the young men, and knocking at the door, to enquire if they were within, and, if no answer was returned, to report them absent. Johnson could not endure this intrusion, and would frequently be silent when the utterance of a word would have insured him from censure; and, farther, to be revenged for being disturbed when he was as profitably employed as perhaps he could be, would join with others of the young men in the college in hunting, as they called it, the servitor, who was thus diligent in his duty; and this they did with the noise of pots and candlesticks, singing to the tune of Chevy-chace, the words in that old ballad,

> To drive the deer with hound and horn, &c

not seldom endangering the life and limbs of the unfortunate victim.

These, and other such levities, marked his behaviour for a short time after his coming to college; but he soon convinced those about him, that he came thither for other purposes than to make sport for either himself or them.

NOTES

Johnson was 'entered a Commoner of Pembroke College on the 31st of October 1728, being then in his nineteenth year' (Boswell). His rooms were at the top of the tower, 'upon the second floor, over the gateway'. Having exhausted his funds, he left without a degree in early December 1729.

1. The Revd William Jorden (d. 1739). Compare Mrs Thrale's version of this incident (*Anecdotes*, p. 22) as related to her by Johnson:

He told me however one day, how, when he was first entered at the university, he passed a morning in compliance with the customs of the place, at his tutor's chambers; but finding him no scholar, went no more. In about ten days after, meeting the same gentleman, Mr Jordan, in the street, he offered to pass by without saluting him; but the tutor stopped, and enquired, not roughly neither, What he had been doing? 'Sliding on the ice', was the reply; and so turned away with disdain. He laughed very heartily at the recollection of his own insolence, and said they endured it from him with wonderful acquiescence, and a gentleness that, whenever he thought of it, astonished himself.

2. Dr William Adams (1706–89) became acquainted with Johnson at Pembroke College, where Adams, three years older, was already a junior fellow, and he remained a lifelong friend. He succeeded Jorden as tutor in 1734, pursued a career in the church, and returned to Pembroke as Master in 1775. Johnson was his guest in Oxford in June 1784, and Adams became one of Boswell's informants. Boswell is properly sceptical concerning Adam's description of Johnson as 'a gay and frolicksome fellow' during his college days, and quotes Johnson as saying, 'Ah, Sir, I was mad and violent. It was bitterness which they mistook for frolick.'

Marriage*

HESTER LYNCH PIOZZI

'I once [said Johnson] chid my wife for beating the cat before the maid, who will now [said I] treat puss with cruelty perhaps, and plead her mistress's example.'

I asked him upon this, if he ever disputed with his wife? (I had heard that he loved her passionately.) 'Perpetually [said he]: my wife had a particular reverence for cleanliness, and desired the praise of neatness in her dress and furniture, as many ladies do, till they become troublesome to their best friends, slaves to their own besoms, and only sigh for the hour of sweeping their husbands out of the house as dirt and useless lumber: a clean floor is *so* comfortable, she would say sometimes, by way of twitting; till at last I told her, that I thought we had had talk enough about the *floor*, we would now have a touch at the *ceiling*.'

On another occasion I have heard him blame her for a fault many people have, of setting the miseries of their neighbours half unintentionally, half wantonly before their eyes, showing them the bad

* *Anecdotes*, pp. 96–9.

side of their profession, situation, &c. He said, 'she would lament the dependence of pupillage to a young heir, &c. and once told a waterman who rowed her along the Thames in a wherry, that he was no happier than a galley-slave, one being chained to the oar by authority, the other by want. I had, however [said he, laughing], the wit to get her daughter on my side always before we began the dispute. She read comedy better than anybody he ever heard [he said]; in tragedy she mouthed too much.'

Garrick told Mr Thrale however, that she was a little painted puppet, of no value at all, and quite disguised with affectation, full of odd airs of rural elegance; and he made out some comical scenes, by mimicking her in a dialogue he pretended to have overheard: I do not know whether he meant such stuff to be believed or no, it was so comical; nor did I indeed ever see him represent her ridiculously, though my husband did. The intelligence I gained of her from old Levett was only perpetual illness and perpetual opium. The picture I found of her at Lichfield was very pretty, and her daughter Mrs Lucy Porter said it was like. Mr Johnson has told me that her hair was eminently beautiful, quite *blonde* like that of a baby; but that she fretted about the colour, and was always desirous to dye it black, which he very judiciously hindered her from doing. His account of their wedding we used to think ludicrous enough – 'I was riding to church [said Johnson], and she following on another single horse: she hung back however, and I turned about to see whether she could get her steed along, or what was the matter. I had, however, soon occasion to see it was only coquetry, and *that I despised*, so quickening my pace a little, she mended hers; but I believe there was a tear or two – pretty dear creature!'

Johnson loved his dinner exceedingly, and has often said in my hearing, perhaps for my edification, 'that wherever the dinner is ill got there is poverty, or there is avarice, or there is stupidity; in short, the family is somehow grossly wrong: for a man seldom thinks with more earnestness of any thing than he does of his dinner; and if he cannot get that well dressed, he should be suspected of inaccuracy in other things.' One day when he was speaking upon the subject, I asked him if he ever huffed[1] his wife about his dinner? 'So often [replied he], that at last she called to me, and said, Nay, hold Mr Johnson, and do not make a farce of thanking God for a dinner which in a few minutes you will protest not eatable.'

When any disputes arose between our married acquaintance however, Mr Johnson always sided with the husband, 'whom [he said] the woman had probably provoked so often, she scarce knew when or how she had disobliged him first. Women give great offence by a contemptuous spirit of non-compliance on petty occasions. The man calls his wife to walk with him in the shade, and she feels a strange desire just at that moment to sit in the sun: he offers to read her a play, or sing her a song, and she calls the children in to disturb them, or advises him to seize that opportunity of settling the family accounts. Twenty such tricks will the faithfullest wife in the world not refuse to play, and then look astonished when the fellow fetches in a mistress. Boarding schools were established for the conjugal quiet of the parents: the two partners cannot agree which child to fondle, or how to fondle them, so they put the young ones to school, and remove the cause of contention. The little girl pokes her head, the mother reproves her sharply: Do not mind your mamma, says the father, my dear, but do your own way. The mother complains to me of this: Madam [said I], your husband is right all the while; he is with you but two hours of the day perhaps, and then you teize him by making the child cry. Are not ten hours enough for tuition? And are the hours of pleasure so frequent in life, that when a man gets a couple of quiet ones to spend in familiar chat with his wife, they must be poisoned by petty mortifications? Put missey to school; she will learn to hold her head like her neighbours, and you will no longer torment your family for want of other talk.'

NOTES

On Mrs Piozzi, see p. 82. Johnson married Mrs Elizabeth ('Tetty') Porter on 9 July 1735. She was the widow of Henry Porter, a Birmingham mercer, who had died in the previous year and by whom she had had two sons and a daughter. She was then 46 and Johnson 25. She died on 17 March 1752.
  1. Scolded, complained to.

The Dictionary*

WILLIAM SHAW

Hitherto, he had tried his genius as a translator, a satirist and a biographer; he was now to appear a philologist. The plan of his Dictionary, which he displays with so much elegance and dignity in an address to the late Earl of Chesterfield, was published as early as the year 1748.[1] This performance promised something so much like what all men of taste had long thought wanting to the purity, stability and perfection of our language, exhibited an object of such magnitude to the public

* *Memoirs of the Life and Writings of the Late Dr Samuel Johnson*, pp. 25–6.

mind, and was itself so exquisite a specimen of the happiest arrangement and most polished diction, that it brought Johnson forward to general attention with peculiar advantage. The eyes of all the world were turned on what part the nobleman thus distinguished would now act in concert with the first writer, and interested by the sketch of a work the most laborious and useful of any which even then had roused the curiosity and excited the wonder of an enlightened age. From a secretary of state, still more illustrious for his elegant accomplishments than for his high birth or official situation, something like substantial encouragement was expected to an undertaking which aimed at no less than a *standard Dictionary of the English tongue.* His lordship was a competent judge of the subject. He acknowledged its importance and necessity. He occupied a sphere in life, an influence among the great, and a character among the learned, which enabled him to do much. His vanity was not inferior to his power; and had the talents of Johnson stooped to the prostituted language of adulation, his toil had probably been considerably alleviated by the taste, the address, the assiduity and the countenance of Chesterfield. But nothing can be conceived more diametrically opposite and irreconcileable than the tempers, the prejudices, the habits, the pursuits and the peculiarities of these contemporary wits. A semblance of intimacy took place, in which it is not likely that either were sincere. The oddities of the author furnished the peer with a fund of ridicule, and the fastidious elegance of the peer excited only the aversion, contempt, and pity of the author. *All the celebrated qualities of Chesterfield* (said Johnson to an intimate friend, to whom he was then in the habit of unbosoming himself on occasion) *are like certain species of fruit which is pleasant enough to the eye, but there is no tasting it without danger.*

In this well written pamphlet it was his ambition to rival the preface to Chambers's Dictionary.[2] How far he succeeded is not easily determined. It will not be denied that he possesses more energy of language, and perhaps a more beautiful arrangement of the multifarious particulars to which he solicits the public attention, but he certainly wants the simplicity, and indeed is proscribed by his subject from displaying the knowledge, of Chambers.

Chesterfield joined in the general applause which followed the exhibition of a design thus replete with utility in the aim, and originality in the execution. He was proud to have attracted the regards of such a man as Johnson, and flattered himself with the hopes of fresh accession of fame, from being the patron of such a work. But the manners of the operator were so disgusting to this Mæcenas of letters, and learned men, that the only concern he took in the matter was saying a few polite things at his table, and congratulating the lovers of grammar on the improvement which that science would derive from the labours of Johnson. It is a disgrace to his memory, and to the age, that the author of an undertaking so arduous and extensive was not placed beyond the recurrence of necessity, and that while his genius was conferring permanency on their language, the exigencies of his situation impelled him to apply to other means for daily subsistence.

The talents requisite for such an undertaking seldom meet in one man. Its magnitude was enough to stagger any resolution less vigorous, to repress any ardour less manly, to derange any intellect less collected than that of Johnson. But his capacity was competent to the object. His reading was chiefly philological, his taste was improved by an intimate acquaintance with all the classical remains of antiquity, his memory retained with exactness whatever his judgment had matured; and he possessed a penetration or discernment characteristically solid, cool and discriminating. It was not a composition that depended on the paroxysms of genius, a vigorous imagination, fertility of invention, originality of conception, or brilliancy of style. Patient industry, laborious attention, a determination of forgetting the lassitude of fatigue by a renewal of the task; and a mind, which notwithstanding a thousand avocations and obstacles, like the water in a river, still returned to the same channel, and pursued the same course; these were some of the qualifications with which Johnson formed the plan, and entered on the compilation of his Dictionary. . . .

Johnson's connection with Chesterfield came to an eclaircissement the moment this great work made its appearance. *Moore*, author of the *World*,[3] and the creature of this nobleman, was employed by him to sound Johnson on the subject of a Dedication. Some time before, Johnson had been refused admittance to his Lordship. This, it was pretended, happened by the mistake of a porter, though it is pretty well known that few servants take such liberties without the connivance of their masters. Johnson, who saw through all the disguises of Chesterfield's pride, never forgave the indignity, and treated every apology which was afterwards suggested by the friends and admirers of this nobleman, as an insult. *Moore*, without touching on that point in the most distant manner, expressed his hopes that Johnson would dedicate his Dictionary to Chesterfield. He received a very pointed and direct negative – 'I am under obligations,' said he, 'to no great man, and of all others, Chesterfield ought to know better than to think me capable of contracting myself into a dwarf, that he may be thought a giant.' You are certainly obliged to his Lordship, said *Moore*, for two very elegant papers in the *World*, and all the influence of his good opinion, in favour of your work. 'You seem totally unacquainted with the true state of the fact,' replied Johnson, 'after making a hazardous and fatiguing voyage round the literary world, I had fortunately got sight of the shore, and was coming into port with a pleasant tide and a fair wind, when my Lord Chesterfield sends out two little cock-boats to tow me in. I know my Lord Chesterfield tolerably well, Mr Moore. He may be a wit among Lords, but I fancy he is no more than a Lord among wits.'

NOTES

On William Shaw, see p. 6.
1. Actually in 1747.
2. Ephraim Chambers, *Cyclopedia* (1728).
3. Edward Moore (1712–57) edited *The World* from 1753 to 1757. Shaw's statement in this sentence seems to be without foundation, and many of his details ought probably to be regarded sceptically.

Johnson Receives the News of his Pension*

ARTHUR MURPHY

We have now travelled through that part of Dr Johnson's life which was a perpetual struggle with difficulties. Halcyon days are now to open upon him. In the month of May 1762, his Majesty, to reward literary merit, signified his pleasure to grant to Johnson a pension of £300 a year. The Earl of Bute[1] was minister. Lord Loughborough, who, perhaps, was originally a mover in the business, had authority to mention it. He was well acquainted with Johnson; but, having heard much of his independent spirit, and of the downfall of Osborne,[2] the bookseller, he did not know but his benevolence might be rewarded with a folio on his head. He desired the author of these memoirs to undertake the task. This writer thought the opportunity of doing so much good the most happy incident in his life. He went, without delay, to the chambers in the Inner Temple Lane, which, in fact, were the abode of wretchedness. By slow and studied approaches, the message was disclosed. Johnson made a long pause: he asked if it was seriously intended? He fell into a profound meditation, and his own definition of a pensioner[3] occurred to him. He was told, 'that he, at least, did not come within the definition'. He desired to meet next day, and dine at the Mitre Tavern. At that meeting he gave up all his scruples. On the following day, Lord Loughborough conducted him to the Earl of Bute. The conversation that passed was in the evening related to this writer by Dr Johnson. He expressed his sense of his Majesty's bounty, and thought himself the more highly honoured, as the favour was not bestowed on him for having dipped his pen in faction. 'No, Sir,' said Lord Bute, 'it is not offered to you for having dipped your pen in faction, nor with a design that you ever should.'

* *An Essay on the Life and Genius of Samuel Johnson, LL.D.* (1792) pp. 92–4.

NOTES

On Arthur Murphy, see p. 22.

1. The third Earl of Bute (1713–92) became First Lord of the Treasury on 26 May 1762. Murphy's dating of the incident as May 1762 is contradicted by various sources, including Johnson's letter of thanks to the Earl of Bute, dated 20 July 1762. George III, who came to the throne in 1760, 'initiated the policy of making public money available, as a matter of principle, to prevent distinguished men from starving and to help them with their work' (John Wain, *Samuel Johnson* (2nd edn, 1980) p. 217).

2. Thomas Osborne (d. 1767), a London bookseller, employed Johnson in 1742 to prepare a catalogue of the Earl of Oxford's library, which he had purchased. According to Johnson's account to Mrs Thrale, 'he was insolent' – presumably he upbraided Johnson for not completing his huge task more quickly – 'and I beat him'. Johnson related the incident in almost identical words to Boswell, but in popular legend the story acquired many graphic but probably fictitious details, including the one ('a folio on his head') referred to by Murphy.

3. In his *Dictionary*, Johnson defines a pensioner as 'a slave of state hired by a stipend to obey his master' and a pension as 'generally understood to mean pay given to a state hireling for treason to his country'.

Part II

Appearance and Habits

'Born a logician'*

ARTHUR MURPHY

His person, it is well known, was large and unwieldy. His nerves were affected by that disorder,[1] for which, at two years of age, he was presented to the royal touch. His head shook, and involuntary motions made it uncertain that his legs and arms would, even at a tea table, remain in their proper place. A person of Lord Chesterfield's delicacy might in his company be in a fever. He would sometimes of his own accord do things inconsistent with the established modes of behaviour. Sitting at table with the celebrated Mrs Cholmondeley,[2] who exerted herself to circulate the subscription for Shakespeare, he took hold of her hand in the middle of dinner, and held it close to his eye, wondering at the delicacy and the whiteness, until with a smile she asked, *Will he give it to me again when he has done with it?* The exteriors of politeness did not belong to Johnson. Even that civility which proceeds, or ought to proceed, from the mind, was sometimes violated. His morbid melancholy had an effect on his temper; his passions were irritable; and the pride of science, as well as of a fierce independent spirit, inflamed him on some occasions above all bounds of moderation. Though not in the shade of academic bowers, he led a scholastic life; and the habit of pronouncing decisions to his friends and visitors gave him a dictatorial manner, which was much enforced by a voice naturally loud, and often overstretched. Metaphysical discussion, moral theory, systems of religion, and anecdotes of literature, were his favourite topics. General history had little of his regard. Biography was his delight. *The proper study of mankind is man.*[3] Sooner than hear of the Punic war, he would be rude to the person that introduced the subject.

Johnson was born a logician; one of those to whom only books of logic are said to be of use. In consequence of his skill in that art, he loved argumentation. No man thought more profoundly, nor with such acute discernment. A fallacy could not stand before him: it was sure to be refuted by strength of reasoning, and a precision both in idea and expression almost unequalled. When he chose by apt illustration to place the argument of his adversary in a ludicrous light, one was almost inclined to think *ridicule the test of truth.* He was surprised to be told, but it is certainly true, that, with great powers of mind, wit and humour were

* *An Essay on the Life and Genius of Samuel Johnson, LL.D.* (1792) pp. 137–41.

his shining talents. That he often argued for the sake of a triumph over his adversary, cannot be dissembled. Dr Rose,[4] of Chiswick, has been heard to tell of a friend of his, who thanked him for introducing him to Dr Johnson, as he had been convinced, in the course of a long dispute, that an opinion which he had embraced as a settled truth, was no better than a vulgar error. This being reported to Johnson, 'Nay,' said he, 'do not let him be thankful, for he was right, and I wrong.' Like his uncle Andrew,[5] in the ring at Smithfield, Johnson, in a circle of disputants, was determined *neither to be thrown nor conquered*. Notwithstanding all his piety, self-government, or the command of his passions in conversation, does not seem to have been among his attainments. Whenever he thought the contention was for superiority, he has been known to break out with violence, and even ferocity. When the fray was over, he generally softened into repentance, and, by conciliating measures, took care that no animosity should be left rankling in the breast of his antagonist. Of this defect he seems to have been conscious. . . . For his own intolerant and overbearing spirit he apologised by observing that it had done some good; obscenity and impiety were repressed in his company.

It was late in life before he had the habit of mixing, otherwise than occasionally, with polite company. At Mr Thrale's he saw a constant succession of well-accomplished visitors. In that society he began to wear off the rugged points of his own character. He saw the advantages of mutual civility, and endeavoured to profit by the models before him. He aimed at what has been called by Swift the *lesser morals*, and by Cicero *minores virtutes*. His endeavour, though new and late, gave pleasure to all his acquaintances. Men were glad to see that he was willing to be communicative on equal terms and reciprocal complacence. The time was then expected when he was to cease being what George Garrick, brother to the celebrated actor, called him the first time he heard him converse, 'a tremendous companion'. He certainly wished to be polite, and even thought himself so; but his civility still retained something uncouth and harsh. His manners took a milder tone, but the endeavour was too palpably seen. He laboured even in trifles. He was a giant gaining a *purchase* to lift a feather.

NOTES

Arthur Murphy (1727–1805), Irish actor, dramatist and journalist, met Johnson in the summer of 1754 and (by his own account) 'enjoyed the conversation and friendship of that excellent man more than thirty years' (*Essay*, p. 3). It was Murphy who, on 9 January 1765, introduced Johnson to the Thrales, having first given Mrs Thrale 'general cautions not to be surprised at his figure, dress or behaviour' (see James L. Clifford, *Hester Lynch Piozzi* (2nd edn, 1952) pp. 54–6).

1. Scrofula, also known as the king's evil (tuberculosis of the lymphatic glands).
2. Mrs Mary Cholmondeley (?1729–1811).
3. Pope's *Essay on Man*, II, line 1.
4. Dr William Rose (1719–86) translator, kept a school at Chiswick from 1758.
5. Andrew Johnson was a Birmingham bookseller who had (according to his nephew's account to Mrs Thrale) at one stage of his career 'kept the ring at Smithfield (where they wrestled and boxed) for a whole year, and never was thrown or conquered'.

'An Irish chairman'*

WILLIAM TEMPLE

To begin with his personal appearance: it does not by any means prejudice one in his favour. He is upwards of six feet, and proportionably large and gross, big-boned, clumsy and awkward. You would rather take him for an Irish chairman, London porter, or one of Swift's Brobdingnaggians,[1] than for a man of letters. His complexion is livid and sallow; he seldom sits still in his chair, but keeps his body in a perpetual rocking motion, shutting or turning up the whites of his eyes in a most disagreeable manner to those present. He is also subject to certain twitches and certain sudden and involuntary gestures, as if he were paralytic, though I believe he is not so in reality; and these contortions and grimaces may be the effect of solitude and low-breeding, to which he was long condemned in the early part of his life. He eats voraciously, and in the most disgusting manner, pawing his meat with his great coarse, sooty hands. Though excessively fond of wine, yet like savages and the vulgar, when he has once tasted it, knowing no moderation, he has renounced it entirely, confining himself to lemonade. This he swallows to a nauseous excess; and wherever he dines, the table is strewed with lemon skins (whose juice has trickled through his dirty fingers) like the bar of a tavern. Tea is another of his favourite beverages, which he always drinks before going to bed, be it ever so late. An old blind lady [Mrs Williams], who owes her support to his humanity, must constantly sit up to make it for him, be the hour ever so unseasonable, and he seldom returns from passing the evening until two or three in the morning.

With regard to his conversation, it can hardly be called by that name:

* *The Character of Doctor Johnson* (1792) pp. 1–5 (published anonymously).

it does not consist of reasonable questions or replies, of apposite narrative, natural and unpremeditated observation and reflection, like that of other men. He seldom speaks unless to contradict with savage rudeness, or to say something which he hopes will be deemed pointed and sententious. But his *most* general manner is to sit silent, rocking his body backwards and forwards, twitching his hands and legs, and rolling his eyes, taking up a knife or fork and looking along it as if it were a spying glass, till he can find an opportunity of making a kind of harangue, which, if spoken by anyone else, would be thought ill-timed, and to have nothing extraordinary in it, but coming from his singular, Colossean figure, in a surly tone of voice, and scholastic phrase, somehow imposes on the hearer. As he is fond of eating, he is frequently invited to the tables of those who affect to admire men of learning; and his enemies say (for he is not generally beloved) that this harangue is the ordinary[2] he pays for his meal.

NOTES

This anonymous publication has been attributed to the Revd William Temple (see F. A. Pottle in *The Times Literary Supplement*, 22 May 1930, p. 434). Temple (1739–96) was a friend and fellow student of Boswell in Edinburgh and London. He met Johnson in 1766.

1. The giants in the second book of *Gulliver's Travels*.
2. Price paid for a set meal at a tavern.

'Continual agitation'*

FANNY BURNEY

[At a social gathering held at the Burney home in St Martin's Street, two of Miss Burney's sisters play a duet; the company includes the Thrales and William Seward.] . . . in the midst of this performance Dr Johnson was announced. He is, indeed, very ill-favoured; is tall and stout; but stoops terribly; he is almost bent double. His mouth is almost continually opening and shutting, as if he was chewing. He has a strange method of frequently twirling his fingers, and twisting his hands. His body is in continual agitation, *see-sawing* up and down; his feet are never a

* C. B. Tinker, *Dr Johnson and Fanny Burney* (1912) pp. 2–5.

moment quiet; and, in short, his whole person is in *perpetual motion*. His dress, too, considering the times, and that he had meant to put on his *best becomes*, being engaged to dine in a large company, was as much out of the common road as his figure; he had a large wig, snuff-colour coat, and gold buttons, but no ruffles to his shirt, dirty fists, and black worsted stockings. He is shockingly near-sighted, and did not, until she held out her hand to him, even know Mrs Thrale. He *poked his nose* over the keys of the harpsichord, until the duet was finished, and then my father introduced Hetty [Esther Burney] to him as an old acquaintance, and he cordially kissed her! When she was a little girl, he had made her a present of *The Idler*.

His attention, however, was not to be diverted five minutes from the books, as we were in the library; he pored over them, shelf by shelf, almost touching the backs of them with his eyelashes, to read to himself, all the time standing at a distance from the company. We were all very much provoked, as we perfectly languished to hear him talk; but it seems he is the most silent creature, when not particularly drawn out, in the world.

My sister then played another duet with my father; but Dr Johnson was so deep in the *Encyclopédie* that, as he is very deaf, I question if he even knew what was going forward. When this was over, Mrs Thrale, in a laughing manner, said, 'Pray, Dr Burney, can you tell me what that song was and whose, which Savoi sung last night at Bach's Concert,[1] and which you did not hear?' . . . wishing to draw Dr Johnson into some conversation, [Dr Burney] told him the question. The Doctor, seeing his drift, good-naturedly put away his book, and said very drolly, 'And pray, Sir, *who is Bach*? Is he a piper?' Many exclamations of surprise, you will believe, followed this question. 'Why you have read his name often in the papers', said Mrs Thrale; and then she gave him some account of his Concert, and the number of the performances she had heard at it.

'Pray,' said he, gravely, 'Madam, what is the expense?'

'Oh!' answered she, 'much trouble and solicitation, to get a Subscriber's Ticket; or else, half a Guinea.'

'Trouble and solicitation,' said he, 'I will have nothing to do with; but I would be willing to give eighteen pence.'

Ha! ha!

Chocolate being then brought, we adjourned to the drawing-room. And here, Dr Johnson being taken from the books, entered freely and most cleverly into conversation; though it is remarkable he never speaks at all, but when spoken to; nor does he ever *start*, though he so admirably *supports*, any subject.

NOTES

On Fanny Burney, see p. 99. The source of the extract is a letter dated 28 March 1778 to Samuel Crisp, a close family friend whom she addressed as 'My Dear Daddy'.

    1. Johann Christian Bach (1735–82), son of J. S. Bach, resided in London from 1759.

'Well, thou art an ugly fellow . . .'*

WILLIAM COOKE

Dr Johnson's face was composed of large coarse features, which, from a studious turn, when composed, looked sluggish, yet awful and contemplative. . . . When the Doctor saw [a] drawing [of his head], he exclaimed, 'Well, thou art an ugly fellow, but still, I believe thou art like the original.'

His face, however, was capable of great expression, both in respect to intelligence and mildness, as all those can witness who have seen him in the flow of conversation, or under the influence of grateful feelings. I am the more confirmed in this opinion, by the authority of a celebrated French Physiognomist, who has, in a late publication on his art,[1] given two different etchings of Dr Johnson's head, to show the correspondence between the countenance and the mind.

In respect to person, he was rather of the heroic stature, being above the middle size; but though strong, broad, and muscular, his parts were slovenly put together. When he walked the streets, what with the constant roll of his head, and the concomitant motion of his body, he appeared to make his way by that motion, independent of his feet.[2] . . .

In his conversation he was learned, various and instructive, oftener in the didactic than in the colloquial line, which might have arisen from the encouragement of his friends, who generally flattered him with the most profound attention – and surely it was well bestowed; for in those moments, the great variety of his reading broke in upon his mind, like mountain floods, which he poured out upon his audience in all the

    * The Life of Samuel Johnson, LL.D. (1785); excerpted in Johnsonian Miscellanies, II, 164–7.

fulness of information – not but he observed Swift's rule, 'of giving every man time to take his share in the conversation'; and when the company thought proper to engage him in the general discussion of little matters, no man threw back the ball with greater ease and pleasantry.

He always expressed himself with clearness and precision, and seldom made use of an unnecessary word – each had its due weight, and stood in its proper place. He was sometimes a little too tenacious of his own opinion, particularly when it was in danger of being wrested from him by any of the company. Here he used to collect himself with all his strength – and here he showed such skill and dexterity in defence, that he either tired out his adversary, or turned the laugh against him, by the power of his wit and irony.

In this place, it would be omitting a very singular quality of his, not to speak of the amazing powers of his memory. The great stores of learning which he laid in, in his youth, were not of that cumbrous and inactive quality, which we meet with in many who are called great scholars; for he could, at all times, draw bills upon this capital with the greatest security of being paid. When quotations were made against him in conversation, either by applying to the context, he gave a different turn to the passage, or quoted from other parts of the same author, that which was more favourable to his own opinion. If these failed him, he would instantly call up a whole phalanx of other authorities, by which he bore down his antagonist with all the superiority of allied force.

But it is not the readiness with which he applied to different authors that proves so much the greatness of his memory, as the extent to which he could carry his recollection upon occasions. I remember one day, in a conversation upon the miseries of old age, a gentleman in company observed that he always thought Juvenal's description of them to be rather too highly coloured – upon which the Doctor replied, 'No, Sir – I believe not; they may not all belong to an individual, but they are collectively true of old age.' Then rolling about his head, as if snuffing up his recollection, he suddenly broke out:

> 'Ille humero, hic lumbis,' etc. . . . .
> down to 'et nigra veste senescant'.
>   (Satire x, 227–45.)

Some time previous to Dr Hawkesworth's publication of his beautiful *Ode on Life*,[3] he carried it down with him to a friend's house in the country to retouch. Dr Johnson was of this party; and as Hawkesworth and the Doctor lived upon the most intimate terms, the former read it to him for his opinion. 'Why, Sir,' says Johnson, 'I can't well determine on a first hearing, read it again, second thoughts are best.' Dr Hawkesworth complied, after which Dr Johnson read it himself, approved of it very highly, and returned it.

Next morning at breakfast, the subject of the poem being renewed, Dr Johnson, after again expressing his approbation of it, said he had but one objection to make to it, which was that he doubted its originality. Hawkesworth, alarmed at this, challenged him to the proof; when the Doctor repeated the whole of the poem, with only the omission of a very few lines; 'What do you say now, Hawkey?' says the Doctor. 'Only this,' replied the other, 'that I shall never repeat any thing I write before you again, for you have a memory that would convict any author of plagiarism in any court of literature in the world.'

I have now the poem before me, and I find it contains no less than *sixty-eight* lines.

NOTES

William Cooke, sometimes spelt Cook (d. 1824), author and dramatist, later known as 'Conversation Cooke' on account of his poem *On Conversation* (1807), was a member of the Essex Head Club. Walter Raleigh dismisses his *Life* as 'a mere trading venture, hastily launched to catch the favourable breeze' (*Six Essays*, p. 41).

1. The reference is to Johann Lavater's *Essay on Physiognomy*, a translation of which appeared in 1793. (Lavater was, in fact, Swiss.)

2. This sentence ('When he walked the streets . . .') is quoted approvingly ('described in a very just and picturesque manner') by Boswell.

3. On Hawkesworth, see p. 83. The poem referred to was published in the *Gentleman's Magazine* in 1747.

'So extremely short-sighted'*

THOMAS PERCY

Johnson was so extremely short-sighted, that he had no conception of rural beauties; and, therefore, it is not to be wondered, that he should prefer the conversation of the metropolis to the silent groves and views of Greenwich; which, however delightful, he could not see. In his Tour through the Highlands of Scotland, he has somewhere observed that one mountain was like another, so utterly unconscious was he of the

* Robert Anderson, *Life of Johnson* (3rd edn, 1815); reprinted in *Johnsonian Miscellanies*, II, 209–10, 215–18.

wonderful variety of sublime and beautiful scenes those mountains exhibited. The writer of this remark was once present when the case of a gentleman was mentioned, who, having with great taste and skill formed the lawns and plantations about his house into most beautiful landscapes, to complete one part of the scenery, was obliged to apply for leave to a neighbour with whom he was not upon cordial terms; when Johnson made the following remark, which at once shows what ideas he had of landscape improvement, and how happily he applied the most common incidents to moral instruction. 'See how inordinate desires enslave man! No desire can be more innocent than to have a pretty garden, yet, indulged to excess, it has made this poor man submit to beg a favour of his enemy.' . . .

Johnson's manner of composing has not been rightly understood. He was so extremely short-sighted, from the defect in his eyes, that writing was inconvenient to him; for whenever he wrote, he was obliged to hold the paper close to his face. He, therefore, never composed what we call a foul draft on paper of anything he published, but used to revolve the subject in his mind, and turn and form every period, till he had brought the whole to the highest correctness and the most perfect arrangement. Then his uncommonly retentive memory enabled him to deliver a whole essay, properly finished, whenever it was called for. The writer of this note has often heard him humming and forming periods, in low whispers to himself, when shallow observers thought he was muttering prayers, etc. But Johnson is well known to have represented his own practice, in the following passage, in his *Life of Pope*. 'Of composition there are different methods. Some employ at once memory and invention; and, with little intermediate use of the pen, form and polish large masses by continued meditation, and write their productions only when, in their own opinion, they have completed them.' . . .

This summer [1764] Johnson paid a visit to Dr Percy at his vicarage house in Easton Maudit, near Wellingborough in Northamptonshire, and spent parts of the months of June, July and August with him, accompanied by his friend Miss Williams, whom Mrs Percy found a very agreeable companion. As poor Miss Williams, whose history is so connected with that of Johnson, has not had common justice done her by his biographers, it may be proper to mention, that, so far from being a constant source of disquiet and vexation to him, although she was totally blind for the last thirty years of her life, her mind was so well cultivated, and her conversation so agreeable, that she very much enlivened and diverted his solitary hours; and though there may have happened some slight disagreements between her and Mrs Desmoulins, which, at the moment, disquieted him, the friendship of Miss Williams contributed very much to his comfort and happiness. For, having been the intimate friend of his wife, who had invited her to his house, she continued to reside with him, and in her he had always a conversible companion; who, whether at his dinners, or at his tea table, entertained his friends with her sensible conversation. And being extremely clean and neat in her person and habits, she never gave the least disgust by her manner of eating; and when she made tea for Johnson and his friends, conducted it with so much delicacy, by gently touching the outside of the cup, to feel, by the heat, the tea as it ascended within, that it was rather matter of admiration than of dislike to every attentive observer.

NOTE

Thomas Percy (1729–1811), remembered as editor of the influential *Reliques of Ancient English Poetry* (1765), was Vicar of Easton Maudit from 1753 and became Bishop of Dromore in 1782. As indicated above, he was Johnson's host when he visited Northamptonshire in 1764. Their close friendship led Johnson to tell Percy various anecdotes of his early years which were duly transmitted to Boswell and used in his *Life*.

'At length he began . . .'*

OZIAS HUMPHRY

The day after I wrote my last letter to you I was introduced to Mr Johnson by a friend: we passed through three very dirty rooms to a little one that looked like an old counting-house, where this great man was sat at his breakfast. The furniture of this room was a very large deal writing-desk, an old walnut-tree table, and five ragged chairs of four different sets. I was very much struck with Mr Johnson's appearance, and could hardly help thinking him a madman for some time, as he sat waving over his breakfast like a lunatic.

He is a very large man, and was dressed in a dirty brown coat and waistcoat, with breeches that were brown also (though they had been crimson), and an old black wig: his shirt collar and sleeves were unbuttoned; his stockings were down about his feet, which had on them, by way of slippers, an old pair of shoes. He had not been up long when we called on him, which was near one o'clock: he seldom goes to bed till near two in the morning; and Mr Reynolds tells me he generally drinks tea about an hour after he has supped. We had been some time with him

* *Johnsonian Miscellanies*, ii, 40–1.

before he began to talk, but at length he began, and, faith, to some purpose! Everything he says is as *correct* as a *second edition*: 'tis almost impossible to argue with him, he is so sententious and so knowing.

NOTE

Ozias Humphry (1742–1810), portrait painter and miniaturist. Boswell quotes three of Johnson's letters to Humphry. The source of the present extract is a letter dated 19 September 1764, at which time Johnson was living in Inner Temple Lane.

'A bountiful disposition'*

THOMAS TYERS

His eyesight was not good; but he never wore spectacles; not on account of such a ridiculous vow as Swift made not to use them, but because he was assured they would be of no service to him. He once declared, that he 'never saw the human face divine'. He saw better with one eye than the other, which however was not like that of Camoens, the Portuguese poet, as expressed on his medal. He chose to say to an observer and inquirer after the apparent blemish of his left eye, that 'he had not seen out of that little scoundrel for a great many years'. 'It is inconceivable,' he used to observe, 'how little light or sight are necessary for the purpose of reading.' Latterly, perhaps, he meant to save his eyes, and did not read so much as he otherwise would. He preferred conversation to books; but when driven to the refuge of reading, by being left alone, he then attached himself to that amusement. 'Till this year,' said he to an intimate, 'I have done tolerably well without sleep, for I have been able to read like Hercules.' But he picked and culled his companions for his midnight hours, 'and chose his author as he chose his friend'. The mind is as fastidious about its intellectual meal as the appetite is as to its culinary one; and it is observable that the dish or the book that palls at one time is a banquet at another. By his innumerable quotations you would suppose, with a great personage, that he must have read more

* 'A Biographical Sketch of Dr Samuel Johnson', *Gentleman's Magazine* (1784); revised and republished as a pamphlet in 1785; reprinted in Brack and Kelley, *Early Biographies*, pp. 66–7, 81–2.

books than any man in England, and have been a mere book-worm; but he acknowledged that supposition was a mistake in his favour. He owned he had hardly ever read a book through. The posthumous volumes of Mr Harris of Salisbury[1] (which treated of subjects that were congenial with his own professional studies) had attractions that engaged him to the end. Churchill[2] used to say, having heard perhaps of his own confession, as a boast, that 'if Johnson had only read a few books, he could not be the author of his own works'. His opinion, however, was, that he who reads most has the chance of knowing most; but he declared that the perpetual task of reading was as bad as the slavery in the mine, or the labour at the oar. He did not always give his opinion unconditionally of the pieces he had even perused, and was competent to decide upon. He did not choose to have his sentiments generally known; for there was a great eagerness, especially in those who had not the pole-star of judgment to direct them, to be taught what to think or to say on literary performances. 'What does Johnson say of such a book?' was the question of every day. Besides, he did not want to increase the number of his enemies, which his decisions and criticisms had created him; for he was generally willing to retain his friends, to whom, and their works, he bestowed sometimes too much praise, and recommended beyond their worth, or perhaps his own esteem. But affection knows no bounds. Shall this pen find a place in the present page to mention that a shameless Aristophanes had an intention of taking him off upon the stage, as the Rehearsal does the great Dryden?[3] When it came to the notice of our exasperated man of learning, he conveyed such threats of vengeance and personal punishment to the mimic, that he was glad to proceed no farther. The reverence of the public for his character afterwards, which was increasing every year, would not have suffered him to be the object of theatrical ridicule. . . .

His benevolence to mankind was known to all who knew him. Though so declared a friend to the Church of England, and even a friend to the Convocation, it assuredly was not in his wish to persecute for speculative notions. He used to say he had no quarrel with any order of men, unless they disbelieved in revelation and a future state. This writer has permission, from Dr Dunbar,[4] to publish this specimen of his pertinacious opinion: for which Mr Hume would have put him into his chapter of bigots. 'That prominent feature in Johnson's character was strongly marked in a conversation one morning with me *tête à tête*. He reproached me in a very serious, though amicable strain, for commending Mr Hume[5] as I had done in my Essays on the History of Mankind. I vindicated myself from the imputation as well as I was able – But he remained dissatisfied; still condemned my praise of Hume; and added: "For my part, sir, I should as soon have praised a *mad dog*." '

Another morning when he expostulated with me on the same offence, I answered, that I had, indeed, commended Mr Hume for talents which really belonged to him; but, by no means for his Scepticism, his

Infidelity, or Irreligion. 'I could not, sir,' said Johnson, 'on any account, have been the instrument of his praise. When I published my Dictionary, I might have quoted *Hobbes*[6] as an authority in language, as well as many other writers of his time: but I scorned, sir, to quote him at all; because I did not like his principles.' . . . His hand and his heart were always open to charity. The objects under his own roof were only a few of the subjects for relief. He was at the head of subscription in cases of distress. His guinea, as he said of another man of a bountiful disposition, was always ready. . . . He implored the hand of benevolence for others, even when he almost seemed a proper object of it himself.

NOTES

Thomas Tyers (1726–87), son of the founder of the pleasure resort at Vauxhall Gardens, of which he became joint manager, was, according to Boswell,

> bred to the law; but having a handsome fortune, vivacity of temper, and eccentricity of mind, he could not confine himself to the regularity of practice. He therefore ran about the world with a pleasant carelessness, amusing everybody by his desultory conversation. He abounded in anecdote, but was not sufficiently attentive to accuracy.

Johnson was fond of 'Tom Tyers' and portrayed him in the *Idler* as 'Tom Restless'. Boswell refers patronisingly to Tyers' brief life of Johnson as 'an entertaining little collection of fragments'.

1. On James Harris, whose posthumous publications include *Philological Inquiries* (1781), see p. 111.
2. Charles Churchill (1731–64), satirist.
3. The Duke of Buckingham's *The Rehearsal* (1672) is a satire on contemporary notions of heroic tragedy.
4. James Dunbar was Professor of Philosophy at King's College, Aberdeen.
5. David Hume (1711–76), philosopher. 'Hume, and other sceptical innovators' (in Boswell's phrase) are the target of Johnson's quip that 'Truth, Sir, is a cow which will yield such people no more milk, and so they are gone to milk the bull.'
6. Thomas Hobbes (1588–1679), political philosopher.

Eating and Tea-drinking*

SIR JOHN HAWKINS

Johnson looked upon [eating] as a very serious business, and enjoyed the pleasure of a splendid table equally with most men. It was, at no time of his life, pleasing to see him at a meal; the greediness with which he ate, his total inattention to those among whom he was seated, and his profound silence in the hour of refection, were circumstances that at the instant degraded him, and showed him to be more a sensualist than a philosopher. Moreover, he was a lover of tea to an excess hardly credible; whenever it appeared, he was almost raving, and by his impatience to be served, his incessant calls for those ingredients which make that liquor palatable, and the haste with which he swallowed it down, he seldom failed to make that a fatigue to every one else, which was intended as a general refreshment.[1] Such signs of effeminacy as these, suited but ill with the appearance of a man, who, for his bodily strength and stature, has been compared to Polyphemus.[2]

NOTES

On Hawkins, see p. 171.

1. The editor of *Johnsonian Miscellanies* cites for comparison the following passage from John Knox's *Tour through the Highlands* (1787) p. 143:

[At Dunvegan] Lady Macleod, who had repeatedly helped Dr Johnson to sixteen dishes or upwards of tea, asked him if a small basin would not save him trouble, and be more agreeable. 'I wonder, Madam,' answered he roughly, 'why all the ladies ask me such impertinent questions. It is to save yourselves trouble, Madam, and not me.' The lady was silent and went on with her task.

2. The one-eyed giant of Greek legend.

* *Life of Samuel Johnson, LL.D.*, p. 355.

'Rather a disgraceful visitor'*

LETITIA HAWKINS

When first I remember Johnson I used to see him sometimes at a little distance from the house, coming to call on my father; his look directed downwards, or rather in such apparent abstraction as to have no direction. His walk was heavy, but he got on at a great rate, his left arm always fixed across his breast, so as to bring the hand under his chin; and he walked wide, as if to support his weight. Getting out of a hackney-coach, which had set him down in Fleet Street, my brother Henry says he made his way up Bolt Court in the zig-zag direction of a flash of lightning; submitting his course only to the deflections imposed by the impossibility of going further to right or left.

His clothes hung loose, and the pocket on the right hand swung violently, the lining of his coat being always visible. I can now call to mind his brown hand, his metal sleeve-buttons, and my surprise at seeing him with plain wristbands, when all gentlemen wore ruffles; his coat-sleeve being very wide showed his linen almost to the elbow. His wig in common was cut and bushy; if by chance he had one that had been dressed in separate curls, it gave him a disagreeable look, not suited to his years or character. I certainly had no idea that this same Dr Johnson, whom I thought rather a disgraceful visitor at our house, and who was never mentioned by ladies but with a smile, was to be one day an honour not only to us but to his country.

I remember a tailor's bringing his pattern-book to my brothers, and pointing out a purple, such as no one else wore, as the doctor's usual choice. We all shouted with astonishment, at hearing that Polypheme,[1] as, shame to say, we had nicknamed him, ever had a new coat; but the tailor assured us he was a good customer. . . .

What the economy of Dr Johnson's house might be under his wife's administration, I cannot tell; but under Miss Williams's management, and, indeed, afterwards, when he was even more at the mercy of those around him, it always exceeded my expectation, as far as the condition of the apartment into which I was admitted could enable me to judge. It

---

* *Memoirs of Letitia Hawkins* (1827); excerpted in *Johnsonian Miscellanies*, II, 139–41.

was not, indeed, his study: amongst his books he probably might bring Magliabecchi[2] to recollection; but I saw him only in a decent drawing-room of a house not inferior to others in the same local situation, and with stout old-fashioned mahogany chairs and tables. I have said that he was a liberal customer to his tailor, and I can remember that his linen was often a strong contrast to the colour of his hands.

NOTES

Letitia Matilda Hawkins was the daughter of Sir John Hawkins.

1. Miss Hawkins's father also uses this family nickname for Johnson: see p. 34.

2. Antonio Magliabechi (1633–1714), 'Florentine bibliophile . . . noted for his great and varied learning' (*Oxford Companion to English Literature*, 4th edn).

'This extraordinary man'*

SIR JOSHUA REYNOLDS

From thirty years' intimacy with Dr Johnson I certainly have had the means, if I had equally the ability, of giving you a true and perfect idea of the character and peculiarities of this extraordinary man. The habits of my profession unluckily extend to the consideration of so much only of character as lies on the surface, as is expressed in the lineaments of the countenance. An attempt to go deeper, and investigate the peculiar colouring of his mind as distinguished from all other minds, nothing but your earnest desire can excuse. Such as it is, you may make what use of it you please. Of his learning, and so much of his character as is discoverable in his writings and is open to the inspection of every person, nothing need be said.

I shall remark such qualities only as his works cannot convey. And among those the most distinguished was his possessing a mind which was, as I may say, always ready for use. Most general subjects had undoubtedly been already discussed in the course of a studious thinking life. In this respect, few men ever came better prepared into whatever company chance might throw him, and the love which he had to society

---

* C. R. Leslie and Tom Taylor, *Life and Times of Sir Joshua Reynolds* (1865); included in *Johnsonian Miscellanies*, II, 218–28.

gave him a facility in the practice of applying his knowledge of the matter in hand in which I believe he was never exceeded by any man. It has been frequently observed that he was a singular instance of a man who had so much distinguished himself by his writings that his conversation not only supported his character as an author, but, in the opinion of many, was superior. Those who have lived with the wits of the age know how rarely this happens. I have had the habit of thinking that this quality, as well as others of the same kind, are possessed in consequence of accidental circumstances attending his life. What Dr Johnson said a few days before his death of his disposition to insanity was no new discovery to those who were intimate with him. The character of Imlac in *Rasselas*, I always considered as a comment on his own conduct, which he himself practised, and as it now appears very successfully, since we know he continued to possess his understanding in its full vigour to the last. Solitude to him was horror; nor would he ever trust himself alone but when employed in writing or reading. He has often begged me to go home with him to prevent his being alone in the coach. Any company was better than none; by which he connected himself with many mean persons whose presence he could command. For this purpose he established a Club at a little ale-house in Essex Street, composed of a strange mixture of very learned and very ingenious odd people. Of the former were Dr Heberden, Mr Windham, Mr Boswell, Mr Stevens and Mr Paradise.[1] Those of the latter I do not think proper to enumerate. By thus living, by necessity, so much in company, more perhaps than any other studious man whatever, he had acquired by habit, and which habit alone can give, that facility, and we may add docility of mind, by which he was so much distinguished. Another circumstance likewise contributed not a little to the power which he had of expressing himself, which was a rule, which he said he always practised on every occasion, of speaking his best, whether the person to whom he addressed himself was or was not capable of comprehending him. 'If,' says he, 'I am understood, my labour is not lost. If it is above their comprehension, there is some gratification, though it is the admiration of ignorance.' And he said those were the most sincere admirers; and quoted Baxter,[2] who made it a rule never to preach a sermon without saying something which he knew was beyond the comprehension of his audience, in order to inspire their admiration. Dr Johnson, by this continual practice, made that a habit which was at first an exertion; for every person who knew him must have observed that the moment he was left out of the conversation, whether from his deafness or from whatever cause, but a few minutes without speaking or listening, his mind appeared to be preparing itself. He fell into a reverie accompanied with strange antic gestures; but this he never did when his mind was engaged by the conversation. [These were] therefore improperly called by ——, as well as by others, convulsions, which imply involuntary contortions;

whereas, a word addressed to him, his attention was recovered. Sometimes, indeed, it would be near a minute before he would give an answer, looking as if he laboured to bring his mind to bear on the question.

In arguing he did not trouble himself with much circumlocution, but opposed, directly and abruptly, his antagonist. He fought with all sorts [of] ludicrous comparisons and similes; [and] if all failed, with rudeness and overbearing. He thought it necessary never to be worsted in argument. He had one virtue which I hold one of the most difficult to practise. After the heat of contest was over, if he had been informed that his antagonist resented his rudeness, he was the first to seek after a reconciliation; and of his virtues the most distinguished was his love of truth.

He sometimes, it must be confessed, covered his ignorance by generals rather than appear ignorant. You will wonder to hear a person who loved him so sincerely speak thus freely of his friend, but, you must recollect I am not writing his panegyric, but as if upon oath, not only to give the truth but the whole truth.

His pride had no meanness in it; there was nothing little or mean about him.

Truth, whether in great or little matters, he held sacred.

From the violation of truth, he said, in great things your character or your interest was affected, in lesser things your pleasure is equally destroyed. I remember, on his relating some incident, I added something to his relation which I supposed might likewise have happened: 'It would have been a better story,' says he, 'if it had been so; but it was not.' Our friend Dr Goldsmith was not so scrupulous; but he said he only indulged himself in white lies, light as feathers, which he threw up in the air, and on whomever they fell, nobody was hurt. 'I wish,' says Dr Johnson, 'you would take the trouble of moulting your feathers.'

I once inadvertently put him in a situation from which none but a man of perfect integrity could extricate himself. I pointed at some lines in the *Traveller*[3] which I told [him] I was sure he wrote. He hesitated a little; during this hesitation I recollected myself, that as I knew he would not lie I put him in a cleft stick, and should have had but my due if he had given me a rough answer; but he only said, 'Sir, I did not write them, but that you may not imagine that I have wrote more than I really have, the utmost I have wrote in that poem, to the best of my recollection, is not more than eighteen lines.' It must be observed there was then an opinion about town that Dr Johnson wrote the whole poem for his friend, who was then in a manner an unknown writer. This conduct appears to me to be in the highest degree correct and refined. If the Doctor's conscience would have let him tell a lie, the matter would have been soon over.

As in his writings not a line can be found which a saint would wish to blot, so in his life he would never suffer the least immorality [or] indecency of conversation, [or any thing] contrary to virtue or piety to proceed without a severe check, which no elevation of rank exempted them from. . . .

Custom, or politeness, or courtly manners has authorised such an Eastern hyperbolical style of compliment, that part of Dr Johnson's character for rudeness of manners must be put to the account of this scrupulous adherence to truth. His obstinate silence, whilst all the company were in raptures, vying with each other who should pepper highest, was considered as rudeness or ill-nature.

During his last illness, when all hope was at an end, he appeared to be quieter and more resigned. His approaching dissolution was always present to his mind. A few days before he died, Mr Langton and myself only present, he said he had been a great sinner, but he hoped he had given no bad example to his friends; that he had some consolation in reflecting that he had never denied Christ, and repeated the text 'Whoever denies me, &c.'[4] We were both very ready to assure him that we were conscious that we were better and wiser from his life and conversation; and that, so far from denying Christ, he had been, in this age, his great champion.

Sometimes a flash of wit escaped him as if involuntary. He was asked how he liked the new man that was hired to watch by him. 'Instead of watching,' says he, 'he sleeps like a dormouse; and when he helps me to bed he is awkward as a turnspit dog the first time he is put into the wheel.'

The Christian religion was with him such a certain and established truth, that he considered it as a kind of profanation to hold any argument about its truth.

He was not easily imposed upon by professions to honesty and candour; but he appeared to have little suspicion of hypocrisy in religion.

His passions were like those of other men, the difference only lay in his keeping a stricter watch over himself. In petty circumstances this wayward disposition appeared, but in greater things he thought it worthwhile to summon his recollection and be always on his guard. . . . [To them that loved him not] as rough as winter; to those who sought his love, as mild as summer many instances will readily occur to those who knew him intimately, of the guard which he endeavoured always to keep over himself.

The prejudices he had to countries did not extend to individuals. The chief prejudice in which he indulged himself was against Scotland, though he had the most cordial friendship with individuals [of that country]. This he used to vindicate as a duty. In respect to Frenchmen he rather laughed at himself, but it was insurmountable. He considered every foreigner as a fool till they had convinced him of the contrary. Against the Irish he entertained no prejudice, he thought they united themselves very well with us; but the Scots, when in England, united and made a party by employing only Scotch servants and Scotch tradesmen. He held it right for Englishmen to oppose a party against them. . . .

The drawback of his character is entertaining prejudices on very slight foundations; giving an opinion, perhaps, first at random, but from its being contradicted he thinks himself obliged always to support [it], or, if he cannot support, still not to acquiesce [in the opposite opinion]. Of this I remember an instance of a defect or forgetfulness in his 'Dictionary'. I asked him how he came not to correct it in the second edition. 'No,' says he, 'they made so much of it that I would not flatter them by altering it!'

From passion, from the prevalence of his disposition for the minute, he was constantly acting contrary to his own reason, to his principles. It was a frequent subject of animadversion with him, how much authors lost of the pleasure and comfort of life by their carrying always about them their own consequence and celebrity. Yet no man in mixed company – not to his intimates, certainly, for that would be an insupportable slavery – ever acted with more circumspection to his character than himself. The most light and airy dispute was with him a dispute on the arena. He fought on every occasion as if his whole reputation depended upon the victory of the minute, and he fought with all the weapons. If he was foiled in argument he had recourse to abuse and rudeness. That he was not thus strenuous for victory with his intimates in tête-à-tête conversations when there were no witnesses, may be easily believed. Indeed, had his conduct been to them the same as he exhibited to the public, his friends could never have entertained that love and affection for him which they all feel and profess for his memory.

But what appears extraordinary is that a man who so well saw, himself, the folly of this ambition of shining, of speaking, or of acting always according to the character [he] imagined [he] possessed in the world, should produce himself the greatest example of a contrary conduct.

Were I to write the Life of Dr Johnson, I would labour this point, to separate his conduct that proceeded from his passions, and what proceeded from his reason, from his natural disposition seen in his quiet hours.

NOTES

Sir Joshua Reynolds (1723–92), the greatest of English portrait painters, was in Italy in 1749–52 and met Johnson soon after his return to London. (The date is uncertain, and may be as late as 1755 or 1756; in any case his reference to 'thirty years' intimacy' must probably be taken as an approximate figure rather than a definite indication that they met in 1754.) Reynolds' circle of friends also included Garrick and Goldsmith. He founded the Literary Club in 1764 in order to provide Johnson with a forum for the exercise of his conversational powers. Reynolds became the first President of the Royal Academy in 1768, and was knighted in the following year. He painted a portrait of Johnson in about 1756 (now in the National Portrait Gallery), another in 1769, another in 1772 (commissioned by Henry Thrale for Streatham Park, and now in the Tate Gallery), and another about 1775.

   1. Dr William Heberden (1710–1801), physician; William Windham (1750–1810), politician; George Stevens (1736–1800), Shakespearean editor; Dr John Paradise (1743–95), linguist.

   2. Richard Baxter (1615–91), Presbyterian divine and author of the *Saint's Everlasting Rest* (1650).

   3. Goldsmith's poem was published in 1764. Johnson contributed nine lines to it (420, 429–34 and 437–8).

   4. Matthew, x, 33.

Johnson and Reynolds*

JAMES NORTHCOTE

Of Johnson's pride, I have heard Reynolds himself observe, that if any man drew him into a state of obligation without his own consent, that man was the first we would affront, by way of clearing off the account. . . .

   [An] anecdote, which I heard related by Miss Reynolds, serves to show how susceptible Johnson's pride was of the least degree of mortification.

   At the time when Mr Reynolds resided in Newport Street, he, one afternoon, accompanied by his sister Frances, paid a visit to the Miss Cotterells,[1] who lived much in the fashionable world. Johnson was also of the party on this tea visit; and at that time being very poor, he was, as might be expected, rather shabbily and slovenly apparelled. The maidservant, by accident, attended at the door to let them in, but did not know Johnson, although he had been a frequent visitor at the house, he having always been attended by the manservant. Johnson was the last of the three that came in; when the servant maid, seeing this uncouth and dirty figure of a man, and not conceiving he could be one of the company who came to visit her mistresses, laid hold of his coat just as he was going up stairs, and pulled him back again, saying, 'You fellow, what is your

* *The Life of Sir Joshua Reynolds* (2nd edn, 1818) I, 71–6, 79–82, 86, 118, 173, 203, 230–3, 235–6, 327–8; II, 93, 143–4, 159–61, 189.

business here? I suppose you intended to rob the house.' This most unlucky accident threw poor Johnson into such a fit of shame and anger, that he roared out like a bull, for he could not immediately articulate, and was with difficulty at last able to utter, 'What have I done? What have I done?' Nor could he recover himself for the remainder of the evening from this mortifying circumstance. . . .

Johnson, it is well known, was as remarkably uncouth in his gait and action as slovenly in his dress, insomuch as to attract the attention of passengers who by chance met him in the street. Once, particularly, he was thus annoyed by an impertinent fellow, who noticed, and insultingly imitated him in derision so ludicrously, that the Doctor could not avoid seeing it, and was obliged to resent the affront, which he did in this manner: 'Ah!' said Johnson, 'you are a very weak fellow, and I will convince you of it.' And then immediately gave him a blow, which knocked the man out of the footpath into the dirty street flat on his back, when the Doctor walked calmly on.

Another circumstance Reynolds used to mention relative to Dr Johnson, gives an idea of the situation and mode of living of that great philosopher in the early part of his life.

Roubiliac,[2] the famous sculptor, desired of Reynolds that he would introduce him to Dr Johnson, at the time when the Doctor lived in Gough Square, Fleet Street. His object was to prevail on Johnson to write an epitaph for a monument, on which Roubiliac was then engaged for Westminster Abbey. Reynolds accordingly introduced the sculptor to the Doctor, they being strangers to each other, when Johnson received him with much civility, and took them up into a garret, which he considered as his library; where, besides his books, all covered with dust, there was an old crazy deal table, and a still worse and older elbow chair, having only three legs. In this chair Johnson seated himself, after having, with considerable dexterity and evident practice, first drawn it up against the wall, which served to support it on that side on which the leg was deficient. He then took up his pen, and demanded what they wanted him to write. On this Roubiliac, who was a true Frenchman, (as may be seen by his works,) began a most bombastic and ridiculous harangue, on what he thought should be the kind of epitaph most proper for his purpose, all which the Doctor was to write down for him in correct language. Johnson, who could not suffer anyone to dictate to him, quickly interrupted him in an angry tone of voice, saying, 'Come, come, Sir, let us have no more of this bombastic, ridiculous rhodomontade, but let me know, in simple language, the name, character, and quality, of the person whose epitaph you intend to have me write.' . . .

Doctor Johnson had a great desire to cultivate the friendship of Richardson,[3] the author of *Clarissa*, and with this view paid him frequent visits. These were received very coldly by the latter; 'but,' observed the Doctor (in speaking of this to a friend), 'I was determined to persist till I had gained my point; because I knew very well, that, when I had once overcome his reluctance and shyness of humour, our intimacy would contribute much to the happiness of both.' The event verified the Doctor's prediction.

It must, however, be remarked that an intimacy with Johnson was always attended with a certain portion of inconvenience to persons whose time was much occupied; as his visits, to those he liked, were long, frequent and very irregular in regard to the hours.

The Doctor's intercourse with Reynolds was at first produced in the same manner as is described in respect to Richardson. He frequently called in the evening, and remained to a late hour, when Mr Reynolds was desirous of going into new company, after having been harassed by his professional occupations the whole day. This sometimes overcame his patience to such a degree, that, one evening in particular, on entering the room where Johnson was waiting to see him, he immediately took up his hat and went out of the house. Reynolds hoped by this means he would have been effectually cured; but Johnson still persisted and at last gained his friendship.

Johnson introduced Mr Reynolds and his sister to Richardson, but hinted to them at the same time, that, if they wished to see the latter in good humour, they must expatiate on the excellencies of his *Clarissa*.

Johnson soon became a frequent visitor at Mr Reynolds's, particularly at Miss Reynolds's tea table, where he had every opportunity of female conversation whilst drinking his favourite beverage.

Indeed, his visits were not alone to Reynolds, but to Miss Reynolds, for whom he had the highest respect and veneration: to such a degree, that, some years afterwards, whilst the company at Mr Thrale's were speculating upon a microscope for the mind, Johnson exclaimed, 'I never saw one that would bear it, except that of my dear Miss Reynolds, and hers is very near to purity itself.'

There is no doubt that Miss Reynolds gained much of his good-will by her good-humoured attention to his extraordinary predilection for tea; he himself saying, that he wished his tea-kettle never to be cold. But Reynolds having once, whilst spending the evening at Mr Cumberland's, reminded him of the enormous quantity he was swallowing, observing, that he had drank eleven cups, Johnson replied, 'Sir, I did not count your glasses of wine, why then should you number up my cups of tea?'

Johnson's extraordinary, or rather extravagant, fondness for this refreshment did not fail to excite notice wherever he went; and it is related, though not by Boswell, that whilst on his Scottish tour, and spending some time at Dunvegan, the castle of the chief of the Macleods, the Dowager Lady Macleod having repeatedly helped him, until she had poured out sixteen cups, she then asked him, if a small basin would not save him trouble and be more agreeable? – 'I wonder, Madam,' answered he roughly, 'why all the ladies ask me such questions! It is to save yourselves trouble, Madam, and not me.' The lady was silent, and resumed her task. Every reader, in this place, will recollect the so often told anecdote of his versification at Mr Reynolds's tea table, when criticising Percy's *Reliques*,[4] and imitating his ballad style:

> Oh! hear it then my Renny dear,
> Nor hear it with a frown –
> You cannot make the tea so fast
> As I can gulp it down.

Doctor Johnson's high opinion of Sir Joshua Reynolds was formed at a very early period of their intimacy, and increased, instead of diminishing, through life. Once at Mr Thrale's, when Reynolds left the room, Johnson observed, 'There goes a man not to be spoiled by prosperity.' And on another occasion he said, 'A story is a specimen of human manners, and derives its sole merit from its truth. When Foote has told me something, I dismiss it from my mind like a passing shadow: when Reynolds tells me something, I consider myself as possessed of an idea the more.' It was about this time, too, that a conversation took place between him and Johnson, which may, in some measure, be considered as a kind of apology on the part of Johnson, for having, in a degree, forced himself into an intimacy; when Johnson said, 'If a man does not make new acquaintance as he advances through life, he will soon find himself alone: a man, Sir, should keep his friendship in constant repair.' . . .

I have heard Reynolds repeat a speech which the Doctor made about this time, and in which he gave himself credit in two particulars: 'There are two things,' said he, 'which I am confident I can do very well: one is an introduction to any literary work, stating what it is to contain, and how it should be executed in the most perfect manner; the other is a conclusion, showing, from various causes, why the execution has not been equal to what the author promised to himself and to the public.' . . .

During [a] pleasant trip to Plymouth, Reynolds, accompanied by Dr Johnson, paid a visit to a neighbouring gentleman, when Johnson's singularity of conduct produced considerable alarm in the mind of their host; who, in order to gratify his guests, had placed before them every delicacy which the house afforded.

On this occasion, the Doctor, who seldom showed much discretion in his feeling, devoured so large a quantity of new honey and of clotted cream, which is peculiar to Devonshire, besides drinking large potations of new cider, that the entertainer found himself much embarrassed between his anxious regard for the Doctor's health, and his fear of breaking through the rules of politeness, by giving him a hint on the subject.

The strength of Johnson's constitution, however, saved him from any unpleasant consequences which might have been expected. . . .

[The] honour of knighthood was highly gratifying to all Sir Joshua's friends. Dr Johnson acknowledged that for years he had not tasted wine, until he was induced to break through his rule of abstemiousness in order to celebrate his friend's elevation. . . .

Miss Frances Reynolds had long lived in the house of Sir Joshua, her brother, which she superintended in its domestic economy; but conceived, on some occasion, that she had not been so kindly treated as she deserved. This occasioned a small degree of coolness between them, and it was her intention to compose a letter, in order to explain to him her supposed grievances; yet the composition of this letter was an affair of great difficulty: she, therefore, consulted with her sage friend Dr Johnson, who participated with her in her troubles, and voluntarily offered to write a letter himself, which when copied should pass as her own. This accordingly he performed; but when this letter was produced by him for her approval, she felt herself obliged to reject it, as the whole contents of it were so very unlike her own diction, and so decidedly like his, that the intended deception would no more have passed with Sir Joshua, than if Johnson had attired himself in her cap and gown, and endeavoured to impose his identical person upon Sir Joshua as his sister.

Dr Johnson being in company with Sir Joshua and his sister, Miss Reynolds, and the conversation turning on morality, Sir Joshua said he did not think there was in the world any man completely wicked.

Johnson answered, 'I do not know what you mean by completely wicked.'

'I mean,' returned Sir Joshua, 'a man lost to all sense of shame,' Dr Johnson replied that 'to be completely wicked a man must be also lost to all sense of conscience'.

Sir Joshua said he thought it was exactly the same – he could see no difference.

'What!' said Johnson, 'can you see no difference? I am ashamed to hear you or anybody utter such nonsense; when the one relates to men, only, the other to God!'

Miss Reynolds then observed that when shame was lost, conscience was nearly gone.

Johnson agreed that her conclusion was very just.

Dr Johnson was displeased if he supposed himself at any time made the object of idle curiosity. When Miss Reynolds once desired him to dine at Sir Joshua's, on a day fixed upon by herself, he readily accepted the invitation; yet having doubts as to the importance of her companions, or of her reasons for inviting him, he added, at the same time, 'But I will not be made a show of.'

James Macardell,[5] the mezzotinto engraver, having taken a very good

print from the portrait of Rubens, came with it one morning to Sir Joshua
Reynolds, to inquire if he could inform him particularly of the many
titles to which Rubens had a right, in order to inscribe them properly
under his print; saying he believed that Rubens had been knighted by the
kings of France, Spain and England; was secretary of state in Flanders,
and of the privy council in Spain; and had been employed in a ministerial
capacity from the court of Madrid to the court of London, to negotiate a
treaty of peace between the two crowns, and that he was also a
magistrate of Antwerp, etc.

Dr Johnson happened to be in the room with Sir Joshua at the time,
and understanding Macardell's inquiry, interfered rather abruptly,
saying, 'Pooh! Pooh! Put his name alone under the print, Peter Paul
Rubens: that is full sufficient, and more that all the rest.'

This advice of the Doctor was accordingly followed.

At the time that Miss Linley[6] was in the highest esteem as a public
singer, Dr Johnson came in the evening to drink tea with Miss Reynolds,
and when he entered the room, she said to him, 'See, Dr Johnson, what a
preference I give to your company; for I had an offer of a place in a box at
the oratorio, to hear Miss Linley: but I would rather sit with you than
hear Miss Linley sing.' 'And I, Madam,' replied Johnson, 'would rather
sit with you than sit upon a throne.'

The Doctor would not be surpassed even in a trifling compliment.

Several ladies being in company with Dr Johnson, it was remarked by
one of them that a learned woman was by no means a rare character in
the present age: when Johnson replied, 'I have known a great many
ladies who, I was told, knew Latin, but very few who know English.'

A lady observed that women surpassed men in epistolary
correspondence. Johnson said, 'I do not know that.' 'At least,' said the
lady, 'they are most pleasing when they are in conversation.' 'No,
Madam,' returned Johnson, 'I think they are most pleasing when they
hold their tongues.'

A friend of Dr Johnson's, in conversation with him, was lamenting the
disagreeable situation in which those persons stood who were eminent
for their witticisms, as they were perpetually expected to be saying good
things – that it was a heavy tax on them.

'It is indeed,' said Johnson, 'a very heavy tax on them; a tax which no
man can pay who does not steal.'

A prosing dull companion was making a long harangue to Dr Johnson
upon the *Punic War*, in which he gave nothing either new or entertaining.
Johnson, afterwards, speaking of the circumstance to a friend, said, 'Sir,
I soon withdrew my attention from him, and thought of Tom Thumb.'

A young gentleman, who was bred to the Bar, having a great desire to
be in company with Dr Johnson, was, in consequence, invited by Miss
Reynolds, Sir Joshua's sister, to meet him at their house. When the
interview took place, they fell into deep conversation on politics, and the

different governments in Europe, particularly that of Venice. Miss Reynolds, who related the anecdote, said that as it was a subject which she neither liked nor understood, she did not attend to the conversation, except to hear that the young man was humbly making his inquiries to gain all possible information from the profound knowledge of Dr Johnson; when her attention was suddenly attracted by the Doctor exclaiming, in a very loud and peremptory tone of voice, 'Yes, Sir, I know very well, that all republican rascals think as you do!' . . .

Dr Johnson knew nothing of the art of painting either in theory or practice, which is one proof that he could not be the author of Sir Joshua's discourses; indeed, his imperfect sight was some excuse for his total ignorance in that department of study. Once being at dinner at Sir Joshua's, in company with many painters, in the course of conversation Richardson's Treatise on Painting[7] happened to be mentioned. 'Ah!' said Johnson, 'I remember, when I was at college, I by chance found that book on my stairs: I took it up with me to my chamber, and read it through, and truly I did not think it possible to say so much upon the art.' Sir Joshua, who could not hear distinctly, desired of one of the company to be informed what Johnson had said; and it being repeated to him so loud that Johnson heard it, the Doctor seemed hurt, and added, 'But I did not wish, Sir, that Sir Joshua should have been told what I then said.'

The latter speech of Johnson denotes a delicacy in him, and an unwillingness to offend; and it evinces a part of his character which he has not had the credit of having ever possessed.

Sir John Hawkins also observes very well of Johnson, that of the beauties of painting, notwithstanding the many eulogiums on the art, which, after the commencement of his friendship with Sir Joshua, he inserted in his writings, he had not the least conception; indeed, he said once to Sir John that in his whole life he was never capable of discerning the least resemblance of any kind, between a picture and the subject it was designed to represent. . .

Soon after Goldsmith's death,[8] certain persons dining with Sir Joshua were commenting rather freely on some part of his works, which, in their opinion, discovered neither talent nor originality. To this, Dr Johnson listened, in his usual growling manner, for some time; when, at length, his patience being exhausted, he rose, with great dignity, looked them full in the face, and exclaimed, 'If nobody was suffered to abuse poor Goldy, but those who could write as well, he would have few censors.'

Yet, on another occasion, soon after the death of Goldsmith, a lady[9] of his acquaintance was condoling with Dr Johnson on their loss, saying, 'Poor Dr Goldsmith! I am exceedingly sorry for him; he was every man's friend!'

'No, Madam,' answered Johnson, 'he was no man's friend!'

In this seemingly harsh sentence, however, he merely alluded to the careless and imprudent conduct of Goldsmith, as being no friend even to himself, and when that is the case a man is rendered incapable of being of any essential service to anyone else.

All the friends of both Johnson and Warton[10] lamented the unhappy disagreement, between them, which almost at once put a period to a warm and long continued friendship of many years. The whole particulars were known only to the parties themselves; but one of the company who overheard part of the wordy conflict begins his account by stating Johnson as saying, 'Sir, I am not used to be contradicted,' to which Dr Warton replied, 'Sir, if you were, our admiration could not be increased, but our love might.' On the interference of the gentleman who overheard this, the dispute ceased, but a coolness always existed afterwards, which, I find stated, was increased by many trifling circumstances that, without the intervention of this contest, might have passed unnoticed by either party. . . .

But Johnson's manners were actually so very uncouth, that he was not fit to dine in public; I remember the first time I ever had the pleasure to dine in company with him, which was at Sir Joshua's table; I was previously advised not to seem to observe him in eating, as his manner was very slovenly at his meals, and he was very angry if he thought it was remarked.

The uncouth manner in which he fed himself was indeed remarkable. I well recollect when dining once at Sir Joshua's with him, he scalded his mouth by hastily and as awkwardly eating some of a beef steak pie when too hot; this, however, he passed off with a smile, saying that 'beef steak pie would be a very good thing if it would ever be cold.' . . .

In the month of June, this year [1783], Johnson sat for his picture to Miss Reynolds, and speaking of this performance in a letter to Mrs Thrale, he says, 'yesterday I sat for my picture to Miss Reynolds, perhaps for the tenth time, and I sat near three hours with the patience of *mortal born to bear*; at last she declared it quite finished, and seems to think it fine'. . . .

This instance may serve to show that perseverance was the rule and practice of Sir Joshua's school; for I have known himself, on some occasions, require as many sittings and as long at each time.

Much as Johnson admired Miss Reynolds's talents, however, he did not compliment her upon that production; but, when finished, told her it was 'Johnson's grimly ghost', and as the picture was afterwards to be engraved, he recommended as an appropriate motto, that stanza from the old ballad of William and Margaret, 'In glided', etc. . . .

We see that Dr Johnson was accustomed to speak the plain truth, by what he said to Miss Reynolds on his portrait, and that he never condescended to give an equivocal answer to any question; of which the following is an instance.

A lady of his acquaintance once asked him how it happened that he was never invited to dine at the tables of the great?

He replied, 'Because, Madam, great lords and ladies do not like to have their mouths stopped!'

Perhaps his abstinence from wine might have induced him to decline many invitations, from a wish not to appear singular; for Sir Joshua informed a friend that he had never seen Dr Johnson intoxicated by hard drinking but once, and that happened at the time they were together in Devonshire, when one night after supper Johnson drank three bottles of wine, which affected his speech so much that he was unable to articulate a hard word which occurred in the course of his conversation. He attempted it three times but failed, yet at last accomplished it, and then said, 'Well Sir Joshua I think it is now time to go to bed.'

I apprehend he afterwards made a vow to abstain from wine entirely, as I recollect that once when I dined in his company at Sir Joshua's table, Miss Reynolds offered to help him to some bread pudding, but he asked if there was any wine in the sauce, and being answered that there was, he refused it. . . .

At another time, Sir Joshua, Dr Johnson and Mr Boswell were dining together, and in the course of conversation, Boswell lamented that he had not been so happy as to have lived at that period which has been called the Augustan age of England, when Swift, Addison, Pope, etc. flourished. Sir Joshua said that he thought Mr Boswell had no reason to complain, as it was better to be alive than dead, as those were whom he named. But Johnson laughing, said, 'No, Sir, Boswell is in the right, as perhaps he has lost the opportunity which he might then have had, of having his name immortalized by being put into the *Dunciad*!' [11]

It was the opinion of Dr Johnson, that the concluding lines of the *Dunciad* were among the finest lines of Pope, and not inferior to those of any poet that ever existed.

NOTES

On Reynolds, see p. 40. James Northcote (1746–1831), painter and author, came to London in 1771, worked as an assistant to Reynolds, and later became a well-known portraitist. The first edition of his *Memoir* appeared in 1813; the second is 'revised and augmented'. William Hazlitt published his *Conversations of James Northcote Esq. R.A.* in 1830. The extracts given here cover the period from 1754.

1. The Miss Cotterells were the daughters of an admiral and lived opposite Johnson in Castle Street, Cavendish Square, in the early 1750s. He met Reynolds at their house.

2. Louis François Roubiliac (d. 1762), French sculptor, settled in London in the 1730s.

3. Samuel Richardson (1689–1761) had published *Clarissa* in 1747–9.

4. See p. 30.

5. James Macardell (?1729–65) engraved over forty plates after paintings by Reynolds.

6. Mary Linley (?1756–87) first appeared in public in 1771.

7. Jonathan Richardson (1665–1745), portrait painter, published an *Essay on the Theory of Painting* (1715) and other critical works.

8. Goldsmith died on 4 April 1774.

9. Identified in a footnote as Miss Frances Reynolds, sister of Sir Joshua.

10. Thomas Warton (1728–90), poet and literary historian. In his well-known verses beginning 'Hermit hoar, in solemn cell' (see p. 101), Johnson parodied Warton's serious attempts to write in the style of the medieval ballads, and Warton was offended. (Boswell dates the parody 1777–9.) They were later reconciled, however, and Warton joined the Literary Club in 1782. For Johnson's visit to Warton in Oxford in 1776, see p. 10.

11. Pope's great satire was published in 1728.

Johnson and Dr Burney*

MADAME D'ARBLAY

Dr Johnson, who had no ear for music, had accustomed himself, like many other great writers who have had that same, and frequently sole, deficiency, to speak slightingly both of the art and of its professors. And it was not until after he had become intimately acquainted with Dr Burney and his various merits that he ceased to join in a jargon so unworthy of his liberal judgment, as that of excluding musicians and their art from celebrity.

The first symptom that he showed of a tendency to conversion upon this subject, was upon hearing the following paragraph read, accidentally, aloud by Mrs Thrale, from the preface to the *History of Music*, while it was yet in manuscript.

'The love of lengthened tones and modulated sounds, seems a passion implanted in human nature, throughout the globe; as we hear of no people, however wild and savage in other particulars, who have not music of some kind or other, with which they seem greatly delighted.'

'Sir,' cried Dr Johnson, after a little pause, 'this assertion I believe may be right.' And then, see-sawing a minute or two on his chair, he forcibly added: 'All animated nature loves music – except myself!'

* *Memoirs of Doctor Burney* (Philadelphia, 1833) pp. 96–7, 99–101, 115–16, 184–5. (This American edition is an abridged version of the edition in three volumes published in London in 1832.)

Some time later, when Dr Burney perceived that he was generally gaining ground in the house, he said to Mrs Thrale, who had civilly been listening to some favourite air that he had been playing: 'I have yet hopes, madam, with the assistance of my pupil, to see yours become a musical family. Nay, I even hope, sir,' turning to Dr Johnson, 'I shall some time or other make you, also, sensible of the power of my art.'

'Sir,' answered the Doctor, smiling, 'I shall be very glad to have a new sense put into me!'

The Tour to the Hebrides being then in hand,[1] Dr Burney inquired of what size and form the book would be. 'Sir,' he replied, with a little bow, 'you are my model!'

Impelled by the same kindness, when the Doctor lamented the disappointment of the public in Hawkesworth's Voyages,[2] – 'Sir,' he cried, 'the public is always disappointed in books of travels – except yours!'

And afterwards, he said that he had hardly ever read any book quite through in his life; but added: 'Chamier and I, sir, however, read all your travels through – except, perhaps, the description of the great pipes in the organs of Germany and the Netherlands!' . . .

The friendship and kindness of heart of Dr Johnson were promptly brought into play by this renewed intercourse. Richard, the youngest son of Dr Burney, born of the second marriage, was then preparing for Winchester School, whither his father purposed conveying him in person. This design was no sooner known at Streatham, where Richard, at that time a beautiful as well as clever boy, was in great favour with Mrs Thrale, than Dr Johnson volunteered an offer to accompany the father to Winchester, that he might himself present the son to Dr Warton,[3] the then celebrated master of that ancient receptacle for the study of youth.

Dr Burney, enchanted by such a mark of regard, gratefully accepted the proposal; and they set out together for Winchester, where Dr Warton expected them with ardent hospitality. The acquaintance of Dr Burney he had already sought with literary liberality, having kindly given him notice, through the medium of Mr Garrick, of a manuscript treatise on music in the Winchester collection. There was, consequently, already an opening to pleasure in their meeting: but the master's reception of Dr Johnson, from the high-wrought sense of the honour of such a visit, was rather rapturous than glad. Dr Warton was always called an enthusiast by Dr Johnson, who, at times, when in gay spirits, and with those with whom he trusted their ebullition, would take off Dr Warton with the strongest humour: describing, almost convulsively, the ecstasy with which he would seize upon the person nearest to him, to hug in his arms, lest his grasp should be eluded, while he displayed some picture, or some prospect; and indicated, in the midst of contortions and gestures that violently and ludicrously shook, if they did not affright his captive, the particular point of view, or of design, that he wished should be noticed.

This Winchester visit, besides the permanent impression made by its benevolence, considerably quickened the march of intimacy of Dr Burney with the great lexicographer, by the *tête-à-tête* journey to and from Winchester; in which there was not only the ease of companionability, to dissipate the modest awe of intellectual super-eminence, but also the certitude of not being obtrusive; since, thus coupled in a post-chaise, Dr Johnson had no choice of occupation, and no one else to whom to turn.

Far, however, from Dr Johnson upon this occasion, was any desire of change, or any requisition for variety. The spirit of Dr Burney, with his liveliness of communication, drew out the mighty stores which Dr Johnson had amassed upon nearly every subject, with an amenity that brought forth his genius in its very essence, cleared from all turbid dregs of heated irritability; and Dr Burney never looked back to this Winchester tour but with recollected pleasure.

Nor was this the sole exertion in favour of Dr Burney, of this admirable friend. He wrote various letters to his own former associates, and to his newer connections at Oxford, recommending to them to facilitate, with their best power, the researches of the musical historian. And some time afterwards, he again took a seat in the chair[4] of Dr Burney, and accompanied him in person to that university; where every head of college, professor, and even general member, vied one with another in coupling, in every mark of civility, their rising approbation of Dr Burney, with their established reverence for Dr Johnson.

Most willingly, indeed, would this great and excellent man have made, had he seen occasion, far superior efforts in favour of Dr Burney; an excursion almost anywhere being, in fact, so agreeable to his taste, as to be always rather a pleasure to him than a fatigue.

His vast abilities, in truth, were too copious for the small scenes, objects, and interests of the little world in which he lived; and frequently must he have felt both curbed and damped by the utter insufficiency of such minor scenes, objects and interests, to occupy powers such as his of conception and investigation. To avow this he was far too wise, lest it should seem a scorn of his fellow-creatures; and, indeed, from his internal humility, it is possible that he was not himself aware of the great chasm that separated him from the herd of mankind, when not held to it by the ties of benevolence or of necessity. . . .

[At an evening party held at Dr Burney's,] the most innocent person of all that went forward was the laurelled chief of the little association, Dr Johnson; who, though his love for Dr Burney made it a pleasure to him to have been included in the invitation, marvelled, probably, by this time, since uncalled upon to distinguish himself, why he had been bidden to the meeting. But, as the evening advanced, he wrapped himself up in his own thoughts, in a manner it was frequently less difficult to him to do than to let alone, and became completely absorbed in silent rumination: sustaining, nevertheless, a grave and composed demeanour, with an air by no means wanting in dignity any more than in urbanity.

Very unexpectedly, however, ere the evening closed, he showed himself alive to what surrounded him, by one of those singular starts of vision, that made him seem at times – though purblind to things in common, and to things inanimate – gifted with an eye of instinct for espying any action or position that he thought merited reprehension: for, all at once, looking fixedly on Mr Greville,[5] who, without much self-denial, the night being very cold, pertinaciously kept his station before the chimney-piece, he exclaimed: 'If it were not for depriving the ladies of the fire, I should like to stand upon the hearth myself.'

A smile gleamed upon every face at this pointed speech. Mr Greville tried to smile himself, though faintly and scoffingly. He tried, also, to hold to his post, as if determined to disregard so cavalier a liberty: but the sight of every eye around him cast down, and every visage struggling vainly to appear serious, disconcerted him; and though, for two or three minutes, he disdained to move, the awkwardness of a general pause impelled him, ere long, to glide back to his chair; but he rang the bell with force as he passed it, to order his carriage.

It is probable that Dr Johnson had observed the high air and mien of Mr Greville, and had purposely brought forth that remark to disenchant him from his self-consequence. . . .

Dr Johnson, while still uninformed of an entanglement it was impossible he should conjecture,[6] attributed [Mrs Thrale's] varying humours to the effect of wayward health meeting a sort of sudden wayward power; and imagined that caprices, which he judged to be partly feminine, and partly wealthy, would soberise themselves away in being unnoticed. He adhered, therefore, to what he thought his post, in being the ostensible guardian protector of the relict and progeny of the late chief of the house; taking no open or visible notice of the alteration in the successor – save only at times, and when they were *tête-à-tête*, to this memorialist; to whom he frequently murmured portentous observations on the woeful, nay, alarming deterioration in health and disposition of her whom, so lately, he had signalised as the gay mistress of Streatham.

But at length, as she became more and more dissatisfied with her own situation, and impatient for its relief, she grew less and less scrupulous with regard to her celebrated guest; she slighted his counsel; did not heed his remonstrances; avoided his society; was ready at a moment's hint to lend him her carriage when he wished to return to Bolt Court; but awaited a formal request to accord it for bringing him back.

The Doctor then began to be stung; his own aspect became altered; and depression, with indignant uneasiness, sat upon his venerable front.

It was at this moment that, finding the memorialist was going one morning to St Martin's Street, he desired a cast thither in the carriage, and then to be set down at Bolt Court.

Aware of his disturbance, and far too well aware how short it was of what it would become when the cause of all that passed should be detected, it was in trembling that the memorialist accompanied him to the coach, filled with dread of offending him by any reserve, should he force upon her any inquiry; and yet impressed with the utter impossibility of betraying a trusted secret.

His look was stern, though dejected, as he followed her into the vehicle; but when his eye, which, however short-sighted, was quick to mental perception, saw how ill at ease appeared his companion, all sternness subsided into an undisguised expression of the strongest emotion, that seemed to claim her sympathy, though to revolt from her compassion; while, with a shaking hand, and pointing finger, he directed her looks to the mansion from which they were driving; and, when they faced it from the coach window, as they turned into Streatham Common, tremulously exclaiming: 'That house – is lost to *me* – for ever!'

During a moment he then fixed upon her an interrogative eye, that impetuously demanded: 'Do you not perceive the change I am experiencing?'

A sorrowing sigh was her only answer.

Pride and delicacy then united to make him leave her to her taciturnity.

He was too deeply disturbed, however, to start or to bear any other subject; and neither of them uttered a single word until the coach stopped in St Martin's Street, and the house and the carriage door were opened for their separation! He then suddenly and expressively looked at her, abruptly grasped her hand, and, with an air of affection, though in a low, husky voice, murmured rather than said: 'Good morning, dear lady!' but turned his head quickly away, to avoid any species of answer.

NOTES

Dr Charles Burney (1726–1814), musician and musicologist, was the father of Fanny Burney, later Madame d'Arblay (see p. 99). He met Johnson in 1755 and they remained lifelong friends, Burney's wide circle also including the Thrales, Burke, Reynolds and Garrick. His *History of Music* (vol. 1, 1776; vol. 2, 1782; vols 3–4, 1789), which brought him fame, has a dedication (to the Queen) by Johnson, who also wrote a dedication for Burney's account of the 1784 commemoration of Handel (published in 1785, after Johnson's death). Burney travelled widely in Europe, and published accounts of his travels in 1771 and 1773, flatteringly referred to by Johnson in the first of the extracts given above. See Percy Scholes, *The Great Dr Burney* (1948); Roger Lonsdale, *Dr Charles Burney* (Oxford, 1965).

1. Johnson's *A Journey to the Western Isles of Scotland* was published in 1775, the journey having been completed on 22 November 1773.

2. Hawkesworth's compilation of accounts of the experiences of Captain Cook and other travellers in the South Seas was published in 1773 and was widely attacked.

3. Joseph Warton (1722–1800), poet and critic, was Headmaster of Winchester College (a 'conspicuously unsuccessful' one, according to the *DNB*) from 1766 to 1793. A longstanding friend of Johnson's, Warton quarrelled with him at Reynolds' house in about 1766, but they were soon reconciled. Warton became a member of the Literary Club in 1773.

4. Chaise (a light carriage drawn by one horse).

5. Possibly Robert Fulke Greville, a patron of Dr Burney in his earlier years and well known for his haughty manners.

6. Between Mrs Thrale and Piozzi. On the former's rupture with Johnson, see p. 82.

Cradock is 'landed'*

JOSEPH CRADOCK

The first time I dined in company with Dr Johnson was at T. Davies's,[1] Russell Street, Covent Garden, as mentioned by Mr Boswell in his *Life of Johnson*. On mentioning my engagement previously to a friend, he said, 'Do you wish to be well with Johnson?' 'To be sure, Sir,' I replied, 'or I should not have taken any pains to have been introduced into his company.' 'Why then, Sir,' says he, 'let me offer you some advice: you must not leave him soon after dinner to go to the play; during dinner he will be rather silent – it is a very serious business with him; between six and seven he will look about him, and see who remains, and, if he then at all likes the party, he will be very civil and communicative.' He exactly fulfilled what my friend had prophesied. Mrs Davies did the honours of the table: she was a favourite with Johnson, who sat betwixt her and Dr Harwood; I sat next, below, to Mr Boswell opposite. Nobody could bring Johnson forward more civilly or properly than Davies. The subject of conversation turned upon the tragedy of *Oedipus*. This was particularly interesting to me, as I was then employed in endeavouring to make such alterations in Dryden's play,[2] as to make it suitable to a revival at Drury Lane theatre. Johnson did not seem to think favourably of it; but I

* *Johnsonian Miscellanies*, II, 61–5, 68–71. Cradock's anecdotes originally appeared in his *Literary and Miscellaneous Memoirs* (1826), and were reprinted, with alterations and additions, in the *Gentleman's Magazine* (January 1828).

ventured to plead that Sophocles wrote it expressly for the theatre, at the public cost, and that it was one of the most celebrated dramas of all antiquity. Johnson said, 'Oedipus was a poor miserable man, subjected to the greatest distress, without any degree of culpability of his own.' I urged that Aristotle, as well as most of the Greek poets, was partial to this character; that Addison considered that, as terror and pity were particularly excited, he was the properest – here Johnson suddenly becoming loud, I paused, and rather apologised that it might not become me, perhaps, too strongly to contradict Dr Johnson. 'Nay, Sir,' replied he, hastily, 'if I had not wished to have heard your arguments, I should not have disputed with you at all.' All went on quite pleasantly afterwards. We sat late, and something being mentioned about my going to Bath, when taking leave, Johnson very graciously said, 'I should have a pleasure in meeting you there.' Either Boswell or Davies immediately whispered to me, 'You're landed.'

The next time I had the pleasure of meeting him was at the Literary Club dinner at the coffee house in St James's Street, to which I was introduced by my partial friend, Dr Percy. Johnson that day was not in very good humour. We rather waited for dinner. Garrick came late, and apologised that he had been to the House of Lords, and Lord Camden insisted on conveying him in his carriage. Johnson said nothing, but he looked a volume. The party was numerous. I sat next Mr Burke at dinner. There was a beef steak pie placed just before us; and I remarked to Mr Burke that something smelt very disagreeable, and looked to see if there was not a dog under the table. Burke with great good humour said, 'I believe, Sir, I can tell you what is the cause; it is some of *my country butter* in the crust that smells so disagreeably.' Dr Johnson just at this time, sitting opposite, desired one of us to send him some of the beef steak pie. We sent but little, which he soon dispatched, and then returned his plate for more. Johnson particularly disliked that any notice should be taken of what he ate, but Burke ventured to say he was glad to find that Dr Johnson was anywise able to relish the beef steak pie. Johnson, not perceiving what he alluded to, hastily exclaimed, 'Sir, there is a time of life when a man requires the repairs of the table!' The company rather talked for victory than social intercourse. I think it was in consequence of what passed that evening, that Dr Goldsmith wrote his *Retaliation*.[3] . . .

Mrs Percy, afterwards nurse to the Duke of Kent, at Buckingham House, told me that Johnson once stayed near a month with them at their dull parsonage at Easton Maudit;[4] that Dr Percy looked out all sorts of books to be ready for his amusement after breakfast, and that Johnson was so attentive and polite to her, that, when Dr Percy mentioned the literature proposed in the study, he said, 'No, Sir, I shall first wait upon Mrs Percy to feed the ducks.' But those halcyon days were about to change – not as to Mrs Percy, for to the last she remained a favourite with him.

I happened to be in London once when Dr Percy returned from Northumberland, and found that he was expected to preach a charity sermon almost immediately. This had escaped his memory, and he said, that, though much fatigued, he had been obliged to sit up very late to furnish out something from former discourses; but, suddenly recollecting that Johnson's fourth *Idler* was exactly to his purpose, he had freely engrafted the greatest part of it. He preached, and his discourse was much admired; but being requested to print it, he most strenuously opposed the honour intended him, until he was assured by the governors that it was absolutely necessary, as the annual contributions greatly depended on the account that was given in the appendix. In this dilemma, he earnestly requested that I would call upon Dr Johnson, and state particulars. I assented, and endeavoured to introduce the subject with all due solemnity; but Johnson was highly diverted with his recital, and, laughing, said, 'Pray, Sir, give my kind respects to Dr Percy, and tell him, I desire he will do whatever he pleases in regard to my *Idler*; it is entirely at his service.' . . .

Admiral Walsingham, who sometimes resided at Windsor, and sometimes in Portugal Street, frequently boasted that he was the only man to bring together miscellaneous parties, and make them all agreeable; and, indeed, there never before was so strange an assortment as I have occasionally met there. At one of his dinners were the Duke of Cumberland, Dr Johnson, Mr Nairn, the optician, and Mr Leoni, the singer: at another, Dr Johnson, etc., and a young dashing officer, who determined, he whispered, to attack the old bear that we seemed all to stand in awe of. There was a good dinner, and during that important time Johnson was deaf to all impertinence. However, after the wine had passed rather freely, the young gentleman was resolved to bait him, and venture out a little further. 'Now, Dr Johnson, do not look so glum, but be a little gay and lively, like others: what would you give, old gentleman, to be as young and sprightly as I am?' 'Why, Sir,' said he, 'I think I would almost be content to be as foolish.'

Johnson, it is well known, professed to recruit his acquaintance with younger persons, and, in his latter days, I, with a few others, were more frequently honoured by his notice. At times he was very gloomy, and would exclaim, 'Stay with me, for it is a comfort to me' – a comfort that any feeling mind would wish to administer to a man so kind, though at times so boisterous, when he seized your hand, and repeated, 'Ay, Sir, but to die and go we know not where', etc. – here his morbid melancholy prevailed, and Garrick never spoke so impressively to the heart. Yet, to see him in the evening (though he took nothing stronger than lemonade), a stranger would have concluded that our morning account was a fabrication. No hour was too late to keep him from the tyranny of his own gloomy thoughts. A gentleman venturing to say to Johnson, 'Sir, I wonder sometimes that you condescend so far as to attend a city club.'

'Sir, the great chair of a full and pleasant club is, perhaps, the throne of human felicity.' . . .

Harris's *Hermes*[5] was mentioned. I said, 'I think the book is too abstruse; it is heavy.' 'It is; but a work of that kind must be heavy.' 'A rather dull man of my acquaintance asked me,' said I, 'to lend him some book to entertain him, and I offered him Harris's *Hermes*, and as I expected, from the title, he took it for a novel; when he returned it, I asked him how he liked it, and, what he thought of it? "Why, to speak the truth," says he, "I was not much diverted; I think all these imitations of *Tristram Shandy*[6] fall far short of the original!"' This had its effect, and almost produced from Johnson a rhinocerous laugh.

One of Dr Johnson's rudest speeches was to a pompous gentleman coming out of Lichfield cathedral, who said, 'Dr Johnson, we have had a most excellent discourse today!' 'That may be,' said Johson, 'but, it is impossible that you should know it.'

Of his kindness to me during the last years of his most valuable life, I could enumerate many instances. One slight circumstance, if any were wanting, would give an excellent proof of the goodness of his heart, and that to a person whom he found in distress. In such a case he was the very last man that would have given even the least momentary uneasiness to any one, had he been aware of it. The last time I saw him was just before I went to France. He said, with a deep sigh, 'I wish I was going with you.' He had just then been disappointed of going to Italy.[7] Of all men I ever knew, Dr Johnson was the most instructive.

NOTES

Joseph Cradock (1742–1826), man of letters and a friend of Garrick, is referred to by Boswell as 'Mr Cradock, of Leicestershire, author of *Zobeide*, a tragedy [based on a play by Voltaire and successfully produced in 1771]'. The occasion referred to in the opening sentence of the extract is dated 12 April 1776 by Boswell, who adds that Cradock was so impressed by Johnson's conversation that he whispered to Boswell, 'O that his words were written in a book!'

1. Thomas (Tom) Davies (?1712–85), actor and bookseller, in the back-parlour of whose shop in Russell Street, Covent Garden, Boswell was introduced to Johnson.

2. Dryden's *Oedipus*, written in collaboration with Nathaniel Lee, was produced in 1678.

3. Cradock's unreliability as a memoirist is suggested by the fact that Goldsmith's poem was published in 1774, two years before Cradock met Johnson. It is only fair to recall, however, that he was probably writing some half-century after the event.

4. See p. 29.

5. See p. 111.

6. Sterne's novel had been published, with great success, in 1759–67.

7. Cradock set off for Italy on 29 October 1783, and 'just then' may be something of an exaggeration. Boswell records that on 11 April 1776, 'A journey to Italy was still in [Johnson's] thoughts', and it was on that occasion that Johnson declared that 'The grand object of travelling is to see the shores of the Mediterranean.' Johnson's letters indicate that he had thoughts – unrealised in the event – of going there in 1780 and 1781, and again in the last year of his life.

A Visit to Johnson*

SARAH MORE

He was no sooner gone, than the most amiable and obliging of women [Miss Reynolds] ordered the coach, to take us to Dr Johnson's *very own house*; yes, Abyssinia's Johnson! Dictionary Johnson! Rambler's, Idler's, and Irene's Johnson! Can you picture to yourselves the palpitation of our hearts as we approached his mansion. The conversation turned upon a new work of his, just going to the press, (the Tour to the Hebrides), and his old friend Richardson. Mrs Williams, the blind poet,[1] who lives with him, was introduced to us. She is engaging in her manners; her conversation lively and entertaining. Miss Reynolds told the doctor of all our rapturous exclamations on the road. He shook his scientific head at Hannah, and said, 'She was a *silly thing*.' When our visit was ended, he called for his hat (as it rained) to attend us down a very long entry to our coach, and not Rasselas could have acquitted himself more *en cavalier*. We are engaged with him at Sir Joshua's, Wednesday evening. What do you think of us?

I forgot to mention, that not finding Johnson in his little parlour when we came in, Hannah seated herself in his great chair, hoping to catch a little ray of his genius; when he heard it, he laughed heartily, and told her it was a chair on which he never sat. He said it reminded him of Boswell and himself when they stopped a night at the spot (as they imagined) where the Weird Sisters appeared to Macbeth: the idea so worked upon their enthusiasm, that it quite deprived them of rest: however, they learnt, the next morning, to their mortification, that they had been deceived, and were quite in another part of the country.

* William Roberts, *Memoirs of the Life and Correspondence of Mrs Hannah More* (1834); the source is a letter written by Sarah More to her sister in 1774, reprinted in *Johnsonian Miscellanies*, II, 180–1.

NOTE

1. On Mrs Anna Williams, see p. 83, note 8. Her *Miscellanies in Prose and Verse*, advertised in 1750, appeared at last in 1766, with a preface and other contributions by Johnson. She is often blamed for contributing to the disharmony of Johnson's household, but her intellectual abilities and conversation must have been some compensation to Johnson for her peevishness. For a favourable view of her, see Thomas Percy's comments on p. 29.

'His intellectual storehouse'*

RICHARD CUMBERLAND

It was on such occasions he was to be seen in his happiest moments; when animated by the cheering attention of friends, whom he liked, he would give full scope to those talents for narration, in which I verily think he was unrivalled both in the brilliancy of his wit, the flow of his humour, and the energy of his language. Anecdotes of times past, scenes of his own life, and characters of humourists, enthusiasts, crack-brained projectors and a variety of strange beings, that he had chanced upon, when detailed by him at length, and garnished with those episodical remarks, sometimes comic, sometimes grave, which he would throw in with infinite fertility of fancy, were a treat, which though not always to be purchased by five and twenty cups of tea, I have often had the happiness to enjoy for less than half the number. He was easily led into topics; it was not easy to turn him from them; but who would wish it? If a man wanted to show himself off by getting up and riding upon him, he was sure to run restive and kick him off; you might as safely have backed Bucephalus, before Alexander had lunged him. Neither did he always like to be over-fondled; when a certain gentleman out-acted his part in this way, he is said to have demanded of him 'What provokes your risibility, Sir? Have I said anything that you understand? Then I ask pardon of the rest of the company.' But this is Henderson's[1] anecdote of him, and I will not swear he did not make it himself. The following apology, however, I myself drew from him, when speaking of his tour I observed to him upon some passages as rather too sharp upon a country and people who had entertained him so handsomely. 'Do you think so, Cumbey?' he replied.

* *Memoirs of Richard Cumberland, Written by Himself* (1807); extract reprinted in *Johnsonian Miscellanies*, II, 76–7.

'Then I give you leave to say, and you may quote me for it, that there are more gentlemen in Scotland than there are shoes.'

The expanse of matter, which Johnson had found room for in his intellectual storehouse, the correctness with which he had assorted it, and the readiness with which he could turn to any article that he wanted to make present use of, were the properties in him which I contemplated with the most admiration. Some have called him a savage; they were only so far right in the resemblance, as that, like the savage, he never came into suspicious company without his spear in his hand and his bow and quiver at his back.

NOTES

Richard Cumberland (1732–1811), dramatist and translator, is mentioned several times by Boswell, who speaks of his 'keen, yet just and delicate pen'; according to G. B. Hill, however, his anecdotes 'must be received with great distrust'. In his journal for 12 January 1826, Sir Walter Scott described Cumberland as 'a great flatterer' who 'carried the poetic jealousy and irritability farther than any man I ever saw'.

1. John Henderson (1747–85), actor. According to Boswell, his impersonation of Johnson was unsuccessful.

Anecdotes of Johnson*

VARIOUS SOURCES

(1)   Mrs Digby told me that when she lived in London with her sister Mrs Brooke, they were every now and then honoured by the visits of Dr Johnson. He called on them one day soon after the publication of his immortal dictionary. The two ladies paid him due compliments on the occasion. Amongst other topics of praise they very much commended the omission of all *naughty* words. 'What, my dears! Then you have been looking for them?' said the moralist. The ladies, confused at being thus caught, dropped the subject of the dictionary.

In early youth I knew Bennet Langton, *of that ilk*, as the Scots say.

* (1) H. D. Best, *Personal and Literary Memorials* (1829), excerpted in *Johnsonian Miscellanies*, ii, 390–1. (2) *European Magazine* (1798), in *Miscellanies*, ii, 394–7. (3) and (4) *Miscellanies*, ii, 404–6.

With great personal claims to the respect of the public, he is known to that public chiefly as a friend of Johnson. He was a very tall, meagre, long-visaged man, much resembling, according to Richard Paget, a stork standing on one leg, near the shore, in Raphael's cartoon of the miraculous draught of fishes. His manners were in the highest degree polished; his conversation mild, equable, and always pleasing. He had the uncommon faculty of being a good reader. I formed an intimacy with his son, and went to pay him a visit at Langton. After breakfast we walked to the top of a very steep hill behind the house. When we arrived at the summit, Mr Langton said, 'Poor, dear Dr Johnson, when he came to this spot, turned to look down the hill, and said he was determined "to take a roll down". When we understood what he meant to do, we endeavoured to dissuade him; but he was resolute, saying, he had not had a roll for a long time; and taking out of his lesser pockets whatever might be in them – keys, pencil, purse, or pen-knife – and laying himself parallel with the edge of the hill, he actually descended turning himself over and over till he came to the bottom.'

The story was told with such gravity, and with an air of such affectionate remembrance of a departed friend, that it was impossible to suppose this extraordinary freak of the great lexicographer to have been a fiction or invention of Mr Langton.

(2)   A gentleman of Lichfield, meeting the Doctor returning from a walk, inquired how far he had been. The Doctor replied that he had gone round Mr Levet's field (the place where the scholars play) in search of a rail that he used to jump over when a boy, 'and', said the Doctor in a transport of joy, 'I have been so fortunate as to find it. I stood gazing upon it some time with a degree of rapture, for it brought to my mind all my juvenile sports and pastimes, and at length I determined to try my skill and dexterity; I laid aside my hat and wig, pulled off my coat, and leapt over it twice.' Thus the great Dr Johnson, only three years before his death, was, without hat, wig or coat, jumping over a rail that he had used to fly over when a schoolboy.

Amongst those who were so intimate with Dr Johnson as to have him occasionally an intimate in their families, it is a well-known fact that he would frequently descend from the contemplation of subjects the most profound imaginable to the most childish playfulness. It was no uncommon thing to see him hop, step and jump; he would often seat himself on the back of his chair, and more than once has been known to propose a race on some grassplat adapted to the purpose. He was very intimate and much attached to Mr John Payne,[1] once a bookseller in Paternoster Row, and afterwards Chief Accountant of the Bank. Mr Payne was of a very diminutive appearance, and once when they were together on a visit with a friend at some distance from town, Johnson in a gaiety of humour proposed to run a race with Mr Payne – the proposal was accepted; but, before they had proceeded more than half of the intended distance, Johnson caught his little adversary up in his arms, and without any ceremony placed him upon the arm of a tree which was near, and then continued running as if he had met with a hard match. He afterwards returned with much exultation to release his friend from the not very pleasant situation in which he had left him.

Dr Johnson, in his tour through North Wales, passed two days at the sea of Colonel Middleton of Gwynagag. While he remained there, the gardener caught a hare amidst some potato plants, and brought it to his master, then engaged in conversation with the Doctor. An order was given to carry it to the cook. As soon as Johnson heard this sentence, he begged to have the animal placed in his arms; which was no sooner done, than approaching the window then half open, he restored the hare to her liberty, shouting after her to accelerate her speed. 'What have you done?' cried the Colonel. 'Why, Doctor, you have robbed my table of a delicacy, perhaps deprived us of a dinner.' 'So much the better, Sir,' replied the humane champion of a condemned hare, 'for if your table is to be supplied at the expense of the laws of hospitality, I envy not the appetite of him who eats it. This, Sir, is not a hare *feræ naturæ*, but one which had placed itself under your protection; and savage indeed must be that man who does not make his hearth an asylum for the confiding stranger.'

(3)   Miss Johnson, one of Sir Joshua's nieces (afterwards Mrs Deane), was dining one day at her uncle's with Dr Johnson and a large party: the conversation happening to turn on music, Johnson spoke very contemptuously of that art, and added, 'that no man of talent, or whose mind was capable of better things, ever would or could devote his time and attention to so idle and frivolous a pursuit'. The young lady, who was very fond of music, whispered to her next neighbour, 'I wonder what Dr Johnson thinks of King David.' Johnson overheard her, and, with great good humour and complacency, said, 'Madam, I thank you; I stand rebuked before you, and promise that, on one subject at least, you shall never hear me talk nonsense again.'

(4)   Mr Williams, the rector of Wellesbourne, in Warwickshire, mentioned having once, when a young man, performed a stagecoach journey with Dr Johnson, who took his place in the vehicle, provided with a little book, which his companion soon discovered to be Lucian:[2] he occasionally threw it aside, if struck by any remark made by his fellow-travellers, and poured forth his knowledge and eloquence in a full stream, to the delight and astonishment of his auditors. Accidentally, the first subject which attracted him was the digestive faculties of dogs, from whence he branched off as to the powers of digestion in various species of animals, discovering such stores of information, that this particular point might have been supposed to have formed his especial study, and

so it was with every other subject started. The strength of his memory was not less astonishing than his eloquence; he quoted from various authors, either in support of his own argument or to confute those of his companions, as readily, and apparently as accurately, as if the works had been in his hands. The coach halted, as usual, for dinner, which seemed to be a deeply interesting business to Johnson, who vehemently attacked a dish of stewed carp, using his fingers only in feeding himself.[3]

NOTES

1. J. Payne (d. 1787) was a friend of Johnson's from 1752 or earlier.
2. Greek satirist.
3. Not as uncouth a habit as it appears, since Johnson explained to Boswell on one occasion that on account of his poor eyesight he could deal with the bones in fish only by resorting to his fingers.

Dr Johnson at the Chelsea China Manufactory*

THOMAS FAULKNER

Mr A. Stephens was told by the foreman of the Chelsea China Manufactory (then in the workhouse of St Luke's, Middlesex) that Dr Johnson had conceived a notion that he was capable of improving on the manufacture of china. He even applied to the directors of the Chelsea China Works, and was allowed to *bake* his compositions in their ovens in Lawrence Street, Chelsea. He was accordingly accustomed to go down with his housekeeper, about twice a week, and stayed the whole day, she carrying a basket of provisions with her. The Doctor, who was not allowed to enter the *mixing* room, had access to every other part of the house, and formed his composition in a particular apartment, without being overlooked by anyone. He had also free access to the oven, and superintended the whole of the process; but completely failed, both as to composition and baking, for his materials always yielded to the intensity of the heat, while those of the company came out of the furnace perfect

* *A Historical and Topographical Account of Chelsea and its Environs* (2nd edn, 1829) I, 273; quoted in Robina Napier, *Johnsoniana* (1884) p. 207.

and complete. The Doctor retired in disgust, but not in despair, for he afterwards gave a dissertation on this very subject in his works; but the overseer assured Mr Stephens, in the spring of 1814, that he was still ignorant of the nature of the operation. He seemed to think that the Doctor imagined one single substance was sufficient, while he, on the other hand, asserted that he always used sixteen, and he must have had some practice, as he had nearly lost his eyesight, by firing batches of china, both at Chelsea and Derby, to which the manufacture was afterwards carried.

Perambulating with Johnson*

MR WICKINS

Deception Walking one day with him in my garden at Lichfield, we entered a small meandering shrubbery, whose 'vista not lengthened to the sight' gave promise of a larger extent. I observed that he might perhaps conceive that he was entering an extensive labyrinth, but that it would prove a deception, though I hoped not an unpardonable one. 'Sir,' said he, 'don't tell me of deception; a lie, Sir, is a lie, whether it be a lie to the eye or a lie to the ear.'

Urns Passing on we came to an urn which I had erected to the memory of a deceased friend. I asked him how he liked that urn – it was of the true Tuscan order. 'Sir,' said he, 'I hate urns; they *are* nothing, they *mean* nothing, convey no ideas but ideas of horror – would they were beaten to pieces to pave our streets!'

Cold Baths We then came to a cold bath. I expatiated upon its salubrity. 'Sir,' said he, 'how do you do?' 'Very well, I thank you, Doctor.' 'Then, Sir, let well alone, and be content. I hate immersion.' . . .

The Venus de Medici Upon the margin stood [a cast of] the Venus de Medici. . . . 'Throw her,' said he, 'into the pond to hide her nakedness, and to cool her lasciviousness.' . . .

* John Wilson Croker's edition of Boswell's *Life of Johnson* (one-volume edition, 1890) pp. 835–6.

Sterne's Sermons   Returning through the house, he stepped into a small study or book room. The first book he laid his hands upon was Harwood's 'Liberal Translation of the New Testament'.[1] The passage which first caught his eye was from that sublime apostrophe in St John, upon the raising of Lazarus, *'Jesus wept'*; which Harwood had conceitedly rendered 'and Jesus, the Saviour of the world, burst into a flood of tears'. He contemptuously threw the book aside, exclaiming 'Puppy!' I then showed him Sterne's Sermons. 'Sir,' said he, 'do you read any others?' 'Yes, Doctor; I read Sherlock, Tillotson, Beveridge and others.' 'Ay, Sir, *there* you drink the cup of salvation to the bottom; here you have merely the froth from the surface.'

NOTES

Wickins, who is not mentioned by Boswell, is identified by Croker as 'a respectable draper in Lichfield' whom Johnson 'was accustomed to call on . . . during his visits to his native town'.

    1. Edward Harwood (1729–94), classical and biblical scholar and a Presbyterian minister, published his translation, of which the portion quoted is a fair sample, in 1768. Boswell records that he dined with Johnson on 12 April 1776.

Part III

The Streatham Years

Life at Streatham I*

HESTER LYNCH THRALE

It was on the 18th day of July 1773 that we were sitting in the blue Room at Streatham and were talking of Writers – Steele's Essays were mentioned – but they are too thin said Mr Johnson; being mere Observations on Life and Manners without a sufficiency of solid Learning acquired from Books, they have the flavour, like the light French Wines you so often hear commended; but having no Body, they cannot keep. Speaking of Mason Gray etc., he said 'The Poems they write must I should suppose greatly delight the Authors; they seem to have attained that which themselves consider as the Summit of Excellence, and Man can do no more: yet surely such unmeaning & verbose Language if in the Morning it appears to be in bloom, must fade before Sunset like Cloe's Wreath.'

Of Swift's Style which I praised as beautiful, he observed that it had only the Beauty of a Bubble, The Colour says he is gay, but the Substance slight.

We talked of Dryden – Buckingham's Play,[1] said I, has hurt the Reputation of that Poet, great as he was; such is the force of ridicule! 'On the contrary, my Dearest,' replied Doctor Johnson. 'The greatness of Dryden's Character is even now the only principle of Vitality which preserves that Play from a State of Putrefaction.'

To Richardson as a Writer he gave the highest Praises, but mentioning his unquenchable Thirst after Applause, That Man said he could not be content to sail gently down the Stream of Fame, unless the Foam was continually dashing in his Face, that he might taste it at Every Stroke of the Oar. We chatted on about Authors until we talked of him himself, when he frankly owned he had never worked willingly in his Life, Man or Boy, nor ever did fairly make an Effort to do his best except three Times whilst he was at School, nor that he ever made it his Custom to read any of his Writings before he sent it to Press. Well now, said I, that will not be believed, even if your Biographer should relate it, which too perhaps he will not. 'I wonder,' said he, 'who will be my Biographer? Goldsmith, to be sure, I replied, if you should go first – and he would do it better than

* *Thraliana: The Diary of Mrs Hester Lynch Thrale (later Mrs Piozzi) 1776–1809*, ed. Katharine C. Balderston (2nd edn, Oxford, 1951) I, 172–3, 167–8, 183–93, 205–8, 492.

anybody. But then he would do maliciously,' says Johnson. As for that, answered I, we should all fasten upon him & make him do Justice in spite of himself. But the worst is the Doctor does not know your Life, nor in Truth can I tell who does, unless it be Taylor of Ashbourne. Why Taylor is certainly,' said he, 'well enough acquainted with my History at Oxford, which I believe he has nearly to himself, but Doctor James can give a better Account of my early Days than most Folks, except Mr Hector of Birmingham & little Doctor Adams.[2] After my coming to London you will be at a Loss again; though Jack Hawkesworth and Baretti both,[3] with whom I lived quite familiarly, can tell pretty nearly all my adventures from the Year 1753. However I intend to disappoint the Dogs, and either outlive them all or write my Life myself.' But for a Johnsoniana, cried I, we will defy you at least; Boswell, & Baretti & myself from Time to Time have a trick of writing down Anecdotes, Bons mots, &c., Doctor Percy will be busy at this work I warrant him. He would, replied Mr Johnson, 'but I have purposely suffered him to be misled, and he has accordingly gleaned up many Things that are not true.'

This Conversation passed on 18 July 1773, I wrote it down that night, as I thought it particularly interesting. . . .

The Story of his calling Lord Bolingbroke a Coward because he charged his Gun to let fly in the face of Christianity, & then paid a hungry Scotsman for drawing the Trigger after his Death has been, I suppose, in every Mouth & in every Jest Book, but one has now & then a coarse Joke of his partly to one's self. For example, poor Miss Owen said meekly enough one Day 'I am sure my Aunt was exceedingly sorry when the Report was raised of Mr Thrale's death.' 'Not sorrier, I suppose,' replied Mr Johnson, 'than the Horse is when the Cow miscarries.' If in short anyone, or even himself had bestowed more Praise on a Person or Thing than he thought they deserved he would instantly rough them, and that in a Manner brutal enough to be sure; at Sir Robert Cotton's Table I once inadvertently commended the Pease – which I have since thought were too little boiled – adding, taste these Pease Mr Johnson do, are not they charming? 'Yes, Madam,' replied he, 'For a Pig.'

It was at Streatham however, & before Murphy Baretti, Lyttelton & *multis aliis*, that he served Sir Joshua Reynolds saucily enough: the Conversation turned upon Painting. 'I am sorry,' says our Doctor, 'to see so much Mind laid out on such perishable Materials. Canvas is so slight a Substance, and your Art deserves to be recorded on more durable Stuff, why do you not paint oftener upon Copper?' Sir Joshua urged the Difficulty of getting a Plate large enough for Historical Subjects, & was going on to raise further Objections, when Mr Johnson, fretting that he had so inflamed his friend's Vanity, I suppose, suddenly and in a surly Tone replied 'What's here to do with such Foppery? Has not Thrale here

got a thousand Tun of Copper? You may paint it all round if you will, it
will be no worse for him to brew in – afterwards.' On the other Hand, if
he had unawares spoken harshly to a modest man, he would strive to
make him amends as in the following Case. A Young Fellow of great
Fortune as he was sitting with a Book in his hand at our House one Day
called to him rather abruptly – & he fancied disrespectfully – Mr
Johnson,' says the Man, 'would you advise me to marry?' 'I would advise
no Man to marry,' answered he, bouncing from his Chair & leaving the
Room in a fret – that is not likely to propagate Understanding. The
young Fellow looked confounded & had barely begun to recover his
Spirits when the Doctor returned with a smiling Countenance and,
joining in the General Prattle of the Party, turned it insensibly to the
Subject of Marriage; where he laid himself out in a Conversation so
entertaining, instructive & gay that nobody remembered the offence
except to rejoice in its Consequences. Nothing indeed seems to flatter
him more than to observe a Person struck with his Conversation whom
he did not expect to be so; & this happened to him particularly in
Company with the famous Daniel Sutton who at that time inoculated
one of my Children and who was a Fellow of very quick Parts, I think,
though as ignorant as dirt both with regard to Books and the World. The
following Thoughts I remember made the Man stare as we call it, and
seemed to throw a new Light upon his Mind. Money chanced to be the
Topic of the Morning Talk, and Mr Johnson observed that it resembled
Poison, as a small Quantity would often produce fatal Effects; but given
in large Doses though it might sometimes prove destructive to a Weak
Constitution, yet it might often be found to work itself off, & leave the
Patient well. He took notice in the Course of the same Conversation that
all Expense was a kind of Game, wherein the Skilful player catches and
keeps what the unskilful suffers to slip out of his Hands. Sutton listened
and grinned and gaped & said at last, half out of Breath, 'I never kept
such Company before and cannot tell how to set about leaving it now.'
The Compliment, though awkward, pleased our Doctor much, & no
wonder; it was likely to please both Vanity & Virtue.

The Piety of Doctor Johnson was exemplary & edifying; yet he had none
of that Turn to religious Mortifications which the Roman Catholic
votaries to Virtue are apt enough to practise. When we were abroad
together I used to talk with him of the hardships suffered in Places of
Seclusion. 'Remember,' says he, 'that Convents are *idle* Places of Course,
& where nothing can be *done*, something must be *suffered*, or the insipidity
of Monastic Life would produce Madness: Mustard has a bad Taste, but
you cannot eat *Brawn* without it.' Of the Claires, Carthusians, he used to
say that they should write upon their Gates what Dante writes upon the
Gates of Hell:

> Lasciate ogni Speranza – voi ch'entrate.[4]

'Religion,' adds Johnson, 'is the highest Exercise of Reason; let us not begin it by turning all reason out of Doors.' I would tell him too, sometimes, that his Morality was easily satisfied, & when I have lamented to him the wickedness of the World, he has often answered 'Prithee, my Dearest, let us have done with Canting, there is very little of gross Iniquity to be seen; & still less of extraordinary Virtue.'

Nothing seemed to disgust Johnson so greatly as Hyperbole; he loved not to hear of Sallies of Excellence. 'Heroic Virtues,' said he one day, 'are the *bons Mots* of Life; they seldom appear, & are therefore, when they do appear, much talked of. But Life is made up of little Things, & that Character is best which does little, but continued Acts of Beneficence; as that Conversation is the best which consists in little, but elegant & pleasing Thoughts; expressed in easy, natural and pleasing Terms.'

He had in his Youth been a great Reader of Mandeville,[5] and was very watchful for the Stains of original Corruption both in himself & others – I mentioned an Event which might have greatly injured Mr Thrale once! If it had happened now, said I, how sorry you would have been! 'I *hope*' replies he gravely, & after a Pause, 'that I should have been *very* sorry.' He was indeed no great sorrower for Events he had himself no Share in; I told him one Day of an Acquaintance who had hanged himself – he was an old Beau – 'Foolish rascal,' says Johnson. 'Why he had better have been airing his Clothes.' Baretti says his Concern for the Loss of Mrs Boothby[6] whom he loved with great Attachment lasted but a Week, & when Dr Bathurst[7] died; whom he professed to love beyond all mortals when I knew him first – I saw no extraordinary Emotion – I believe, however, now I think on it, he was dead before I knew Mr Johnson. 'Bathurst,' says he the other day, 'was a fine fellow! He hated a fool, & he hated a rogue, & he hated a whig. He was a very good Hater!'

Mr Johnson has more Tenderness for Poverty than any other Man I ever knew; and less for other Calamities: the person who loses a Parent, Child or Friend he pities but little. 'These,' says he, are the Distresses of Sentiment, which a Man who is *indeed* to be pitied has no leisure to feel. The want of Food & Raiment is so common in London', adds Johnson, 'that one who lives there has no Compassion to spare for the Wounds given only to Vanity or Softness.'

In consequence of these Principles he has *now* in his house whole Nests of People who would, if he did not support them, be starving I suppose: A Blind woman & her Maid, a Blackamoor and his Wife, a Scots Wench who has her Case as a Pauper depending in some of the Law Courts; a Woman whose Father once lived at Lichfield & whose Son is a strolling Player, and a superannuated Surgeon to have Care of the whole *Ship's Company*.[8] Such is the present State of Johnson's Family resident in Bolt Court, an Alley in Fleet Street, which he gravely asserts to be the best Situation in London; and thither when he is at home he keeps a sort of odd Levee for distressed Authors, breaking Booksellers, & in short everybody that has even the lowest Pretensions to Literature in Distress. Meanwhile he has a Cousin at Coventry[9] who is wholly maintained by him and a Female Cousin, a Mrs Herne,[10] I forget where to whom he regularly remits £10 a Year, & she is, I think, his cheapest Dependent. Mr Johnson has, of Course, ways enough to spend his Income which he is willing to increase by doing now & then a Job for Booksellers; & I believe few People know better how to make their Bargains, 'for,' says he, 'I do not love to beat down the price of Learning'. His Friends often prevailed on him to write Prefaces, Dedications, &c., for them, but he did not love it – one would rather says he one Day give anything than that which one is used to sell. 'Would not you, Sir,' – to Mr Thrale – 'rather give a Man Money than Porter.' The Doctor, however, was no good refuser, and you might coax him out of anything except out of a Visit, which I think he has been very backward in paying of late Years, unless he is asked to Dinner. But to return to his Notions concerning the Poor, he really loved them as nobody else does, with a Desire they should be happy. 'What signifies?' says somebody giving Money to common Beggars. 'They lay it out only in Gin or Tobacco.' 'And why should they not,' says our Doctor. 'Why should everybody else find Pleasure necessary to their Existence and deny the poor every possible Avenue to it? Gin & Tobacco are the only Pleasures in their Power; let them have the Enjoyments within their reach without Reproach.' Mr Johnson's own Pleasures – except those of Conversation – were all coarse ones: he loves a good Dinner dearly, eats it voraciously, & his notions of a good Dinner are nothing less than delicate: a Leg of Pork boiled until it drops from the bone almost, a Veal Pie with Plums & Sugar, & the outside Cut of a Buttock of Beef, are his favourite Dainties, though he loves made Dishes, Soups, &c., souses his Plum Pudding with melted Butter, & pours Sauce enough into every Plate to drown all Taste of the Victuals. With regard to Drink, his liking is for the *strongest*, as it is not the Flavour but the Effect of Wine which he even professes to desire, and he used often to pour Cappillaire into his Glass of Port when it was his Custom to drink Wine, which he has now left wholly off. To make himself amends for this Concession, he drinks Chocolate liberally, & puts in large Quantities of Butter or of Cream: he loves Fruit exceedingly, & though I have seen him eat of it immensely, he says he never had his Bellyful of Fruit but twice – once at our House and once at Ombersly, the Seat of my Lord Sandys.

I was saying this Morning that I did not love Goose much: one smells it so, says I. 'But you, Madam,' replies Johnson, 'have always had your hunger forestalled by Indulgence, & do not know the Pleasure of smelling one's Meat before hand.' A Pleasure, answered I, that is to be had in Perfection by all who walk through *Porridge Island* of a Morning! 'Come, come,' says the Doctor gravely, 'let us have done laughing at what is serious to so many. Hundreds of your Fellow Creatures, dear

Lady, turn another way that they may not be tempted by the Luxuries of *Porridge Island*[11] to hope for Gratifications they are not able to obtain.'

These Notions – just as they doubtless are – seem to me the fæculancies[12] of his low Birth, which I believe has never failed to leave its *Stigma* indelible in every human Creature, however exalted by Rank or polished by Learning. No Varnish, though strong, can totally cover primæval meanness, nor can any Situation of Life remove it out of the Sight even of a cursory & casual Observer.

As no Man better liked to be genteely Complimented than Johnson, so no Man ever had the power of Complimenting with a better Grace; for he always contrived to raise the Person he commended without lowering himself. It is, however, somewhat remarkable that no Flattery was so welcome to him as that which told him he had the Mind or Manners of a *Gentleman*, which he always said was the most complete & the most difficult to obtain: one said an Officer had commonly the Manner of a Gentleman. 'On the contrary,' says Johnson, 'he is generally branded very deeply with the mark of his Profession, now it is the Essence of A Gentleman's Character to have no professional Mark whatever.' 'An Officer,' added he, 'is seldom *bright* indeed, but he is almost always *smooth*. Talking on upon this Subject, he named Mr Berenger[13] as particularly elegant in his Carriage and Behaviour, but on my objecting his resemblance to the Gentlemen in Congreve's Comedies, and that he rather seemed to *play* the Man of Fashion than to *be* it, he changed him for Tom Hervey[14] who is dead & gone, and was doubtless as completely a Gentleman as one shall ever know.

Mr Johnson used to say that bright Parts were like Gold, common Sense like Iron, but more of this in the *Idler*. The *Idlers* came out without his name to them, & without Mottoes; he talks of publishing them sometime with Mottoes and bid me choose proper ones; I did fit about 20 Numbers in some Humour, & wrote them on a Card which I have now lost, and so the Scheme like many a greater, dropped to nothing. Here is another of his Schemes which will fall to nothing: 'My heart,' says he yesterday, 'is set upon seeing the Chartreuse in company with my Mistress.' We *will* go sometime, that's certain.' Then, replied I – whose Heart is set on very different Projects – we must write Verses to leave behind us. 'Well,' returned he, 'few People's Verses will be better than ours, we need not stay at home for want of *poetical* Powers: but are you willing to go?' No, Sir, said I gravely: are you unwilling? 'Yes, Sir,' in the same Accent. 'Then,' says he, 'I'll work up my Master to make you go, for go we will.' Johnson was in some Respects a very good Travelling Companion: The Rain & the Sun, the Night and the Day, were the same to him, and he had no Care about Food, Hours or Accommodations; but then he expected that nobody else should have any neither, and felt no sort of Compassion for one's Fatigue, or uneasiness, or Confinement in the Carriage, 'for nobody ever talks of such Stuff,' says he, 'except the

People who have nothing else to say, & if one *said* nothing, why it is because you *feel* nothing to be sure,' says he.

Mr Johnson had, ever since I knew him, an enthusiastic fondness for Poetry, indeed for all sorts of Literature; and had a respect for a Club he belonged to, that was little less than ridiculous. 'Our Club, Madam,' said he, 'is a Society which can scarcely be matched in the World. We have Reynolds for Painting, Goldsmith for Poetry, Percy for Antiquities, Nugent for Physic; Chamier for Trade, Politics and all Money Concerns; Mr Burke for Oratory, Mr Beauclerk for Polite Literature, Dyer for Modern History & Travels, Chambers for the Law, Langton for Ecclesiastical History & indeed all Branches of Learning, Sir John Hawkins for Judicature & ancient Music.[15] I have forgotten the other Members & his Eulogiums upon them; but many are dead, & new members have come in – I suppose against his Consent – for he now says the Club is spoiled. He had, however, no Taste for Modern Poetry – Gray, Mason[16] &c. – 'Modern Poetry,' says he one day at our house, 'is like Modern Gardening, everything now is raised by a hot bed; everything therefore is forced, & everything tasteless.'

One may therefore, without much difficulty, conceive how his Friend Grierson must have offended him when he observed that a Cook was a more excellent & useful Being than a Poet. 'Ay,' replies Johnson, 'and in that Opinion, all the Dogs in the Town will join with you.' *A propos* to Gardening, he once advised me to buy myself some famous Book upon the Subject, 'and read it,' says he, 'attentively, but do not believe it; use the World likewise as a large book, but use it with the same Restriction.' One cannot be sorry for the Rebuff given to Grierson, but it was cruel to Mrs Langton when she showed him her grotto, & asked if he did not think it a pretty convenient habitation? 'Yes, Madam,' replied he, 'for a Toad.' The Abbé Renard or Reinel[17] I forget his Name, who had published some Infidel Writings, was at a house and in a Room with Johnson – I think it was Paradise's. 'Sir,' says the Master of the Family, 'will you permit me to introduce to you the Abbé Reinel – he had the Man in his hand too. '*No, Sir,*' replies the Doctor, & turns away in a Huff. In the same spirit, when young Cholmondeley rode up to our Carriage as we drove through Derbyshire, Mr Thrale, seeing him address Johnson in a Style civilly familiar, & knowing them to be acquainted, tapped the Doctor, who was reading, & said 'Sir, that is Mr Cholmondeley.' 'Well, Sir,' replies Johnson, raising His Eyes from the Book, 'and *what if it is* Mr Cholmondeley!'

Mr Johnson's bodily Strength & Figure has not yet been mentioned; his Height was five Foot eleven without Shoes, his Neck short, his Bones large & His Shoulders broad: his Leg & Foot eminently handsome, his hand handsome too, in spite of Dirt, & of such Deformity as perpetually picking his Fingers necessarily produced. His Countenance was rugged, though many People pretended to see a benignity of Expression when he was in Good humour. Garrick tells a Story how at a strolling Play in some Country Town, a young Fellow took away Johnson's Chair which he had quitted for five minutes, & seated himself in it on the Stage. When the original Possessor returned, he desired him to leave his Chair, which he refused, & claimed it as his own. Johnson did not offer to dispute the Matter, but, lifting up Man & Chair, and all together in his Arms, took & threw them at one Jerk into the Pit. Beauclerk tells a Story of him that he had two large Pointers brought into the Parlour on some Occasion to show his Company, and they immediately fastening on one another alarmed the People present not a little with their ferocity, till Johnson gravely laying hold on each Dog by the Scuff of the Neck, held them asunder at Arm's length, and said 'Come, Gentlemen, where is your difficulty? Put one of them out at one Door, & the other out of the other. & let us go on with our Conversation.' He confirmed these two Stories himself to me before I would write them down. I saw him myself once throw over a Bathing Tub full of Water, which two of the Footmen had tried in vain to overturn, 'but,' says he, 'these Fellows have no more strength than Cats'. As an Instance of his Activity, I will only mention that one day after riding very hard for fifty Miles after Mr Thrale's Foxhounds – they were sitting and talking over the Chase when Dinner was done in our blue Room at Streatham – I mentioned some Leap they spoke of as difficult. 'No more,' says Johnson, 'than leaping over that stool' – it was a Cabriolet that stood between the Windows – which, says I, would not be a very easy Operation to you, I believe, after fifty Miles Galloping – & in Boots too. He said no more, but jumped fairly over it, & so did Mr Thrale, who is however full twenty Years younger than the Doctor. Johnson loved a Frolic or a Joke well enough, though he had strange serious Rules about them too, and very angry was he always at poor me for being merry at improper times and Places. 'You care for nothing,' says he, 'so you can crack your Joke.' One Day, to be sure, I was saucy in that way & he was very much affronted: my friend Mrs Strickland and he were entered into a Dispute on whose Dress was most expensive – a Gentleman's or a Lady's. Mrs Strickland instanced Lady Townsend's Extravagance, & said She knew of her having a new Cloak of eight Guineas Value every three Months. 'A Cloak, Madam!' cries Johnson, & was going to make a serious Answer. Why, Lord bless me, what does a Young Girl marry an old Lord *for*, said I, but for a *Cloak*? He did not like to be served so.

In the same manner, when a foolish Fellow had fretted him one day at Chester, showing him the Curiosities of the place, & yet running from Thing to thing, so that he had no Time to see any distinctly: 'What is this Gentleman's Name?' says Johnson to me gravely. His Name is Harold, I understand, replied I, and I fancy for my Part that we should call him *Harold Harefoot*. 'That Joke is so good,' says the Doctor, 'that you are Glad he has plagued us so – to bring it in.'

Mr Johnson had a consummate Knowledge of Figures and an uncommon delight in Arithmetical Speculations; he had too a singular Power of withdrawing his Attention from the prattle he heard round him, and would often sit amusing himself with calculating Sums while there was a Noise in the room enough to perplex any common Mortal, & prevent their Thinking at all: he used indeed to be always tormenting one with showing how much Time might be lost by squandering two hours a day, how much Money might be saved by laying up five Shillings a day, how many Lines might be written by putting down only ten every day with a hundred such-like Propositions. One Time that he was greatly indisposed at our house with the Spasms in his Stomach, which tormented him so long, he found himself unable to bear Company, & so sat alone in the next Room, & made an odd Calculation: no other than that the National Debt, setting it at 130 Millions Sterling would, if converted into Silver make a Meridian of that metal for the real Globe of the Earth – this might be called the *Meridian* of *London* very properly. I mentioned to him one day Soame Jennings's Refutation of Paschal, as thus: 'Infinity', says the French Geometrician, 'though on all sides astonishing, is most so when connected with numbers; for the Idea of infinite Number – & infinite number we know *there is* – can hardly find room in the human Mind, but stretches it still more than the Idea of infinite Space.' Our English Philosopher on the other hand exclaims – I mean Soame Jennings[18] – 'Let no man give his tongue leave to talk of infinite Number, for infinite Number is a Contradiction in Terms; if [it] is Numbered, it is not infinite I'll warrant it.' What do *you* say to these contenders, Mr Johnson? 'Why, *I* say,' replied he, 'that *Numeration* is infinite, for eternity might be employed in adding Figure to Figure, or if you will better comprehend me, Unit to Unit; but each Number is *finite*, which the possibility of doubling it easily proves; besides, stop where you will; you will find yourself as far from Infinitude as ever.' So much for his Arithmetic.

With regard to Virtue, I can only say that he was uniformly, not capriciously good; nor thought it right to load Life with unnecessary Scruples. 'Scruples,' says he, 'seldom make a Man good, but they certainly make him miserable.' He had, however, very piously and judiciously scrupled among the various Authorities he quotes in his *Dictionary* ever to give one from an immoral or an Infidel Writer, 'lest,' says he, 'the Quotation should send People to look in an Author that might taint their Virtue, or poison their Principles.' Somebody complimented Mr Johnson on his *Dictionary*, & said he had done more than forty Frenchmen. 'Why, what could you expect,' replied he, 'from Fellows that eat Frogs?' I dare say this is mentioned before, but I write from Memory, & can neither recollect every Trifle, nor turn back to see whether it is down or no. I know not whether I put it into this Book or no, but Johnson always hated his Schoolmaster – a Mr Hunter of

Stourbridge, I think his name was, and I have heard him say that the hatred was reciprocal – he left that Hunter at the Age of 18, and spent a Year at Oxford where he felt, I find, and I am sure he *expressed*, most sovereign Contempt for his Instructors. I must here have a Stroke at his Political Opinions, though God knows he has not left them dubious until *now*. He is a Tory in what he calls the truest sense of the Word, and is strongly attached to the notion of Divine & Hereditary Right inherent in Kings: he was therefore a *Jacobite* while *Jacob* existed, or any of his Progeny was likely to sit on the Throne: he is now however firmly attached to the present Royal Family; not from change of Principles, but difference of Situations, and he is as zealous that *this* King should maintain his Prerogatives, as if he belonged to the exiled Family. His Aversion to a Presbyterian is great, to a consistent, Whig as he often calls a Deist, it is still greater, we mentioned Alderman Trecothick's[19] having behaved oddly on some Occasion: 'Is he not a Citizen of London, a Native of North America, a *Whig?*' says Mr Johnson. 'Let him be absurd, I beg of you. When a Monkey is *too* like a Man, he shocks one.' A Contempt for small Matters – & he thinks few great – is, however, a Characteristick of Mr Johnson in all Things, Politics not excepted; so that now the popular Clamour runs so high about our Disgraces in America, our Debt at home, our Terrors of a Bankruptcy, & Fears of a French War. 'What signifies all this Canting?' says the Doctor. 'The World goes on just as it did; who eats the less? Or who sleeps the worse? Or where is all this *Consternation* you talk of – but in the News papers. Nobody is thinking or feeling about the matter, otherwise than it is somewhat to talk about.' I was one Day exalting the Character of a Statesman, & expatiating on the Skill required to direct the different departments, reconcile the jarring Interests, &c. 'Thus,' replies Mr Johnson, 'a *Mill* is a curious Construction enough, but the Water is no part of the Workmanship.'

I was, in another Humour, lamenting how all public Business was left to Clerks – Jerry Sneyd, said I, & Tom Cotton – pretty Fellows to have any Direction in State Affairs. 'You may as well,' answered he, 'complain that the Account of Time should be kept by the Clock; for to be sure he is no considerable Chronologer.' Of the Conduct of Lord Chatham, he observed the other day that Ambition in its last ramifications ends in Vanity, as an Old Oak at last puts forth nothing but Twigs & Leaves.

A propos to Johnson's contempt of Trifles, in November 1769 a female Servant in Our house was suspected of murdering her Bastard. The same Day, Baretti was taken up for killing a Man in the streets.[20] Our Gentlemen were running from Coroner to Coroner, when Seward observed how licentious the Times were grown, for see now, says he, if the Bird catchers be not out though it is Sunday. Since this Speech was made, I hardly ever dare lament Distresses of which the Consequences

are at least distant, if not uncertain; for if I do, Mr Johnson is sure to
remind me of the Iniquity of catching Birds on a Sunday.

One Evening, as I was giving my Tongue Liberty to praise Mr Johnson
to his Face, a favour he would not often allow me, he said in high good
humour, 'come! You shall draw up my Character your own Way, &
show it me; that I may see what you will say of me when I am gone.' At
Night I wrote as follows.

   It is usual, I know not why, when a Character is given, to begin with a
Description of the Person: that which contained the Soul of Mr Johnson,
deserves to be particularly described. His Stature was remarkably high,
and his Limbs exceedingly large; his Strength was more than common, I
believe, & his Activity was greater than his Size gave one Cause to
expect. His Features were strongly marked, though his Complexion was
fair, a Circumstance somewhat unusual; his Sight was near, and
otherwise imperfect, yet his Eyes, though of a light blue Colour, were so
wild, so piercing, and at Times so fierce; that Fear was, I believe, the first
Emotion in the hearts of all his Beholders.

   His Mind was so Comprehensive that no Language but his own could
have expressed its Contents, & so ponderous was his Language that
Sentiments less lofty & less solid than his would have been encumbered,
not adorned by it. Mr Johnson was, however, no pompous Converser, &
though he was accused of using big Words, it was only when little ones
would not express his meaning as clearly, or when the Elevation of the
thought would have been disgraced by a Dress less superb. He used to
say that the size of a man's Understanding might always be known by his
Mirth, and his own was never contemptible: he would laugh at a Stroke
of Absurdity, or a Saillie of genuine Humour more heartily than I almost
ever saw a man, and though the Jest was often such as few felt besides
himself, yet his Laugh was irresistible, & was observed immediately to
produce that of the Company, not merely from the notion that it was
proper to laugh when he did, but purely for want of Power to forbear it.
He was no Enemy to Splendour of Apparel, or Pomp of Equipage. 'Life,'
he would say sometimes, 'is but too barren with all her Trappings; let us
therefore be cautious how we strip her.' Mr Johnson had indeed, when I
knew him first, looked on Life until he was weary; for as a Mind slow in
its own nature, or unenlivened by Information, will contentedly read in
the same Book for twenty Times perhaps, the very Effort of reading it
being more than half the business, & every Period being at every
Reading better understood; while a Mind more active or more skilful to
comprehend its meaning is made sincerely sick at the second Perusal; so
a Soul like his, acute to discern the Truth, vigorous to embrace, and
powerful to retain it, soon sees enough of the World's dull Prospect,
which at first, like that of the Sea, pleases by its Extent, but soon, like that
too, fatigues from its Uniformity: a Calm and a Storm being the only

Variations which the Nature of either will admit of. Of Mr Johnson's Learning the World has been the Judge, and were I to produce a score of his sayings as a Proof of his Wit, it would be like showing a handful of Oriental pearl to evince the Riches of the great Mogul. Suffice it at once that he was great on all Occasions, and like a Cube in Architecture you beheld him on each Side, & his Size still appeared undiminished. The heart of this Man was, however, not a hard one, but susceptible of Gratitude, & of every kind impression. Yet though he had refined his Sensibility, he had not endangered his quiet by encouraging in himself a Solicitude about Trifles, which he treated with the neglect they Deserve. It is well known that Mr Johnson had a roughness in his Manner which subdued the saucy & terrified the Meek; this was, when I knew him, the prominent Part of a Character, which few durst venture to approach so nearly, & which was for that Reason in many Respects so grossly, and so frequently mistaken, & it was perhaps peculiar to him that the noble Consciousness of Superiority which animated his Looks, and raised his Voice in Conversation, cast likewise an impenetrable Veil over him when he said nothing. His talk had therefore commonly the Complexion of Arrogance, his Silence of Superciliousness: he was, however, seldom inclined to be silent when any Moral or Literary Subject was proposed, & it was on such occasions that like the Sage in Rasselas he spoke & Attention watched his Lips; he reasoned and Conviction closed his periods.[21] If Poetry was talked of, his Quotations were the readiest; & had he not been eminent for more solid & brilliant Qualities, Mankind would have united to extol his extraordinary Memory. His manner of repeating, too, deserves to be described, though at the same time it defeats all Power of Description. His Equity in giving the Character of another ought not undoubtedly to be omitted in his own, whence Partiality and Prejudice were totally excluded; a Steadiness of Conduct the more to be commended, as no Man had stronger Likings or Aversions. His Veracity was, indeed, on all occasions strict even to severity; he scorned to embellish a Story with fictitious Circumstances which he used to say took off from its real Value. 'A Story,' says Johnson, 'should be a Specimen of Life and Manners; but if the surrounding Circumstances are false, as it is no longer any Representation of Reality it is no longer worthy of our Attention'.

For the rest; that Beneficence which during his Life increased the Comforts of so many, may after his Death be ungratefully forgotten; but that Piety which dictated the serious Papers in the *Rambler* will be forever remembered, forever, I think, revered. That ample Repository of religious Truth, moral Wisdom & accurate Criticism breathes indeed the genuine Emanations of its Author's Mind; expressed, too, in a Style so natural to him, & so much like his common Mode of conversing, that I was myself not much astonished when he told me that he had scarcely read over one of those inimitable Essays before they were sent to the Press. I shall add one peculiarity before I finish his Character. Though a man of obscure Birth, His partiality to People of Family was visible on every Occasion; his Zeal for Subordination warm even to Bigotry; his hatred for Innovation & Reverence for the old feudal Times, apparent whenever any possible means of showing them occurred. I have spoken of his Piety, his Charity & his Truth; the Enlargement of his Heart, & the Delicacy of his Sentiments; & when I search for the Blemishes in a Character so complete, none will present itself to my Sight, but Pride modified differently, as different Opportunities showed it in different Forms; yet his Pride was ever nicely purified at once from meanness and from Vanity. The mind of Mr Johnson was indeed expanded beyond the common Limits of human Nature, & stored with such variety of Knowledge that I used to think it resembled a Royal Pleasure Ground, where every Tree, of every Name & Nation, flourished in the full perfection of their Nature; where though lofty Woods & falling Cataracts first caught the Eye, & fixed the Attention of Beholders, yet neither the trim Parterre, nor the pleasing Shrubbery; nor even the antiquated Evergreens were denied a Place in some fit Corner of the happy Valley. When I showed him his Character next day – for he would see it – he said it was a very fine Piece of Writing, and that I had improved upon *Young*, who he saw was my *Model*, he said; for my Flattery was still stronger than *his*, & yet somehow or other less *hyperbolical*.

Streatham 1 May 1781] I have now appointed three Days a Week to attend at the counting house, & wish I could defecate my Mind of Borough Dirt, when I pass the Laystalls at the Stones End; but it will not be yet, it will not be:

> The *vile* Ideas where I fly pursue:
> Rise in the *Grove*, even in the *Thicket* rise,
> *Stain* all my Soul, and *grovel* in my Eyes.[22]

  If an Angel from Heaven had told me 20 Years ago, that the Man I knew by the Name of *Dictionary Johnson* should one Day become Partner with me in a great Trade, & that we should jointly or separately sign Notes, Draughts, &c., for 3 or 4 Thousand Pounds of a Morning, how unlikely it would have seemed ever to happen! Unlikely is no Word though – it would have seemed incredible: neither of us then being worth a Groat, God knows, & both as immeasurably removed from Commerce as Birth, Literature & Inclination could set us. Johnson, however, who desires above all other Good the Accumulation of new Ideas, is but too happy with his present Employment; & the Influence I have over him added to his own solid Judgment and Regard for Truth, will at last find it *in a small degree* difficult to win him from the dirty Delight of seeing his Name in a new Character flaming away at the bottom of Bonds & Leases.

NOTES

Mrs Hester Lynch Thrale (1741–1821), née Salusbury, subsequently Mrs Piozzi, married the wealthy gentleman-brewer Henry Thrale (?1729–81) against her inclinations in 1763. She became a well-known hostess and met Johnson on 9 or 10 January 1765. The Thrales' country home at Streatham Park (demolished 1863), which stood in an estate of 89 acres, became a favourite resort of his; he had his own room there and spent a good deal of time with the Thrales from 1765. He also accompanied them on their tours of Wales (1774) and France (1775): see pp. 131 and 132. After Thrale's death, to Johnson's distress and disgust, Mrs Thrale married Gabriel Piozzi, an Italian musician and a Roman Catholic. The Streatham period was one of great happiness for Johnson: living during his visits there in considerable luxury, and surrounded by admirers, he was able to give full rein to his gifts for sociability and conversation. For a full account, see J. L. Clifford, *Hester Lynch Piozzi* (2nd edn, 1952).

Thraliana is a compound of anecdotes, sayings and quotations – in the words of its editor, both 'a wit's catch-all' and 'a private record of her life'. It contains much of interest concerning Johnson, in connection with whom Mrs Thrale seems to have been collecting and writing down stories from at least as early as 1768. (Boswell asked her, no doubt in vain, on 30 August 1776 to 'transmit to me sometimes a few of the admirable sayings which you collect'.) Mrs Piozzi was living in Milan with her new husband when Johnson died, and the news did not reach her until late January 1785. As Professor Balderston has shown, she evidently had *Thraliana* with her there, and used it as a basis for her *Anecdotes of Dr Johnson* (excerpted in this volume), which were begun within a few weeks and finished by September of the same year.

There are grounds for believing that the account of Johnson given in the *Anecdotes* was subjected to some retouching, and that a more authentic record is to be found in *Thraliana*. There are certainly some significant variations: to cite only one small example, in *Thraliana* she has Johnson declare, on the subject of his biographers, that he will 'either outlive them all or write my Life myself' (dated 18 July 1773 and written down 'that night'); in the *Anecdotes* this becomes 'and either make you write the life . . . or, which is better, do it myself'. Professor Balderston's conclusion is that 'Boswell's charge of inaccuracy against the *Anecdotes* is, in the narrow sense, amply sustained by the evidence' (p. xxvii). In a few instances, both versions of an episode or speech – the earlier one of *Thraliana* and the later one of *Anecdotes* – have been given in the selections included in the present volume in order to suggest the modifications that were introduced.

1. See p. 33, note 3.

2. Dr J. Taylor (1711–88), 'a wealthy well-beneficed clergyman' (Boswell) of Ashbourne in Derbyshire, had been at school with Johnson, who visited him in March 1776. Dr R. James (1705–76), another schoolfellow of Johnson's, became

a physician and published a *Medicinal Dictionary* (1743), for which Johnson wrote the dedication. On Hector and Adams, see pp. 9 and 12.

3. Dr John Hawkesworth (?1715–73) was, according to Boswell, a 'warm admirer' of Johnson and 'a studious imitator of his style' who 'lived in great intimacy with him' in about 1752, and was an original member of the first of Johnson's clubs, held at the King's Head in Ivy Lane. Johnson contributed to Hawkesworth's periodical *The Adventurer* (1752–4), which was modelled on his own *Rambler*.

4. 'Abandon hope all ye who enter' (Dante, *Inferno*, iii, 9).

5. Bernard de Mandeville (1670–1733), author of *The Fable of the Bees* (1714) and other works.

6. Miss Hill Boothby (1708–56), a friend of Johnson's youth.

7. Dr Richard Bathurst, a member of the Ivy Lane Club, was an army physician who died in Havana in 1762.

8. These members of Johnson's household are, respectively, Mrs Anna Williams ('a blind woman') (1706–83), a friend of Johnson's wife who remained in his home and served as his housekeeper for over thirty years (see also p. 60, note 1); Francis (Frank) Barber ('a Blackamoor') (?1745–1801), Johnson's negro servant, who attended him in his last illness and became his residuary legatee; Poll Carmichael; Mrs Desmoulins (b. 1716), daughter of Johnson's godfather, Dr Swinfen (with Frank Barber, she was at Johnson's bedside when he died; on her son John, one of the witnesses of Johnson's will, see p. 163, note 14); Robert Levet (or Levett or Levit) (1705–82), whose death was the occasion for one of the finest of Johnson's shorter poems ('Condemned to hope's delusive mine'). Johnson's charity and forbearance were not lessened by what Boswell nicely calls 'the perpetual jarring' of the inmates of his home: Boswell quotes Johnson as saying (in a letter to Mrs Thrale) that 'Williams hates every body; Levet hates Desmoulins, and does not love Williams; Desmoulins hates them both; Poll loves none of them'.

9. Thomas Johnson (d. 1779), son of Andrew Johnson.

10. Elizabeth Herne, actually a second cousin, was a lunatic and Johnson contributed to her maintenance in an asylum at Bethnal Green.

11. An alley situated between Chandos Street and the Strand, well known for its cooks' shops catering for lower-class customers.

12. Residue, waste matter.

13. Richard Berenger (d. 1782), gentleman of the horse to George iii for many years and, according to the *DNB*, 'famous in his day for his charm in social life'.

14. The Hon. Thomas Hervey (1699–1775), second son of the Earl of Bristol; his brother Henry was an early friend of Johnson's.

15. Under the date February 1764, Boswell lists the original nine members of the Literary Club, which was formed at that time and met weekly at the Turk's Head in Gerrard Street. Among the founding members were Dr Christopher Nugent (d. 1775), physician; Topham Beauclerk (1739–80), a man of means and aristocratic family who had met Johnson in 1757; Anthony Chamier (1725–80), later an MP and under-secretary of state; and Bennet Langton (1737–1801), a classical scholar whom Johnson visited in Oxford in 1759. Samuel Dyer (1725–72), translator, and Sir Robert Chambers (1737–1803), Indian judge, were among those who joined later. The others named by Mrs Thrale are the subject of notes elsewhere or are too well-known to need explanation.

16. The Revd William Mason (1724–97), poet and biographer of Gray.

17. The Abbé du Resnel (or Raynal) published *Analyse de l'histoire philosophique et politique des établissements et du commerce des Européens dans les deux Indes* (1770).

18. Soame Jenyns (1704–87): the reference is to his *A Free Enquiry into the Nature and Origin of Evil* (1757), which Johnson had attacked in a review in the *Literary Magazine,* Jenyns' optimism being profoundly uncongenial to his own view of human suffering.

19. Trecothick, a merchant involved in trading with America, was not in fact an American. G. B. Hill suggests that Mrs Thrale has given his name in error for that of William Lee (1739–95), a Virginian, who met Johnson on 15 May 1776 and to whose lamentation (reported by Boswell) that 'Poor old England is lost', Johnson replied, 'Sir, it is not so much to be lamented that Old England is lost, as that the Scots have found it'.

20. See p. 88.

21. The reference is to chap. 18 of Johnson's *Rasselas*.

22. Adapted from Pope's *Eloisa to Abelard*, lines 264–6.

Life at Streatham II*

THOMAS CAMPBELL

16 [March 1775] – a fair day – dined with Mr Thrale along with Dr Johnson and Baretti.... Johnson, you are the very man Lord Chesterfield describes. A Hottentot indeed.[1] And though your abilities are respectable, you never can be respected yourself. He has the aspect of an idiot – without the faintest ray of sense gleaming from any one feature. With the most awkward garb & unpowdered grey wig on one side only of his head, he is forever dancing the devil's jig, & sometimes he makes the most drivelling effort to whistle some thought in his absent paroxisms. He came up to me & took me by the hand – then sat down on a sofa, & mumbled out that he had heard two papers had appeared against him in the course of this week – one of which was that he was to go to Ireland next Summer in order to abuse the hospitality of that place also, &c. His awkwardness at table is just what Chesterfield described, & his roughness of manners kept pace with that. When Mrs Thrale quoted something from *Foster's Sermons*[2] he flew in a passion & said that Foster was a man of mean ability, & of no original thinking. All which though I took to be most true yet I held it not meet to have it to set down. He said that he looked upon Burke to be the author of Junius,[3] & that though he would

* *Dr Campbell's Diary of a Visit to England in 1775,* ed. James L. Clifford (Cambridge, 1947) pp. 53–5, 67–9, 76–7.

not take him *contra mundum*, yet he would take him against any man –
Baretti was of the same mind, though he mentioned a fact which made
against the opinion; which was that a paper having appeared against
Junius, as on this day, a Junius came out in answer to that the very next –
when (everybody knew) Burke was in Yorkshire. But all the Junius's
were evidently not written by the same hand. Burke's brother is a good
writer, though nothing like Edmund. The Doctor – as he drinks no wine
– retired soon after dinner – & Baretti, who, I see, is a sort of literary
toad-eater to Johnson, told me that he was a man nowise affected by
praise or dispraise & that the journey to the Hebrides would never have
been published but for himself. The Doctor, however, returned again, &
with all the fond anxiety of an author I saw him cast out all his nets to
know the sense of the town about his last pamphlet *Taxation no Tyranny*[4] –
which he said did not sell. Mr Thrale told him such & such members of
both houses admired it. 'And why did you not tell me this?' quoth
Johnson. Thrale asked him what Sir Joshua Reynolds said of it: 'Sir
Joshua,' quoth the Doctor, 'has not read it.' 'I suppose,' quoth Thrale,
'he has been busy of late.' 'No!' says the Doctor, 'but I never look at his
pictures, so he won't read my writings.' Was this like a man insensible to
glory? Thrale then asked him if he had got Miss Reynolds's opinion – for
she, it seems, is a politician. 'As to that,' quoth the Doctor, it is no great
matter, for she could not tell, after she had read it, on which side of the
question Mr Burke's speech was.' NB: We had a great deal of
conversation about A[rch] D[eacon] Congreve[5] – who was his
classfellow at Lichfield School. He talked of him as a man of great
coldness of mind, who could be two years in London without letting him
know it, until a few weeks ago, & then apologising by saying that he did
not know where to enquire for him. This plainly raised his indignation,
for he swelled to think that his celebrity should not be notorious to every
porter in the street. The Arch Deacon, he told me, has a sermon upon the
nature of moral good & evil preparing for the press, & should he die
before publication, he leaves £50 for that purpose. He said he read some
of it to him, but that as he had interrupted him to make some remarks, he
hopes never to be troubled with another rehearsal. . . .

April 1 – a fair day. Dined at Mr Thrale's – whom in proof of the
magnitude of London I cannot help remarking, no coachman (& this is
the third) I have called, could find without inquiry. – But this by the
way. – There was Murphy, Boswell & Baretti – the two last, as I learned,
just before they entered, are mortal foes so much so that Murphy & Mrs
Thrale agreed that Boswell expressed a desire that Baretti should be
hanged upon that unfortunate affair of his killing, &c.[6] Upon this hint, I
went, & without any sagacity, it was easily discernable for upon Baretti
entering, Boswell did not rise, & upon Baretti's descry of Boswell, he
grinned a perturbed glance. Politeness, however, smoothes the most

hostile brows – and theirs were smoothed. Johnson was the subject both before & after dinner – for it was the boast of all (but myself) that under that roof were the Doctor's first friends. His *bons mots* were retailed in such plenty that they like a surfeit could not lie upon my memory – Boswell arguing in favour of a chearful glass, adduced the maxim *in vino veritas* – 'well,' says Johnson, '& what then unless a man has lived a lye.' – Boswell then urged that it made a man forget all his cares. 'That to be sure,' says Johnson, 'might be of use if a man sat by such a person as *you*.' Boswell confessed that he liked a glass of whiskey in the Highland tour & used to take it – at length says Johnson 'let me try *wherein the pleasure of a Scotsman consists*', & so tips off a brimmer of whiskey. But Johnson's abstemiousness is new to him, for within a few years he would swallow two bottles of port without any apparent alteration, & once in the company with whom I dined this day he said: 'Pray, Mr Thrale, give us another bottle.' It is ridiculous to pry so nearly into the movements of such men – yet Boswell carries it to a degree of superstition. The Doctor, it seems, has a custom of putting the peel of oranges into his pocket, & he asked the Doctor what use he made of them. The Doctor's reply was that his dearest friend should not know that. This has made poor Boswell unhappy, & I verily think he is as anxious to know the secret as a green sick girl, &c. NB: The book wherewith Johnson presented the highland lady was Cocker's *Arithmetick* – Murphy gave it (on Garrick's authority) that when it was asked what was the greatest pleasure, Johnson answered f——g & the second was drinking. And therefore he wondered why there were not more drunkards, for all could drink though all could not f——k. But Garrick is his most intimate friend – they came to London together – & he is very correct in both his conduct & language. As a proof of this, they all agreed in a story of him & Dr James (who is, it seems, a very lewd fellow, both *verbo & facto*). James, it seems, in a coach with his whore, took up Johnson & set him down at a given place. Johnson, hearing afterward what the lady was, attacked James where next he met him, for carrying him about in such company. James apologised by saying that he always took a swelling in his stones[7] if he abstained a month, &c. 'Damn the rascal,' says Johnson, 'he is past sixty, the swelling would have gone no farther'.

Boswell, desirous of setting his native country off to the best advantage, expatiated upon the beauty of a certain prospect, particularly, upon a view of the sea. 'O, Sir,' says Johnson, *'the sea is the same everywhere.'* . . .

April 8 – very cold & some rain, but not enough to allay the blowing of the dust. Dined with Thrale where Dr Johnson was & Boswell (& Baretti as usual). The Doctor was not in as good spirits as he was at Dilly's. He had supped the night before with Lady ——, Miss Jeffrys, one of the maids of honour, Sir Joshua Reynolds, &c at Mrs Abbington's. He said

LIFE AT STREATHAM II

Sir C. Thompson & some others who were there spoke like people who had seen good company, & so did Mrs Abbington herself – who could not have seen good company.

He seems fond of Boswell, & yet he is always abusing the Scots before him, by way of joke. Talking of their nationality, he said they were not singular, the negroes & Jews being so too. Boswell lamented there was no good map of Scotland. 'There never can be a good of Scotland,' says the Doctor, sententiously. This excited Boswell to ask wherefore. 'Why, Sir, to measure land a man must go over it; but who could think of going over Scotland?'

When Dr Goldsmith was mentioned & Dr Percy's intention of writing his life, he expressed his approbation strongly, adding that Goldsmith was the best writer he ever knew upon every subject he wrote upon.

He said that Kendric[8] had borrowed all his *Dictionary* from him. 'Why,' says Boswell, 'every man who writes a dictionary must borrow.' 'No! Sir,' says Johnson, 'that is not necessary.' 'Why,' says Boswell, 'have not you a great deal in common with those who wrote before you?' 'Yes, Sir,' says Johnson, 'I have the words. But my business was not to *make* words but to explain them.'

NOTES

Thomas Campbell (1733–95), Irish clergyman, visited England in 1775 and met Johnson at the Thrales' house on 16 March of that year. His diary for the period 23 February–9 May contains many references to Johnson. He visited England again in 1776–7 and in 1781, and saw Johnson on both occasions. By the time of his fourth visit in 1786, Johnson was dead. Campbell's diary of his first visit turned up in Sydney over half a century after his own death, and was published, with expurgations, as *Diary of a Visit to England in 1775, by an Irishman . . .* (Sydney, 1854). When copies reached England, Macaulay judged it genuine and found it interesting; later, Benjamin Jowett dismissed it as a forgery. Campbell's animus against Johnson is sometimes obvious, and his reliability in reporting conversations may be of no higher standard than his spelling. Boswell's *Life* contains half-a-dozen references to 'the Irish Dr Campbell'.

  1. The allusion is to one of Chesterfield's letters, in which the character of 'a respectable Hottentot' was, as Boswell says, 'generally understood to be meant for Johnson'.

  2. Dr James Foster (1697–1753), celebrated preacher.

  3. Junius was the pseudonym of the author (still not definitively identified) of a series of letters on political topics published in 1769–72. Burke was one of numerous persons to whom their authorship was at various times attributed.

  4. Johnson's pamphlet on the question of American taxation and representation had appeared earlier in the year.

  5. The Revd Charles Congreve (1708–77). Johnson saw him again in his later years: for his amusing account of Congreve's valetudinarian state, see Boswell's narrative under 22 March 1776.

6. Joseph (Giuseppi) Baretti (1719–89) came to London from Turin, published an English–Italian dictionary with a dedication by Johnson (1760), and was a regular visitor at Streatham Park as well as a tutor to the Thrale children. He accompanied the Thrales and Johnson to France in 1768. When in 1769 he was charged with killing a man in a street fight, Johnson was among those who visited him in Newgate and appeared as character witnesses at his trial on 20 October 1769 (he was acquitted).

7. Testicles.

8. William Kenrick (?1725–79) published an English dictionary in 1773; he had earlier attacked Johnson's edition of Shakespeare.

Life at Streatham III*

FANNY BURNEY

[The first extract is dated August 1778; most of the others are from the same year, except the last three, which belong to 1782.]

When we were summoned to dinner, Mrs Thrale made my father and me sit on each side of her. I said that I hoped I did not take Dr Johnson's place; for he had not yet appeared.

'No,' answered Mrs Thrale, 'he will sit by you, which I am sure will give him great pleasure.'

Soon after we were seated, this great man entered. I have so true a veneration for him, that the very sight of him inspires me with delight and reverence, notwithstanding the cruel infirmities to which he is subject; for he has almost perpetual convulsive movements of his hands, lips, feet or knees, and sometimes of all together.

Mrs Thrale introduced me to him, and he took his place. We had a noble dinner, and a most elegant dessert. Dr Johnson, in the middle of dinner, asked Mrs Thrale what was in some little pies that were near him.

'Mutton,' answered she, 'so I don't ask you to eat any, because I know you despise it.'

'No, madam, no,' cried he; 'I despise nothing that is good of its sort; but I am too proud now to eat of it. Sitting by Miss Burney makes me very proud to-day!'

'Miss Burney,' said Mrs Thrale, laughing, 'you must take great care of

* *Diary and Letters of Madame d'Arblay (1778–1840)*, ed. Charlotte Barrett (1904) i, 55–9, 67–72, 81–3, 111–15, 147, 245–7; ii, 107–9, 114–15, 159–60.

your heart if Dr Johnson attacks it; for I assure you he is not often
successless.'

'What's that you say, madam?' cried he; 'are you making mischief
between the young lady and me already?'

A little while after he drank Mrs Thrale's health and mine, and then
added: ''Tis a terrible thing that we cannot wish young ladies well,
without wishing them to become old women!'

'But some people,' said Mr Seward,[1] 'are old and young at the same
time, for they wear so well that they never look old.'

'No, sir, no,' cried the Doctor, laughing; 'that never yet was; you might
as well say they are at the same time tall and short. I remember an
epitaph to that purpose, which is in ——.' (I have quite forgot what, and
also the name it was made upon, but the rest I recollect exactly):

> —— lies buried here;
> So early wise, so lasting fair,
> That none, unless her years you told,
> Thought her a child, or thought her old.

Mrs Thrale then repeated some lines in French, and Dr Johnson some
more in Latin. An epilogue of Mr Garrick's to *Bonduca*[2] was then
mentioned, and Dr Johnson said it was a miserable performance, and
everybody agreed it was the worst he had ever made.

'And yet,' said Mr Seward, 'it has been very much admired; but it is in
praise of English valour, and so I suppose the subject made it popular.'

'I don't know, sir,' said Dr Johnson, 'anything about the subject, for I
could not read on till I came to it; I got through half a dozen lines, but I
could observe no other subject than eternal dullness. I don't know what
is the matter with David; I am afraid he is grown superannuated, for his
prologues and epilogues used to be incomparable.'

'Nothing is so fatiguing,' said Mrs Thrale, 'as the life of a wit: he and
Wilkes[3] are the two oldest men of their ages I know; for they have both
worn themselves out, by being eternally on the rack to give
entertainment to others.'

'David, madam,' said the Doctor, 'looks much older than he is; for his
face has had double the business of any other man's; it is never at rest;
when he speaks one minute, he has quite a different countenance to what
he assumes the next; I don't believe he ever kept the same look for half an
hour together, in the whole course of his life; and such an eternal,
restless, fatiguing play of the muscles, must certainly wear out a man's
face before its real time.'

'Oh yes,' cried Mrs Thrale, 'we must certainly make some allowance
for such wear and tear of a man's face.'

The next name that was started, was that of Sir John Hawkins: and
Mrs Thrale said, 'Why now, Dr Johnson, he is another of those whom

you suffer nobody to abuse but yourself; Garrick is one, too; for if any other person speaks against him, you browbeat him in a minute!'

'Why, madam,' answered he, 'they don't know when to abuse him, and when to praise him; I will allow no man to speak ill of David that he does not deserve; and as to Sir John, why really I believe him to be an honest man at the bottom: but to be sure he is penurious, and he is mean, and it must be owned he has a degree of brutality, and a tendency to savageness, that cannot easily be defended.'

We all laughed, as he meant we should, at this curious manner of speaking in his favour, and he then related an anecdote that he said he knew to be true in regard to his meanness. He said that Sir John and he once belonged to the same club, but that as he ate no supper after the first night of his admission, he desired to be excused paying his share.

'And was he excused?'

'Oh yes; for no man is angry at another for being inferior to himself! We all scorned him, and admitted his plea. For my part I was such a fool as to pay my share for wine, though I never tasted any. But Sir John was a most *unclubable* man!'

[How delighted was I to hear this master of languages so unaffectedly and sociably and good-naturedly make words, for the promotion of sport and good humour.]

'And this,' continued he, 'reminds me of a gentleman and lady with whom I travelled once; I suppose I must call them gentleman and lady, according to form, because they travelled in their own coach and four horses. But at the first inn where we stopped, the lady called for – a pint of ale! And when it came, quarrelled with the waiter for not giving full measure. Now, Madame Duval[4] could not have done a grosser thing!'

Oh, how everybody laughed! And to be sure I did not glow at all, nor munch fast, nor look on my plate, nor lose any part of my usual composure! But how grateful do I feel to this dear Dr Johnson, for never naming me and the book as belonging one to the other, and yet making an allusion that showed his thoughts led to it, and, at the same time, that seemed to justify the character as being natural! But, indeed the delicacy I met with from him, and from all the 'Thrales, was yet more flattering to me than the praise with which I have heard they have honoured my book. . . .

Indeed, the freedom with which Dr Johnson condemns whatever he disapproves, is astonishing; and the strength of words he uses would, to most people, be intolerable; but Mrs Thrale seems to have a sweetness of disposition that equals all her other excellences, and far from making a point of vindicating herself, she generally receives his admonitions with the most respectful silence. . . .

But to return. Mrs Thrale then asked whether Mr Langton took any better care of his affairs than formerly?

'No, madam,' cried the Doctor, 'and never will; he complains of the ill effects of habit, and rests contentedly upon a confessed indolence. He told his father himself that he had "no turn to economy"; but a thief might as well plead that he had "no turn to honesty".'

Was not that excellent?

At night, Mrs Thrale asked if I would have anything? I answered, 'No'; but Dr Johnson said, 'Yes: she is used, madam, to suppers; she would like an egg or two, and a few slices of ham, or a rasher – a rasher, I believe, would please her better.'

How ridiculous! However, nothing could persuade Mrs Thrale not to have the cloth laid: and Dr Johnson was so facetious, that he challenged Mr Thrale to get drunk!

'I wish,' said he, 'my master would say to me, Johnson, if you will oblige me, you will call for a bottle of Toulon, and then we will set to it, glass for glass, till it is done; and after that, I will say, Thrale, if you will oblige me, you will call for another bottle of Toulon, and then we will set to it, glass for glass, till that is done: and by the time we should have drunk the two bottles, we should be so happy, and such good friends, that we should fly into each other's arms, and both together call for the third!'

I ate nothing, that they might not again use such a ceremony with me. Indeed, their late dinners forbid suppers, especially as Dr Johnson made me eat cake at tea, for he held it till I took it, with an odd or absent complaisance.

He was extremely comical after supper, and would not suffer Mrs Thrale and me to go to bed for near an hour after we made the motion. . . .

Now for this morning's breakfast.

Dr Johnson, as usual, came last into the library; he was in high spirits, and full of mirth and sport. I had the honour of sitting next to him: and now, all at once, he flung aside his reserve, thinking, perhaps, that it was time I should fling aside mine.

Mrs Thrale told him that she intended taking me to Mr T——'s.

'So you ought, madam,' cried he, "tis your business to be Cicerone to her.'

Then suddenly he snatched my hand, and, kissing it, 'Ah!' he added, 'they will little think what a tartar you carry to them!'

'No, that they won't!' cried Mrs Thrale; 'Miss Burney looks so meek and so quiet, nobody would suspect what a comical girl she is; but I believe she has a great deal of malice at heart.'

'Oh, she's a toad!'[5] cried the Doctor, laughing – 'a sly young rogue! With her Smiths and her Branghtons!'

'Why, Dr Johnson,' said Mrs Thrale, 'I hope you are very well this morning! If one may judge by your spirits and good humour, the fever you threatened us with is gone off.'

He had complained that he was going to be ill last night.

'Why no, madam, no,' answered he, 'I am not yet well; I could not sleep at all; there I lay restless and uneasy, and thinking all the time of Miss Burney. Perhaps I have offended her, thought I; perhaps she is angry; I have seen her but once, and I talked to her of a rasher! Were you angry?'

I think I need not tell you my answer.

'I have been endeavouring to find some excuse,' continued he, 'and, as I could not sleep, I got up, and looked for some authority for the word; and I find, madam, it is used by Dryden: in one of his prologues, he says 'And snatch a homely rasher from the coals'.[6] So you must not mind me, madam; I say strange things, but I mean no harm.'

I was almost afraid he thought I was really idiot enough to have taken him seriously; but, a few minutes after, he put his hand on my arm, and shaking his head, exclaimed, 'Oh, you are a sly little rogue! what a Holborn beau have you drawn!'

'Ay, Miss Burney,' said Mrs Thrale, 'the Holborn beau is Dr Johnson's favourite; and we have all your characters by heart, from Mr Smith up to Lady Louisa.'

'Oh, Mr Smith, Mr Smith is the man!' cried he, laughing violently. 'Harry Fielding never drew so good a character! Such a fine varnish of low politeness! Such a struggle to appear a gentleman! Madam, there is no character better drawn anywhere – in any book or by any author.'

I almost poked myself under the table. Never did I feel so delicious a confusion since I was born! But he added a great deal more, only I cannot recollect his exact words, and I do not choose to give him mine. . . .

And now let me try to recollect an account he gave us of certain celebrated ladies of his acquaintance: an account which, had you heard from himself, would have made you die with laughing, his manner is so peculiar, and enforces his humour so originally.

It was begun by Mrs Thrale's apologising to him for troubling him with some question she thought trifling – Oh, I remember! We had been talking of colours, and of the fantastic names given to them, and why the palest lilac should be called a *soupir étouffé*; and when Dr Johnson came in, she applied to him.

'Why, madam,' said he with wonderful readiness, 'it is called a stifled sigh because it is checked in its progress, and only half a colour.'

I could not help expressing my amazement at his universal readiness upon all subjects, and Mrs Thrale said to him, 'Sir, Miss Burney wonders at your patience with such stuff; but I tell her you are used to me, for I believe I torment you with more foolish questions than anybody else dares do.'

'No, madam,' said he, 'you don't torment me; you tease me, indeed, sometimes.'

'Ay, so I do, Dr Johnson, and I wonder you bear with my nonsense.'

'No, madam, you never talk nonsense; you have as much sense, and more wit, than any woman I know!'

'Oh,' cried Mrs Thrale, blushing, 'it is my turn to go under the table this morning, Miss Burney!'

'And yet,' continued the Doctor, with the most comical look, 'I have known all the wits, from Mrs Montagu down to Bet Flint!'[7]

'Bet Flint!' cried Mrs Thrale; 'pray who is she?'

'Oh, a fine character, madam! She was habitually a slut and a drunkard, and occasionally a thief and a harlot.'

'And, for Heaven's sake, how came you to know her?'

'Why, madam, she figured in the literary world, too! Bet Flint wrote her own life, and called herself Cassandra, and it was in verse. It began:

When Nature first ordained my birth,
A diminutive I was born on earth:
And then I came from a dark abode,
Into a gay and gaudy world.

'So Bet brought me her verses to correct; but I gave her half-a-crown, and she liked it as well. Bet had a fine spirit; she advertised for a husband, but she had no success, for she told me no man aspired to her! Then she hired very handsome lodgings and a footboy; and she got a harpsichord, but Bet could not play; however, she put herself in fine attitudes and drummed.'

Then he gave an account of another of these geniuses, who called herself by some fine name, I have forgotten what.

'She had not quite the same stock of virtue,' continued he, 'nor the same stock of honesty as Bet Flint; but I suppose she envied her accomplishments, for she was so little moved by the power of harmony, that while Bet Flint thought she was drumming very divinely, the other jade had her indicted for a nuisance!'

'And pray what became of her, sir?'

'Why, madam, she stole a quilt from the man of the house, and he had her taken up: but Bet Flint had a spirit not to be subdued; so when she found herself obliged to go to jail, she ordered a sedan chair, and bid her footboy walk before her. However, the boy proved refractory, for he was ashamed, though his mistress was not.'

'And did she ever get out of jail again, sir?'

'Yes, madam; when she came to her trial the judge acquitted her. "So now," she said to me, "the quilt is my own, and now I'll make a petticoat of it." Oh, I loved Bet Flint!'

Oh, how we all laughed! . . .

At tea time the subject turned upon the domestic economy of Dr Johnson's own household. Mrs Thrale has often acquainted me that his house is quite filled and overrun with all sorts of strange creatures, whom he admits for mere charity, and because nobody else will admit them – for his charity is unbounded – or, rather, bounded only by his circumstances.

The account he gave of the adventures and absurdities of the set was highly diverting, but too diffused for writing, though one or two speeches I must give. I think I shall occasionally theatricalise my dialogues.

Mrs Thrale – Pray, sir, how does Mrs Williams like all this tribe?

Dr Johnson – Madam, she does not like them at all; but their fondness for her is not greater. She and De Mullin [Mrs Desmoulins] quarrel incessantly; but as they can both be occasionally of service to each other, and as neither of them have any other place to go to, their animosity does not force them to separate.

Mrs T – And pray, sir, what is Mr Macbean?[8]

Dr J – Madam, he is a Scotchman: he is a man of great learning, and for his learning I respect him, and I wish to serve him. He knows many languages, and knows them well; but he knows nothing of life. I advised him to write a geographical dictionary; but I have lost all hopes of his ever doing anything properly, since I found he gave as much labour to Capua as to Rome.

Mr T – And pray who is clerk of your kitchen, sir?

Dr J – Why, sir, I am afraid there is none; a general anarchy prevails in my kitchen, as I am told by Mr Levat [Levett] who says it is not now what it used to be!

Mrs T – Mr Levat, I suppose, sir, has the office of keeping the hospital in health? For he is an apothecary.

Dr J – Levat, madam, is a brutal fellow, but I have a good regard for him; for his brutality is in his manners, not his mind.

Mr T – But how do you get your dinners drest?

Dr J – Why, De Mullin has the chief management of the kitchen; but our roasting is not magnificent, for we have no jack.

Mr T – No jack? Why, how do they manage without?

Dr J – Small joints, I believe, they manage with a string, and larger are done at the tavern. I have some thoughts (with a profound gravity) of buying a jack, because I think a jack is some credit to a house.

Mr T – Well, but you'll have a spit, too?

Dr J – No, sir, no; that would be superfluous; for we shall never use it; and if a jack is seen, a spit will be presumed!

Mrs T – But pray, sir, who is the Poll[9] you talk of? She that you used to abet in her quarrels with Mrs Williams, and call out, 'At her again, Poll! Never flinch, Poll'?

Dr J – Why, I took to Poll very well at first, but she won't do upon a nearer examination.

Mrs T – How came she among you, sir?

Dr J – Why, I don't rightly remember, but we could spare her very well from us. Poll is a stupid slut; I had some hopes of her at first; but when I talked to her tightly and closely, I could make nothing of her; she was wiggle-waggle,[10] and I could never persuade her to be categorical. I wish Miss Burney would come among us; if she would only give us a week, we should furnish her with ample materials for a new scene in her next work.

A little while after he asked Mrs Thrale who had read *Evelina* in his absence?

'Who?' cried she; 'why, Burke! – Burke sat up all night to finish it; and Sir Joshua Reynolds is mad about it, and said he would give fifty pounds to know the author. But our fun was with his nieces – we made them believe I wrote the book, and the girls gave me the credit of it at once.'

'I am sorry for it, madam,' cried he, quite angrily. 'You were much to blame; deceits of that kind ought never to be practised; they have a worse tendency than you are aware of.'

Mrs T – Why, don't frighten yourself, sir; Miss Burney will have all the credit she has a right to, for I told them whose it was before they went.

Dr J – But you were very wrong for misleading them a moment; such jests are extremely blamable; they are foolish in the very act, and they are wrong, because they always leave a doubt upon the mind. What first passed will be always recollected by those girls, and they will never feel clearly convinced which wrote the book, Mrs Thrale or Miss Burney.

Mrs T – Well, well, I am ready to take my Bible oath it was not me; and if that won't do, Miss Burney must take hers too.

I was then looking over the *Life of Cowley*,[11] which he had himself given me to read, at the same time that he gave to Mrs Thrale that of Waller. They are now printed, though they will not be published for some time. But he bade me put it away.

'Do,' cried he, 'put away that now, and prattle with us; I can't make this little Burney prattle, and I am sure she prattles well; but I shall teach her another lesson than to sit thus silent before I have done with her.'

'To talk,' cried I, 'is the only lesson I shall be backward to learn from you, sir.'

'You shall give me,' cried he, 'a discourse upon the passions: come, begin! Tell us the necessity of regulating them, watching over and curbing them! Did you ever read Norris's *Theory of Love*?'[12]

'No, sir,' said I, laughing, yet staring a little.

Dr J – Well, it is worth your reading. He will make you see that inordinate love is the root of all evil: inordinate love of wealth brings on avarice; of wine, brings on intemperance; of power, brings on cruelty; and so on. He deduces from inordinate love all human frailty.

Mrs T – Tomorrow, sir, Mrs Montagu dines here, and then you will have talk enough.

Dr Johnson began to see-saw, with a countenance strongly expressive of inward fun, and after enjoying it some time in silence, he suddenly, and with great animation, turned to me and cried, 'Down with her, Burney! Down with her! Spare her not! Attack her, fight her, and down with her at once! You are a rising wit, and she is at the top; and when I was beginning the world, and was nothing and nobody, the joy of my life was to fire at all the established wits! And then everybody loved to halloo me on. But there is no game now; everybody would be glad to see me conquered: but then, when I was new, to vanquish the great ones was all the delight of my poor little dear soul! So at her, Burney – at her, and down with her!'

Oh, how we were all amused! . . .

The P——— family came in to tea; and . . . when they were gone, Mrs Thrale complained that she was quite worn out with that tiresome silly woman, who had talked of her family and affairs till she was sick to death of hearing her.

'Madam,' said the Doctor, 'why do you blame the woman for the only sensible thing she could do – talking of her family and her affairs? For how should a woman who is as empty as a drum, talk upon any other subject? If you speak to her of the sun, she does not know it rises in the east; if you speak to her of the moon, she does not know it changes at the full; if you speak to her of the queen, she does not know she is the king's wife; how, then, can you blame her for talking of her family and affairs?' . . .

And now I cannot resist telling you of a dispute which Dr Johnson had with Mrs Thrale, the next morning, concerning me, which that sweet woman had the honesty and good sense to tell me. Dr Johnson was talking to her and Sir Philip Jennings of the amazing progress made of late years in literature by the women. He said he was himself astonished at it, and told them he well remembered when a woman who could spell a common letter was regarded as all accomplished; but now they vied with the men in everything.

'I think, sir,' said my friend Sir Philip, 'the young lady we have here is a very extraordinary proof of what you say.'

'So extraordinary, sir,' answered he, 'that I know none like her, nor do I believe there is, or there ever was, a man who could write such a book so young.'

They both stared – no wonder, I am sure! – and Sir Philip said, 'What do you think of Pope, sir? Could not Pope have written such a one?'

'Nay, nay,' cried Mrs Thrale, 'there is no need to talk of Pope; a book may be a clever book, and an extraordinary book, and yet not want a Pope for its author. I suppose he was no older than Miss Burney when he wrote *Windsor Forest*; and I suppose *Windsor Forest* is equal to *Evelina*!'

'*Windsor Forest*,' repeated Dr Johnson, 'though so delightful a poem, by no means required the knowledge of life and manners, nor the accuracy of observation, nor the skill of penetration, necessary for composing such a work as *Evelina*: he who could ever write *Windsor Forest*, might as well write it young as old. Poetical abilities require not age to mature them; but *Evelina* seems a work that should result from long experience, and deep and intimate knowledge of the world; yet it has been written without either. Miss Burney is a real wonder. What she is, she is intuitively. Dr Burney told me she had had the fewest advantages of any of his daughters, from some peculiar circumstances. And such has been her timidity, that he himself had not any suspicion of her powers.' . . .

[Mr Pepys][13] entered into an argument [with Dr Johnson] upon some lines of Gray, and upon Pope's definition of wit, in which he was so roughly confuted, and so severely ridiculed, that he was hurt and piqued beyond all power of disguise, and, in the midst of the discourse, suddenly turned from him, and, wishing Mrs Thrale goodnight, very abruptly withdrew.

Dr Johnson was certainly right with respect to the argument and to reason; but his opposition was so warm, and his wit so satirical and exulting, that I was really quite grieved to see how unamiable he appeared, and how greatly he made himself dreaded by all, and by many abhorred. What pity that he will not curb the vehemence of his love of victory and superiority!

The sum of the dispute was this. Wit being talked of, Mr Pepys repeated,

> True wit is Nature to advantage dress'd,
> What oft was thought, but ne'er so well express'd.[14]

'That, sir,' cried Dr Johnson, 'is a definition both false and foolish. Let wit be dressed how it will, it will equally be wit, and neither the more nor the less for any advantage dress can give it.'

Mr P – But, sir, may not wit be so ill expressed, and so obscure, by a bad speaker, as to be lost?

Dr J – The fault, then, sir, must be with the hearer. If a man cannot distinguish wit from words, he little deserves to hear it.

Mr P – But, sir, what Pope means –

Dr J – Sir, what Pope means, if he means what he says, is both false and foolish. In the first place, 'what oft was thought', is all the worse for being often thought, because to be wit, it ought to be newly thought.

Mr P – But, sir, 'tis the expression makes it new.

Dr J – How can the expression make it new? It may make it clear, or may make it elegant; but how new? You are confounding words with things.

Mr P – But, sir, if one man says a thing very ill, may not another man say it so much better that –

Dr J – That other man, sir, deserves but small praise for the amendment; he is but the tailor to the first man's thoughts.

Mr P – True, sir, he may be but the tailor; but then the difference is as great as between a man in a gold lace suit and a man in a blanket.

Dr J – Just so, sir, I thank you for that: the difference is precisely such, since it consists neither in the gold lace suit nor the blanket, but in the man by whom they are worn.

This was the summary; the various contemptuous sarcasms intermixed would fill, and very unpleasantly, a quire.[15] . . .

I happened to be standing by Dr Johnson when all the ladies came in; but, as I dread him before strangers, from the staring attention he attracts both for himself and all with whom he talks, I endeavoured to change my ground. However, he kept prating a sort of comical nonsense that detained me some minutes whether I would or not; but when we were all taking places at the breakfast table I made another effort to escape. It proved vain; he drew his chair next to mine, and went rattling on in a humorous sort of comparison he was drawing of himself to me – not one word of which could I enjoy, or can I remember, from the hurry I was in to get out of his way. In short, I felt so awkward from being thus marked out, that I was reduced to whisper a request to Mr Swinerton to put a chair between us, for which I presently made a space: for I have often known him stop all conversation with me, when he has ceased to have me for his next neighbour. Mr Swinerton, who is an extremely good-natured young man, and so intimate here that I make no scruple with him, instantly complied, and placed himself between us.

But no sooner was this done, than Dr Johnson, half seriously, and very loudly, took him to task.

'How now, sir! What do you mean by this? Would you separate me from Miss Burney?'

Mr Swinerton, a little startled, began some apologies, and Mrs Thrale winked at him to give up the place; but he was willing to oblige me, though he grew more and more frightened every minute, and coloured violently as the Doctor continued his remonstrance, which he did with rather unmerciful raillery, upon his taking advantage of being in his own house to thus supplant him, and *crow*; but when he had borne it for about ten minutes, his face became so hot with the fear of hearing something worse, that he ran from the field, and took a chair between Lady De Ferrars and Mrs Thrale.

I think I shall take warning by this failure, to trust only to my own expedients for avoiding his public notice in future. . . .

I dined with Mrs Thrale and Dr Johnson, who was very comic and good-humoured. Susan Thrale had just had her hair turned up, and powdered and has taken to the womanly robe. Dr Johnson sportively gave her instructions how to increase her consequence, and to 'take upon her' properly.

'Begin,' said he, 'Miss Susy, with something grand – something to surprise mankind! Let your first essay in life be a warm censure of *Cecilia*.[16] You can no way make yourself more conspicuous. Tell the world how ill it was conceived, and how ill executed. Tell them how little there is in it of human nature, and how well your knowledge of the world enables you to judge of the failings in that book. Find fault without fear; and if you are at a loss for any to find, invent whatever comes into your mind, for you may say what you please, with little fear of detection, since of those who praise *Cecilia* not half have read it, and of those who have read it, not half remember it. Go to work, therefore, boldly; and particularly mark that the character of Albany is extremely unnatural, to your own knowledge, since you never met with such a man at Mrs Cummyn's School.'

This stopped his exhortation, for we laughed so violently at this happy criticism that he could not recover the thread of his harangue.

NOTES

Frances (Fanny) Burney (1752–1840), novelist and diarist, was the daughter of Dr Charles Burney (see p. 54); she is also known as Madame d'Arblay, having married a French refugee, General d'Arblay, in 1793. Her first novel, *Evelina*, was published anonymously in January 1778 and was a brilliant success. Johnson, who learned the secret of its authorship from Mrs Thrale (who had had it from Dr Burney), admired it, quoted it freely, and declared that parts of it 'might do honour to Richardson'. Frances met Johnson at her father's house towards the end of March 1778: for her first impressions of him, see p. 24. Thereafter, she saw him frequently at the Thrales' home at Streatham. Her accounts of his visits to Streatham in 1778–9 provide a vivid and delightful picture of how Johnson struck an intelligent and observant young woman exhilarated by the success of her first book and her recent entry into the fashionable literary world. She memorably records both his physical peculiarities and the power of his conversation: his 'universal readiness upon all subjects', the 'freedom' and 'strength' (i.e. frankness and vehemence) of his speech, his 'love of victory and superiority', the fact that he could at times be 'unamiable', but also his 'jocosity' and gallantry. However, as the extracts given also suggest, her pleasure at Johnson's flattering and almost flirtatious attentions later gave way to occasional intolerance and embarrassment at his eccentricities and hectoring style of argument, though her affection was revived in the closing stages of his life (see p. 140). Boswell plays down Fanny Burney's relationship with Johnson: his first reference to her is under the date 26 May 1783. The fact is that during the heyday of their relationship, they enjoyed an intimacy that meant a good deal to both of them: Johnson became fond of her, referring to her as 'my dear little Burney', and she of him ('dear Dr Johnson'). In May 1781 she wrote, 'Dr Johnson was charming, both in spirits and humour. I really think he grows gayer and gayer daily, and more *ductile* and pleasant.' It was not everyone who was capable of finding these qualities in Johnson, or of eliciting them from him. More seriously, after Thrale's death she had 'very often . . . long and melancholy discourses with Dr Johnson, about our dear deceased master, whom, indeed, he regrets incessantly'. See Joyce Hemlow, *Fanny Burney* (1958). C. B. Tinker's *Dr Johnson and Fanny Burney* (1912) conveniently assembles 'the Johnsonian passages from the works of Madame d'Arblay'.

1. William Seward (1747–99), a Fellow of the Royal Society and a friend of the Thrales as well as of Dr Johnson. He later published *Anecdotes of Some Distinguished Persons* (1795–7) and supplied Boswell with some material for his biography.

2. Beaumont and Fletcher's tragedy was produced in July 1778 in an adaptation by George Colman the Elder, Garrick supplying a prologue (not an epilogue).

3. John Wilkes (1727–97), politician. Johnson attacked his views and described him as 'an abusive scoundrel' as well as disparaging his reputation for wit. Boswell contrived a meeting between them in 1776.

4. A character in Fanny Burney's *Evelina*.

5. Toad: the word is, as the *OED* says, usually applied 'opprobriously' to human beings, but the intention here is clearly facetiously teasing.

6. The line is from *All for Love* (1678).

7. Boswell records that on 8 May 1781, Johnson 'gave us an entertaining account of *Bet Flint*, a woman of the town'; some of the details given by Boswell are very close to Fanny Burney's.

8. Alexander Macbean (d. 1784); Johnson wrote a preface for his *Dictionary of Ancient Geography* (1773).

9. Miss Carmichael, one of the numerous objects of Johnson's unobtrusive charity.

10. 'Wiggle-waggle': vacillating (the *OED* cites this instance).

11. The first of Johnson's *Lives of the Poets*, completed before the end of 1777.

12. John Norris, *The Theory and Regulation of Love* (1688).

13. Presumably William Weller Pepys (1740–1820).

14. Pope, *Essay on Criticism*, lines 297–8.

15. Two days later (31 October 1782), Fanny Burney records that the party, with the single exception of Johnson, have been invited to visit Lady Rothes, sister-in-law of Mr Pepys, who was 'tortured' by Johnson in the above argument. On 2 November she notes: 'We went to Lady Shelley's, Dr Johnson, again, excepted in the invitation. He is almost constantly omitted, either from too much respect or too much fear. I am sorry for it, as he hates being alone.'

16. Fanny Burney's second novel, published in 1782.

Life at Streatham IV*

HESTER LYNCH PIOZZI

Some of the old legendary stories put in verse by modern writers provoked [Johnson] to caricature them thus one day at Streatham; but they are already well-known, I am sure.

> The tender infant, meek and mild,
>   Fell down upon the stone;
> The nurse took up the squealing child,
>   But still the child squeal'd on.

A famous ballad also, beginning *Rio verde, Rio verde*, when I commended the translation of it, he said he could do it better himself – as thus:

> Glassy water, glassy water,
> Down whose current clear and strong,
> Chiefs confus'd in mutual slaughter,
> Moor and Christian roll along.

But Sir, said I, this is not ridiculous at all. 'Why no [replied he], why should I always write ridiculously? Perhaps because I made these verses to imitate such a one, naming him:

> Hermit hoar, in solemn cell,
> Wearing out life's evening gray;
> Strike thy bosom sage! and tell,
> What is bliss, and which the way?

> Thus I spoke, and speaking sigh'd,
> Scarce repress'd the starting tear,
> When the hoary Sage reply'd,
> Come, my lad, and drink some beer.'[1]

I could give another comical instance of caricatura imitation. Recollecting some day, when praising these verses of Lopez de Vega,[2]

---

* *Anecdotes of Samuel Johnson*, pp. 45–7, 52–3, 130–2, 64–5, 145–6, 152–3.

> *Se a quien los leones vence*
> *Vence una muger hermosa*
> *O el de flaco averguençe*
> *O ella di ser mas furiosa,*

more than he thought they deserved, Mr Johnson instantly observed, 'that they were founded on a trivial conceit; and that conceit ill-explained, and ill-expressed beside. The lady, we all know, does not conquer in the same manner as the lion does: 'Tis a mere play of words [added he], and you might as well say, that

> If the man who turnips cries,
> Cry not when his father dies,
> 'Tis a proof that he had rather
> Have a turnip than his father.'

And his humour is of the same sort with which he answered the friend who commended the following line:

> Who rules o'er freemen should himself be free.

'To be sure [said Dr Johnson],

> Who drives fat oxen should himself be fat.'

This readiness of finding a parallel, or making one, was shown by him perpetually in the course of conversation. When the French verses of a certain pantomime were quoted thus,

> *Je suis Cassandre descendiie des cieux,*
> *Pour vous fair entendre, mesdames et messieurs,*
> *Que je suis Cassandre descendiie des cieux,*

he cried out gaily and suddenly, almost in a moment,

> I am Cassandra come down from the sky,
> To tell each by-stander what none can deny,
> That I am Cassandra come down from the sky.

The pretty Italian verses too, at the end of Baretti's book called *Easy Phraseology*,[3] he did *all' improviso*, in the same manner:

> *Viva! viva la padrona!*
> *Tutta bella, e tutta buona,*
> *La padrona è un angiolella*
> *Tutta buona e tutta bella;*

Tutta bella e tutta buona;
Viva! viva la padrona!

Long may live my lovely Hetty!
Always young and always pretty,
Always pretty, always young,
Live my lovely Hetty long!
Always young and always pretty;
Long may live my lovely Hetty!

The famous distich too, of an Italian *improvisatore*, who, when the Duke of Modena ran away from the comet in the year 1742 or 1743,

Se al venir vestro i principi sen' vanno
Deh venga ogni di—durate un anno;

'which [said he] would do just as well in our language thus:

If at your coming princes disappear,
Comets! come every day – and stay a year.'

Mr Johnson's health had been always extremely bad since I first knew him, and his over-anxious care to retain without blemish the perfect sanity of his mind, contributed much to disturb it. He had studied medicine diligently in all its branches; but had given particular attention to the diseases of the imagination, which he watched in himself with a solicitude destructive of his own peace, and intolerable to those he trusted. Dr Lawrence[4] told him one day, that if he would come and beat him once a week he would bear it; but to hear his complaints was more than *man* could support. 'Twas therefore that he tried, I suppose, and in eighteen years contrived to weary the patience of a *woman*. When Mr Johnson felt his fancy, or fancied he felt it, disordered, his constant recurrence was to the study of arithmetic; and one day that he was totally confined to his chamber, and I enquired what he had been doing to divert himself, he showed me a calculation which I could scarce be made to understand, so vast was the plan of it, and so very intricate were the figures: no other indeed than that the national debt, computing it at one hundred and eighty millions sterling, would, if converted into silver, serve to make a meridian of that metal, I forget how broad, for the globe of the whole earth, the real *globe*. . . .

Promptitude of thought indeed, and quickness of expression, were among the peculiar felicities of Johnson: his notions rose up like the dragon's teeth sowed by Cadmus all ready clothed, and in bright armour too, fit for immediate battle. He was therefore (as somebody is said to have expressed it) a tremendous converser, and few people ventured to try their skill against an antagonist with whom contention was so hopeless. One gentleman however, who dined at a nobleman's house in his company and that of Mr Thrale, to whom I was obliged for the anecdote, was willing to enter the lists in defence of King William's character, and having opposed and contradicted Johnson two or three times petulantly enough; the master of the house began to feel uneasy, and expect disagreeable consequences: to avoid which he said, loud enough for the Doctor to hear, 'Our friend here has no meaning now in all this, except just to relate at club to-morrow how he teased Johnson at dinner today – this is all to do himself *honour*.' 'No, upon my word,' replied the other, 'I see no *honour* in it, whatever you may do.' 'Well, Sir!' returned Mr Johnson sternly, 'if you do not *see* the *honour*, I am sure I *feel* the *disgrace*.'

A young fellow, less confident of his own abilities, lamenting one day that he had lost all his Greek – 'I believe it happened at the same time, Sir,' said Johnson, 'that I lost all my large estate in Yorkshire.'

But however roughly he might be suddenly provoked to treat a harmless exertion of vanity, he did not wish to inflict the pain he gave, and was sometimes very sorry when he perceived the people to smart more than they deserved. How harshly you treated that man today, said I once, who harangued us so about gardening – 'I am sorry,' said he, 'if I vexed the creature, for there certainly is no harm in a fellow's rattling a rattle-box, only don't let him think that he thunders.' The Lincolnshire lady who showed him a grotto she had been making, came off no better as I remember: 'Would it not be a pretty cool habitation in summer?' said she, 'Mr Johnson!' 'I think it would, Madam,' replied he, 'for a toad.'

All desire of distinction indeed had a sure enemy in Mr Johnson. We met a friend driving six very small ponies, and stopped to admire them. 'Why does nobody [said our Doctor] begin the fashion of driving six spavined horses, all spavined of the same leg? It would have a mighty pretty effect, and produce the distinction of doing something worse than the common way.' . . .

I have sometimes indeed been rather pleased than vexed when Mr Johnson has given a rough answer to a man who perhaps deserved one only half as rough, because I knew he would repent of his hasty reproof, and make us all amends by some conversation at once instructive and entertaining, as in the following cases. A young fellow asked him abruptly one day, 'Pray, Sir, what and where is Palmira? I heard somebody talk last night of the ruins of Palmira.' ''Tis a hill in Ireland,' replies Johnson, 'with palms growing on the top, and a bog at the bottom, and so they call it *Palm-mira*.'[5] Seeing, however, that the lad thought him serious, and thanked him for the information, he undeceived him very gently indeed; told him the history, geography and chronology of Tadmor in the wilderness, with every incident that literature could furnish I think, or eloquence express, from the building of Solomon's palace to the voyage of Dawkins and Wood.

On another occasion, when he was musing over the fire in our drawing-room at Streatham, a young gentleman called to him suddenly, and I suppose he thought disrespectfully, in these words. 'Mr Johnson, would you advise me to marry?' 'I would advise no man to marry, Sir,' returns for answer, in a very angry tone, Dr Johnson, 'who is not likely to propagate understanding', and so left the room. Our companion looked confounded, and I believe had scarce recovered the consciousness of his own existence, when Johnson came back, and drawing his chair among us, with altered looks and a softened voice, joined in the general chat, insensibly led the conversation to the subjet of marriage, where he laid himself out in a dissertation so useful, so elegant, so founded on the true knowledge of human life, and so adorned with beauty of sentiment, that no one ever recollected the offence, except to rejoice in its consequences. He repented just as certainly, however, if he had been led to praise any person or thing by accident more than he thought it deserved; and was on such occasions comically earnest to destroy the praise or pleasure he had unintentionally given. . . .

The strangest applications in the world were certainly made from time to time towards Mr Johnson, who by that means had an inexhaustible fund of anecdote, and could, if he pleased, tell the most astonishing stories of human folly and human weakness that ever were confided to any man not a confessor by profession.

One day when he was in a humour to record some of them, he told us the following tale. 'A person had for these last five weeks often called at my door, but would not leave his name, or other message; but that he wished to speak with me. At last we met, and he told me that he was oppressed by scruples of conscience: I blamed him gently for not applying, as the rules of our church direct, to his parish priest or other discreet clergyman; when, after some compliments on his part, he told me, that he was clerk to a very eminent trader, at whose warehouses much business consisted in packing goods in order to go abroad: that he was often tempted to take paper and packthread enough for his own use, and that he had indeed done so so often, that he could recollect no time when he ever had bought any for himself. But probably (said I), your master was wholly indifferent with regard to such trivial emoluments; you had better ask for it at once, and so take your trifles with consent. Oh, Sir! replies the visitor, my master bid me have as much as I pleased, and was half angry when I talked to him about it. Then pray, Sir (said I), tease me no more about such airy nothings; and was going on to be very angry, when I recollected that the fellow might be mad perhaps; so I asked him when he left the counting-house of an evening? At seven o'clock, Sir. And when do you go to bed, Sir? At twelve o'clock. Then (replied I) I have at least learned thus much by my new acquaintance; that five hours of the four-and-twenty unemployed are enough for a man to go mad in; so I would advise you Sir, to study algebra, if you are not an adept already in it: your head would get less *muddy*, and you will leave off tormenting your neighbours about paper and packthread, while we all live together in a world that is bursting with sin and sorrow. It is perhaps needless to add, that this visitor came no more.' . . .

Dr Johnson was always exceeding fond of chemistry; and we made up a sort of laboratory at Streatham one summer, and diverted ourselves with drawing essences and colouring liquors. But the danger Mr Thrale found his friend in one day when I was driven to London, and he had got the children and servants round him to see some experiments performed, put an end to all our entertainment; so well was the master of the house persuaded, that his short sight would have been his destruction in a moment, by bringing him close to a fierce and violent flame. Indeed, it was a perpetual miracle that he did not set himself on fire reading a-bed, as was his constant custom, when exceedingly unable even to keep clear of mischief with our best help; and accordingly the fore-top of all his wigs were burned by the candle down to the very net-work. Mr Thrale's valet-de-chambre, for that reason, kept one always in his own hands, with which he met him at the parlour-door when the bell had called him down to dinner, and as he went up stairs to sleep in the afternoon, the same man constantly followed him with another.

Future experiments in chemistry, however, were too dangerous, and Mr Thrale insisted that we should do no more towards finding the philosophers stone.

Mr Johnson's amusements were thus reduced to the pleasures of conversation merely: and what wonder that he should have an avidity for the sole delight he was able to enjoy? No man conversed so well as he on every subject; no man so acutely discerned the reason of every fact, the motive of every action, the end of every design. He was, indeed, often pained by the ignorance or causeless wonder of those who knew less than himself, though he seldom drove them away with apparent scorn, unless he thought they added presumption to stupidity.

NOTES

On Mrs Piozzi (formerly Mrs Thrale), and the relationship of her *Anecdotes* to her *Thraliana*, see p. 82.

1. See p. 50, note 10.

2. Lope de Vega (1562–1635), Spanish dramatist.

3. Johnson wrote a preface for Baretti's *Phraseology for the Use of Young Ladies Who Intend to Learn the Colloquial Part of the Italian Language* (1775).

4. Dr Thomas Lawrence (1711–83), President of the Royal College of Physicians (1767–74), described by Boswell as Johnson's 'intimate friend and physician', and by Johnson himself as 'one of the best men whom I have known' and 'a learned, intelligent, and communicative companion' (19 March 1782). Boswell quotes one of Johnson's letters to Lawrence, written in Latin and describing his symptoms.

5. Fanny Burney's diary dates this conversation 26 August 1778 and gives the following version of Johnson's reply: 'Palmyra, sir?' said the Doctor; 'why, it is a hill in Ireland, situated in a bog, and has palm trees at the top, whence it is called Palm-mire.'

Life at Streatham V*

FRANCES REYNOLDS

On the praises of Mrs Thrale, he used to dwell with a peculiar delight, a paternal fondness, expressive of conscious exultation in being so intimately acquainted with her. One day, in speaking of her to Mr Harris, author of *Hermes*,[1] and expatiating on her various perfections – the solidity of her virtues, the brilliancy of her wit, and the strength of her understanding, &c. – he quoted some lines, a stanza, I believe, but from what author I know not, with which he concluded his most eloquent eulogium, and of these I retained but the two last lines:

> Virtues – of such a generous kind,
> Good in the last recesses of the mind.

Dr Johnson had a most sincere and tender regard for Mrs Thrale, and no wonder; she would with much apparent affection overlook his foibles. One Day at her own Table, before a large company, he spoke so very roughly to her, that every person present was surprised how she could bear it so placidly; and on the Ladies withdrawing, one of them expressed great astonishment how Dr Johnson could speak in such harsh terms to her! But to this she said no more than 'Oh! Dear good man!' This short reply appeared so strong a proof of her *generous virtues* that the Lady took the first opportunity of communicating it to him, repeating

* *Johnsonian Miscellanies*, II, 272–9.

her own animadversion that had occasioned it. *He seemed much delighted* with this intelligence, and sometime after, as he was lying back in his Chair, seeming to be half asleep, but more evidently musing on this pleasing incident, he repeated in a loud whisper, *'Oh! Dear good man!'* This was a common habit of his, when anything very flattering, or very extraordinary ingrossed his thoughts, and I rather wonder that none of his Biographers have taken any notice of it, or of his praying in the same manner; at least I do not know that they have.

Nor has any one, I believe, described his extraordinary gestures or antics with his hands and feet, particularly when passing over the threshold of a Door, or rather before he would venture to pass through *any* doorway. On entering Sir Joshua's house with poor Mrs Williams, a blind lady who lived with him, he would quit her hand, or else whirl her about on the steps as he whirled and twisted about to perform his gesticulations; and as soon as he had finished, he would give a sudden spring, and make such an extensive stride over the threshold, as if he was trying for a wager how far he could stride, Mrs Williams standing groping about outside the door, unless the servant or the mistress of the House more commonly took hold of her hand to conduct her in, leaving Dr Johnson to perform at the Parlour Door much the same exercise over again.

But the strange positions in which he would place his feet (generally I think before he began his straddles, as if necessarily preparatory) are scarcely credible. Sometimes he would make the back part of his heels to touch, sometimes the extremity of his toes, as if endeavouring to form a triangle, or some geometrical figure, and as for his gestures with his hands, they were equally as strange; sometimes he would hold them up with some of his fingers bent, as if he had been seized with the cramp, and sometimes at his Breast in motion like those of a jockey on full speed; and often would he lift them up as high as he could stretch over his head, for some minutes. But the manoeuvre that used the most particularly to engage the attention of the company was his stretching out his arm with a full cup of tea in his hand, in every direction, often to the great annoyance of the person who sat next him, indeed to the imminent danger of their clothes, perhaps of a Lady's Court dress; sometimes he would twist himself round with his face close to the back of his chair, and finish his cup of tea, breathing very hard, as if making a laborious effort to accomplish it.

What could have induced him to practise such extraordinary gestures, who can divine! His head, his hands and his feet were often in motion at the same time. Many people have supposed that they were the natural effects of a nervous disorder, but had that been the case he could not have sat still when he chose, which he did, and so still indeed when sitting for his picture, as often to have been complimented with being a pattern for sitters, no slight proof of his complaisance or his good nature. I remember a lady told him he sat like Patience on a monument smiling at grief,[2] which made him laugh heartily at the ridiculous coincidence of the idea with his irksome situation; for irksome it doubtless was to him, restraining himself as he did, even from his common and most habitual motion of see-sawing, the more difficult for him to effect because the most habitual.

It was not only at the entrance of a Door that he exhibited his gigantic straddles, but often in the middle of a Room, as if trying to make the floor to shake; and often in the street, even with company, who would walk on at a little distance until he had finished his ludicrous beat, for fear of being surrounded with a mob; and then he would hasten to join them, with an air of great satisfaction, seeming totally unconscious of having committed any impropriety.

I remember to have heard Sir Joshua Reynolds relate, that being with Dr Johnson at Dorchester on their way to Devonshire, they went to see Corfe Castle. I believe that neither of them was sufficiently known to Mr Banks to introduce themselves as visitors to him; however that might be, he showed them great civility, politely attending them through the apartments, &c., in the finest of which Dr Johnson began to exhibit his antics, stretching out his legs alternately as far as he could possibly stretch; at the same time pressing his foot on the floor as heavily as he could possibly press, as if endeavouring to smooth the carpet, or rather perhaps to rumple it, and every now and then collecting all his force, apparently to effect a concussion of the floor. Mr Banks, regarding him for some time with silent astonishment, at last said, 'Dr Johnson, I believe the floor is very firm', which immediately made him desist, probably without making any reply. It would have been difficult indeed to frame an apology for such ridiculous manoeuvres.[3]

It was amazing, so dim-sighted as Dr Johnson was, how very observant he was of appearances in Dress, in behaviour, and even of the servants, how they waited at table, &c.; *the more particularly, so seeming as he did to be stone-blind to his own*. One day as his man Frank was waiting at Sir Joshua's table, he observed with some emotion that he had the salver under his arm. Nor would the behaviour of the company on some occasions escape his animadversions, particularly for their perversion of the idea of refinement in the use of a water-glass, a very strange perversion indeed he thought it, as some people use it. He had also a great dislike to the use of a pocket-handkerchief at meals, when, if he wanted one, I have seen him rise from his Chair, and go at some distance with his back towards the company, performing the operation as silently as possible.

Dr Johnson's sight was so very defective that he could scarcely distinguish the Face of his most intimate acquaintance at a half yard's distance from him, and, in general, it was observable that his critical remarks on dress, &c. were the result of a very close inspection of the object; partly, perhaps, excited by curiosity, and partly from a desire of exacting admiration of his perspicacity, of which it was remarkable he was not a little ambitious.

That Dr Johnson possessed the essential principles of politeness and of good taste, which I suppose are the same, at least concomitant, none who knew his virtues and his genius will, I imagine, be inclined to dispute. But why they remained with him, like gold in the ore, unfashioned and unseen, except in his literary capacity, no person that I know of has made any enquiry, though in general it has been spoken of as an unaccountable inconsistency in his character. But a little reflection on the disqualifying influence of blindness and deafness would suggest many apologies for Dr Johnson's want of politeness. The particular instance I have just mentioned, of his inability to discriminate the features of any one's face, deserves perhaps more than any other to be taken into consideration, wanting, as he did, the aid of those intelligent signs, or insinuations, which the countenance displays in social converse; and which, in their slightest degree, influence and regulate the manners of the polite, even of the common observer.

And to his defective hearing, perhaps, his unaccommodating manners may be equally ascribed, which precluded him not only from the perception of the expressive tones of the voice of others, but from hearing the boisterous sound of his own.

Under such disadvantages, it was not much to be wondered at that Dr Johnson should have committed many blunders and absurdities, and excited surprise and resentment in company; one in particular I remember to have heard related of him many years since. Being in company with Mr Garrick and some others, who were unknown to Dr Johnson, he was saying something tending to the disparagement of the character or of the works of a gentleman present – I have forgot the particulars; on which Mr Garrick touched his foot under the table; but he still went on, and Garrick, much alarmed, touched him a second time, and, I believe, the third. At last Johnson exclaimed, 'David, David, is it you? What makes you tread on my toes so?' This little anecdote, perhaps, indicates as much the want of prudence in Dr Johnson as the want of sight. But had he at first seen Garrick's expressive countenance, and (probably) the embarrassment of the rest of the company on the occasion, it doubtless would not have happened.

Dr Johnson was very ambitious of excelling in common acquirements, as well as the uncommon, and particularly in feats of activity. One day, as he was walking in Gunisbury Park (or Paddock) with some gentlemen and ladies, who were admiring the extraordinary size of some of the trees, one of the gentlemen said that, when he was a boy, he made nothing of climbing (swarming, I think, was the phrase) the largest there. 'Why, I can swarm it now,' replied Dr Johnson, which excited a hearty laugh (he was then, I believe, between fifty and sixty); on which he ran to the tree, clung round the trunk, and ascended to the branches, and, I believe, would have gone in amongst them, had he not been very earnestly entreated to descend; and down he came with a triumphant air, seeming *to make nothing of it.*

At another time, at a gentleman's seat in Devonshire, as he and some company were sitting in a saloon, before which was a spacious lawn, it was remarked as a very proper place for running a Race. A young lady present boasted that she could outrun any person; on which Dr Johnson rose up and said, 'Madam, you cannot outrun me'; and, going out on the Lawn, they started. The lady at first had the advantage; but Dr Johnson happening to have slippers on much too small for his feet, kicked them off up into the air, and ran a great length without them, leaving the lady far behind him, and, having won the victory, he returned, leading Her by the hand, with looks of high exultation and delight.

It was at this place where the lady of the House before a large company at Dinner addressed herself to him with a very audible voice, 'Pray, Dr Johnson, what made you say in your Dictionary that the Pastern of a Horse was the knee of a Horse?' 'Ignorance, madam, ignorance,' answered Johnson. And I was told that at another time at the same table, when the lady was pressing him to eat something, he rose up with his knife in his hand, and loudly exclaimed, 'I vow to God I cannot eat a bit more', to the great terror, it was said, of all the company. I did not doubt of the gentleman's veracity who related this. But I was rather surprised at this expression from Johnson; for never did I know any person so cautious in mentioning that awful name on common occasions, and I have often heard him rebuke those who have unawares interjectionally made use of it.

It was about this time when a lady was travelling with him in a post-chaise near a village Churchyard, in which she had seen a very striking object of maternal affection, a little verdant flowery monument, raised by the Widowed Mother over the grave of her only chld, and had heard some melancholy circumstances concerning them, and as she was relating them to Dr Johnson, she heard him make heavy sighs, indeed sobs, and turning round she saw his Dear Face bathed in tears.

NOTES

Frances Reynolds (1729–1807), the youngest sister of Sir Joshua Reynolds and herself a painter, painted Johnson's portrait in 1783. Johnson was fond of her and called her his 'Renny dear'.

1. James Harris (1709–80), whose *Hermes* is subtitled 'A Philosophical Inquiry concerning Universal Grammar'.

2. *Twelfth Night*, II, iv, 116–17.

3. Johnson's 'extraordinary gestures or antics' are described by several observers. Boswell refers to his 'convulsive cramps' and enumerates his habitual involuntary movements; Fanny Burney notes that 'his vast body is in constant agitation' and, like Miss Reynolds, speaks of his 'see-sawing'; and Thomas Tyers states that 'he was to the last a convulsionary'. For an interesting discussion from a medical standpoint, see Russell Brain, *Some Reflections on Genius* (1960) pp. 69–91.

Part IV

Travelling with Johnson

Oxford, Cambridge, Aberdeen*

THOMAS TYERS

In 1750, we find Johnson at Oxford (which he visited almost every year) during the instalment of Lord Westmorland, the chancellor of the university: on which occasion he wore his academical gown in the theatre, 'where,' says he, 'I have clapped my hands, till they are sore, at Dr King's speech.' From hence he transmitted a periodical *Idler*, during the *Idler* season, and whilst his visits were at this place. Like Erasmus, he carried his powers of composition with him wherever he went. University College was frequently his home; and he often expressed his wishes for an apartment in Pembroke College, which were rather discouraged, for whatever reasons. That college might have had, until they were weary of each other, this most respectable layman to itself, where, like Father Paul, in his monastic cell, he might have enjoyed his meditations, and been consulted, like that Venetian oracle, on all points and cases whatsoever.

In 1765, Johnson was at Cambridge, with Mr Beauclerk, 'where he drank his large potations of tea [says Dr Sharp,[1] in a letter, and who styles him Caliban], interrupted by many an indignant contradiction, and many a noble sentiment'. He displayed some instances of his tenacious memory, talked learnedly on sonnet-writing, which subject arose from the sonnet compositions of Milton. 'At twelve,' says the letter, 'he began to be very great, stripped poor Mrs Macauley[2] to the very skin, then gave her for his toast, and drank her in two bumpers.'

Though his predilection for the English establishments for learning was always conspicuous, yet he could find praise for the literary seminaries of the North. For when he was on his tour [in 1773], with Mr Boswell, his *fidus Achates*,[3] the scene at Aberdeen had made such an impression upon him that he often said, on his return to London, to Dr Dunbar,[4] that if he ever removed from the capital, he would incline to fix at Aberdeen. 'What,' said the professor, 'in preference to Oxford?' 'Yes, sir,' replied Johnson, 'for Aberdeen is not only a seat of learning, but a seat of commerce, which would be particularly agreeable.' This he so often repeated that Dunbar used to tell him he had secured apartments

* Brack and Kelley, *Early Biographies*, pp. 89–90.

for him in the King's College, which flattered him much. If he had taken a residence at this university, we possibly might have heard of the walk of Johnson at Aberdeen, as of Erasmus at Cambridge, *Localities* have charms for everybody.

NOTES

On Thomas Tyers, see p. 33.

1. Dr John Sharp (d. 1792) was a Fellow of Trinity College, Cambridge, and later became Archdeacon of Northumberland. His letter, from which Boswell also quotes, appeared in the *Gentleman's Magazine* (1785) and is reprinted in G. B. Hill's edition of Boswell's *Life*, i, 517. The passage referring to Milton is as follows:

> We were puzzled about one of the sonnets, which we thought was not to be found in Newton's edition [1752], and differed from all the printed ones. But Johnson cried, 'No, no!', repeated the whole sonnet instantly, *memoriter*, and shewed it us in Newton's book. After which, he learnedly harangued on sonnet-writing, and its different numbers.

2. Mrs Catherine Macaulay (1731–91), historian and controversialist. According to Boswell, when Johnson was told that she resorted to rouge, he replied, 'She is better employed at her toilet, than using her pen. It is better she should be reddening her own cheeks, than blackening other people's characters.'

3. Faithful companion (Achates was the companion of Aeneas in Virgil's *Aeneid*).

4. See p. 33.

Cambridge (1765)*

B. N. TURNER

My first introduction to Dr Johnson was owing to the following circumstance. [The Revd J. Lettice] and I had agreed upon attempting a new translation of Plutarch's Lives; but previously, as I was just then going to town, my friend wished me to consult Johnson about it, with whom he himself was well acquainted. In consequence, when in town, I procured an interview with Levett,[1] who willingly next morning

* *The New Monthly Magazine*, x (1 December 1818) 385–91.

introduced me to breakfast with the great man. His residence was then in
some old-fashioned rooms called, I think, Inner Temple Lane, no. 1. At
the top of a few steps the door opened into a dark and dingy looking old
wainscoted anteroom, through which was the study, and into which a
little before noon, came rolling, as if just roused from his cabin, the truly
uncouth figure of our literary Colossus, in a strange black wig, too little
for him by half, but which, before our next interview, was exchanged for
that very respectable brown one in which his friend, Sir Joshua, so
faithfully depicted him. I am glad, however, I saw the queer black bob,
as his biographers have noticed it, and as it proved that the lustre of
native genius can break through the most disfiguring habiliments. He
seemed pleased to see a young Cantab in his rooms, and on my
acquainting him with the business on which I had taken the liberty of
consulting him, he rather encouraged our undertaking than otherwise;
though after working at it for a few months we found the work too tedious
and incompatible with other pursuits, and were obliged to relinquish it.
After this, the great man questioned me about Cambridge, and whatever
regarded literature, and attended to my answers with great
complacency. The situation of these apartments I well remember. I
called once more before I left town, but the Doctor was absent, and when
Francis Barber, his black servant, opened the door to tell me so, a group
of his African countrymen were sitting round a fire in the gloomy
anteroom; and on their all turning their sooty faces at once to stare at me
they presented a curious spectacle. I repeatedly afterwards visited him,
both in Johnson's Court and Bolt Court.

  Though I meant at first to confine myself solely to his Cambridge
excursion, yet, that we may not lose, as Garrick says, 'one drop of this
immortal man', permit me to say a few words respecting these different
calls. When alone he sometimes asked me to take tea with him; and I can
truly say, that I never found him morose or overbearing, though I freely
contradicted him, with which he seemed pleased, and in order to lead a
young man into a sort of controversy or discussion, he would now and
then advance what he did not think. He has been aptly compared to a
ghost, as he would seldom speak first, but would sit librating[2] in his chair
until a question was asked, upon which he would promptly and fluently
dilate. The reason for this seems, as a first-rate genius, who feels himself
equally prepared to discuss whatever subject may be started, must deem
it more to his own honour that he should not choose the topic himself.
When I saw the Doctor again, after we had given up Plutarch, I told him
that my friend and Professor Martyn[3] had undertaken to give an edition
in English, with the plates, of the Herculaneum Antiquities. Johnson:
'They don't know what they have undertaken; the engravers will drive
them mad, Sir.' And this perhaps, with other reasons, might prevent
their executing more than one volume. At another time, he said, 'that Mr
Farmer,[4] of your College, is a very clever man, indeed, Sir.' And on my

asking him whether he knew the fact with respect to the learning of Shakespeare, before that gentleman's publication, Johnson said 'Why, yes, Sir. I knew in general that the fact was as he represents it; but I did not know it, as Mr Farmer has now taught it me, by *detail*, Sir.' I was several times the bearer of messages between them; and my suggesting and expressing a hope that we should some time or other have the pleasure of seeing him at Cambridge when I should be most happy to introduce them to each other, might somewhat conduce to his taking the journey I am about to describe.

The last time I called upon him was long after the Cambridge visit, and I found with him Mr Strahan, his son, the Vicar of Islington, and two or three other gentlemen, one of whom was upon his legs taking leave, and saying, 'Well Doctor, as you know I shall set off tomorrow, what shall I say for you to Mrs Thrale, when I see her?' Johnson: 'Why, Sir, you may tell her how I am: but noa, Sir, noa, she knows that already; and so when you see Mrs Thrale, you will say to her what it is predestined that you are to say to her, Sir.' Amidst the general laugh occasioned by this sally the gentleman retired; and the Doctor joining in the merriment, proceeded, 'for you know, Sir, when a person has said or done any thing, it was plainly predestinated that he was to say or do that particular thing, Sir.' I recollect but one more interview with him in town, but to describe that would lead me so far out of my way at present, that I believe I must defer this to some future communication.

Of the journey I principally intended to describe, there is, as I observed, a short account by Dr Sharp in the *Gentleman's Magazine* for March 1785, in which he there addresses his friend, 'I have had Johnson in the chair in which I am now writing. He came down on Saturday with a Mr Beauclerk, who has a friend at Trinity (a Mr Lester, or Leicester). Caliban, you may be sure, was not roused from his lair until next day noon. He was not heard of until Monday afternoon, when I was sent for home to two gentlemen unknown. He drank his large potations of tea with me, interrupted by many an indignant contradiction and many a noble sentiment, &c. He had a better wig than usual, but one whose curls were not, like Sir Cloudesley's, formed for 'eternal buckle'. He went to town next morning; but as it began to be known that he was in the University, several persons got into his company the last evening at Trinity'. And then his conclusion is equally foolish and indecent; 'where about twelve he began to be very great, stripped poor Mrs Macauley to the skin, then gave her for a toast, and drank her in two bumpers'. Who these several persons were will appear in the sequel.

When I mentioned a wish to introduce him to our common friend Farmer, the Doctor did not seem disinclined to the proposal; and it was on a Saturday in the beginning of March 1765, that having accepted the offer of Topham Beauclerk, esq., to drive him down in his phaeton, they arrived at the Rose Inn, Cambridge. My friend, of Sidney [Sussex

College], had the honour to be the only gownsman sent for by the great man to spend the first evening with him, though Mr Beauclerk had probably also his friend from Trinity. Next morning, though Caliban, as Sharp saucily calls him, might have been time enough out of his lair, yet I admire his prudence and good sense in not appearing that day at St Mary's, to be the general gaze during the whole service. Such an appearance at such a time and place might have turned, as it were, a Christian church into an idol temple; but vanity consorts not with real excellence. He was however heard of that day, for he was with the above party, with the addition perhaps of another friend of his, our respectable Greek Professor, Dr Lort;[5] but whether or not I was myself of my friend's Sunday party, we can neither of us clearly recollect. To my enquiries concerning this Sidney symposium, my friend has returned the following short, but lively description of it: 'Our distinguished visitor shone gloriously in his style of dissertation on a great variety of subjects. I recollect his condescending to as earnest a care of the animal as of the intellectual man, and after doing all justice to my College bill of fare, and without neglecting the glass after dinner, he drank sixteen dishes of tea. I was idly curious enough to count them, from what I had remarked, and heard Levett mention of his extraordinary devotion to the tea-pot.'

Before I close my account of the Sidney dinner, let me observe, that though my friend could not recollect any of the Doctor's *bons mots* at that time, yet the enquiry brought to his mind a former one of our literary hero, so well authenticated and perhaps so little known, that though it has no reference to our present story, I shall take this opportunity of recording it. From the year 1768 to 1771, my friend was Chaplain to his Majesty's Minister, at the court of Denmark, Sir R. Gunning, and tutor to his children. One of the latter, a very accomplished young lady, became in process of time the Hon. Mrs Digby, who related to her former tutor the following anecdote. This lady was present at the introduction of Dr Johnson at one of the late Mrs Montagu's literary parties, when Mrs Digby herself, with several still younger ladies, almost immediately surrounded our Colossus of literature (an odd figure sure enough) with more wonder than politeness, and while contemplating him, as if he had been some monster from the deserts of Africa, Johnson said to them 'Ladies, I am tame; you may stroke me.' 'A happier, or more deserved reproof,' Mrs D. said, 'could not have been given!'

I now hasten to redeem my pledge by describing the first meeting of our two great luminaries, Johnson and Farmer. . . . On Monday morning I met the former at Sidney with the view of conducting him to the latter at Emmanuel. As the Doctor was a stranger at Cambridge, we took a circuitous route to give him a cursory glimpse of some of the colleges. We passed through Trinity, which he admired in course, and then said to me, 'And what is this next?' 'Trinity Hall.' 'I like that college.' 'Why so, Doctor?' 'Because I like the science that they study there.' Hence he walked, or rather, perhaps, rolled or waddled, in a manner not much unlike Pope's idea of 'a dab chick waddling through the copse', either by or through Clare Hall, King's College, Catherine Hall, Queen's, Pembroke and Peterhouse, to the place of our destination.

The long-wished-for interview of these unknown friends was uncommonly joyous on both sides. After the salutations, said Johnson, 'Mr Farmer, I understand you have a large collection of very rare and curious books.' Farmer: 'Why yes, sir, to be sure I have plenty of all such reading as was never read.' Johnson: 'Will you favour me with a specimen, sir?' Farmer, considering for a moment, reached down 'Markham's Booke of Armorie', and turning to a particular page, presented it to the Doctor, who, with rolling head, attentively perused it. . . .

What I have next to relate occurred during the visit, but at what period of it is uncertain. If the great man left us on Tuesday morning, as Sharp asserts, and I think correctly, then it must have been on Sunday afternoon, which will prove that I *was* of the Sidney party, and went with the rest, conducted by Mr Leicester, into Trinity library. On our first entering, Johnson took up, on the right-hand side, not far from the door, a folio, which proved to be the Polyhistor of Morhof, a German genius of great celebrity in the 17th century. On opening this he exclaimed 'Here is the book upon which all my fame was originally founded: when I had read this book I could teach my tutors!' 'And now that you have acquired such fame, Doctor,' said Mr Leicester, 'you must feel exquisite delight in your own mind.' Johnson: 'Why noa, sir, noa, I have no such feeling on that account, as you have attributed to me, sir.' Whether the sincerity of Johnson's declaration be allowed or not, the anecdote may perhaps supply a useful hint to future aspiring geniuses ambitious of emulating so great a man.

Monday, then, we may say, was probably that *last evening* on which the symposium took place, of which Sharp has attempted to give so ridiculous an account. That some strangers crowded about him was the absurd notion of Sharp; but the plain truth is, that on this *last evening* there was assembled at the chambers of Mr Leicester, in Nevell's Court, Trinity College, the very same company as before – viz. Mr L. the entertainer, Mr Beauclerk, Drs Johnson and Lort, my friend and myself, with the addition only of Farmer, on whose account principally the journey was undertaken.

During our conviviality nothing occurred that was at all like an *indignant contradiction*, though the Doctor was himself sometimes purposely contradicted to elicit the sparks of his genius by collision. There was, however, no lack of *noble sentiments*; and on any subject being stated, he would instantly give a sort of treatise upon it in miniature. Long before 12 o'clock our hero *began to be very great*; for on his entering the room, having a pain in his face he bent it down to the fire, archly observing, with a smile, 'This minority cheek of mine is warring against the general constitution.' 'Nay, Doctor,' said Beauclerk, who well knew how to manage him, 'you musn't talk against the minority, for they tell you, you know, that they are your friends, and wish to support your *liberties*, and save you from oppression.' Johnson: 'Why yes, sir, just as wisely, and just as necessarily as if they were to build up the interstices of the cloisters at the bottom of this court, for fear the library should fall upon our heads, sir.' He was brilliant, therefore, from the very first; and might not the above be accepted as a lively and decisive answer to minority politics in general, during the whole of the present reign?

Kit Smart[6] happening to be mentioned, and that he had broken out of a house of confinement: 'He was a fool for that,' said Beauclerk; 'for within two days they meant to have released him.' Johnson: 'Whenever poor Kit could make his escape, sir, it would always have been within two days of his intended liberation.' He then proceeded to speak highly of the parts and scholarship of poor Kit; and to our great surprise, recited a number of lines out of one of Smart's Latin Triposes; and added, 'Kit Smart was mad, sir.' Beauclerk: 'What do you mean by mad, Doctor?' Johnson: 'Why, sir, he could not walk the streets without the boys running after him.' Soon after this, on Johnson's leaving the room, Beauclerk said to us 'What he says of Smart is true of himself', which well agrees with my observations during the walk I took with him that very morning. Beauclerk also took the same opportunity to tell us of that most astonishing, and scarcely credible two days and a night, and then travelling down with the price to support his sick mother! But Boswell says this was done after her decease, to pay her debts and funeral expenses. In either case, what parts! What piety!

On the Doctor's return, Beauclerk said to him, 'Doctor, why do you keep that blind woman in your house?' Johnson: 'Why, sir, she was a friend to my poor wife, and was in the house with her when she died. And so, sir, as I could not find in my heart to desire her to quit my house, poor thing! she has remained in it ever since, sir.' It appears, however that the friendship and conversation of the intelligent Anna Williams, proved in general highly gratifying to him, and he feelingly lamented her loss, in 1703. . . .

In the height of our convivial hilarity, our great man exclaimed 'Come, now, I'll give you a test: now I'll try who is a true antiquary amongst you. Has any one of this company ever met with the History of Glorianus and Gloriana?' Farmer, drawing the pipe out of his mouth, followed by a cloud of smoke, instantly said 'I've got the book.' 'Gi' me your hand, gi' me your hand,' said Johnson; 'you are the man after my own heart.' And the shaking of two such hands, with two such happy faces attached to them, could hardly, I think, be matched in the whole annals of literature!

Such was the rapid appearance and disappearance, the very transient visit of this great man, to an University supereminently famous in itself for the production of great men. It was a visit, however, of which he spoke afterwards in town, to the writer of this account, with very pleasing recollections. Though he must have been well known to many of the heads and doctors at this seat of learning, yet he seemed studious to preserve a strict incognito; his only aim being an introduction to his favourite scholar – his brother patriot, and antiquary, who was then Mr but afterwards Dr Farmer, and master of his college, and who finally declined episcopacy. Merit like Johnson's seeks not publicity; it follows not fame, but leaves fame to follow it. Had he visited Cambridge at the commencement, or on some public occasion, he would doubtless have met with the honours due to the bright luminary of a sister University; and yet, even these honours, however genuine and desirable, the modesty of conscious excellence seems rather to have prompted him to avoid.

NOTES

Baptist Noel Turner's essay, titled 'Account of Dr Johnson's Visit to Cambridge, in 1765', is dated 17 October 1818 – that is, more than fifty-three years after the visit described.

1. See p. 83.

2. Swaying to and fro – a characteristic described by many observers. See also p. 112, note 3.

3. Thomas Martyn (1735–1825) was Professor of Botany at Cambridge from 1762 until his death.

4. Richard Farmer (1735–97) was a tutor at Emmanuel College from 1760 and became Master in 1775. He published his *Essay on the Learning of Shakespeare*, which reaches the conclusion that Shakespeare's knowledge was largely 'confined to Nature and his own Language', in 1767.

5. Michael Lort (1725–90) was Professor of Greek at Cambridge 1759–71.

6. Christopher Smart (1722–71), poet, was acquainted with Johnson during his years of obscurity in London. Boswell reports Johnson as saying on 24 May 1763 that 'My poor friend Smart shewed the disturbance of his mind, by falling upon his knees, and saying his prayers in the street, or in any other unusual place.'

Scotland (1773)*

JAMES BOSWELL

[In Edinburgh, 16 August 1773] He seemed to me to have an unaccountable prejudice against Swift; for I once took the liberty to ask him if Swift had personally offended him, and he told me, he had not. He said today, 'Swift is clear, but he is shallow.[1] In coarse humour, he is inferior to Arbuthnot;[2] in delicate humour, he is inferior to Addison. So he is inferior to his contemporaries; without putting him against the whole world. I doubt if the "Tale of a Tub" was his: it has so much more thinking, more knowledge, more power, more colour, than any of the works which are indisputably his. If it was his, I shall only say, he was *impar sibi*.'[3]

We gave him as good a dinner as we could. Our Scotch muir-fowl, or grouse, were then abundant, and quite in season; and, so far as wisdom and wit can be aided by administering agreeable sensations to the palate, my wife took care that our great guest should not be deficient.

Sir Adolphus Oughton, then our Deputy Commander in Chief, who was not only an excellent officer, but one of the most universal scholars I ever knew, had learned the Erse language, and expressed his belief in the authenticity of Ossian's Poetry.[4] Dr Johnson took the opposite side of that perplexed question; and I was afraid the dispute would have run high between them. But Sir Adolphus, who had a very sweet temper, changed the discourse, grew playful, laughed at Lord Monboddo's[5] notion of men having tails, and called him a Judge *à posteriori*, which amused Dr Johnson; and thus hostilities were prevented.

[In St Andrews, 19 August 1773] Mr Nairne introduced us to Dr Watson, whom we found a well-informed man, of very amiable manners. Dr Johnson, after they were acquainted, said, 'I take great delight in him.' His daughter, a very pleasing young lady, made breakfast. Dr Watson observed that Glasgow University had fewer home-students, since trade increased, as learning was rather incompatible with it. Johnson: 'Why, sir, as trade is now carried on by subordinate hands, men in trade have as much leisure as others; and now learning itself is a

* 'Journal of a tour to the Hebrides', in *Boswell's Life of Johnson*, ed. G. B. Hill, revised by L. F. Powell (Oxford, 1934) v, 44–5, 58–61, 72–3, 208–9, 214–17, 230–1, 306–7.

trade. A man goes to a bookseller, and gets what he can. We have done with patronage. In the infancy of learning, we find some great man praised for it. This diffused it among others. When it becomes general, an author leaves the great, and applies to the multitude.' Boswell: 'It is a shame that authors are not now better patronised.' Johnson: 'No, sir. If learning cannot support a man, if he must sit with his hands across till somebody feeds him, it is as to him a bad thing, and it is better as it is. With patronage, what flattery! What falsehood! While a man is in equilibrio, he throws truth among the multitude, and lets them take it as they please: in patronage, he must say what pleases his patron, and it is an equal chance whether that be truth or falsehood.' Watson: 'But is not the case now, that, instead of flattering one person, we flatter the age?' Johnson: 'No, sir. The world always lets a man tell what he thinks, his own way. I wonder however, that so many people have written, who might have let it alone. That people should endeavour to excel in conversation, I do not wonder; because in conversation praise is instantly reverberated.'

We talked of change of manners. Dr Johnson observed that our drinking less than our ancestors was owing to the change from ale to wine. 'I remember,' said he 'when all the *decent* people in Lichfield got drunk every night, and were not the worse thought of. Ale was cheap, so you pressed strongly. When a man must bring a bottle of wine, he is not in such haste. Smoking has gone out. To be sure, it is a shocking thing, blowing smoke out of our mouths into other people's mouths, eyes and noses, and having the same thing done to us. Yet I cannot account, why a thing which requires so little exertion, and yet preserves the mind from total vacuity, should have gone out. Every man has something by which he calms himself: beating with his feet, or so. I remember when people in England changed a shirt only once a week: a Pandour,[6] when he gets a shirt, greases it to make it last. Formerly, good tradesmen had no fire but in the kitchen; never in the parlour, except on Sunday. My father, who was a magistrate of Lichfield, lived thus. They never began to have a fire in the parlour, but on leaving off business, or some great revolution of their life.' Dr Watson said the hall was as a kitchen, in old squires' houses. Johnson: 'No, sir. The hall was for great occasions, and never was used for domestic refection.' We talked of the Union, and what money it had brought into Scotland. Dr Watson observed, that a little money formerly went as far as a great deal now. Johnson: 'In speculation, it seems that a smaller quantity of money, equal in value to a larger quantity, if equally divided, should produce the same effect. But it is not so in reality. Many more conveniences and elegancies are enjoyed where money is plentiful, than where it is scarce. Perhaps a great familiarity with it, which arises from plenty, makes us more easily part with it.'

[Montrose, 20 August 1773] He said our judges had not gone deep in the question concerning literary property. I mentioned Lord Monboddo's opinion, that if a man could get a work by heart, he might print it, as by such an act the mind is exercised. Johnson: 'No, sir; a man's repeating it no more makes it his property, than a man may sell a cow which he drives home.' I said printing an abridgement of a work was allowed, which was only cutting the horns and tail off the cow. Johnson: 'No, sir; 'tis making the cow have a calf.'

About eleven at night we arrived at Montrose. We found but a sorry inn, where I myself saw another waiter put a lump of sugar with his fingers into Dr Johnson's lemonade, for which he called him 'rascal!' It put me in great glee that our landlord was an Englishman. I rallied the Doctor upon this, and he grew quiet. Both Sir John Hawkins's and Dr Burney's History of Music had then been advertised.[7] I asked if this was not unlucky: would not they hurt one another? Johnson: 'No, sir. They will do good to one another. Some will buy the one, some the other, and compare them; and so a talk is made about a thing, and the books are sold.'

He was angry at me for proposing to carry lemons with us to Skye, that he might be sure to have his lemonade. 'Sir, I do not wish to be thought that feeble man who cannot do without anything. Sir, it is very bad manners to carry provisions to any man's house, as if he could not entertain you. To an inferior, it is oppressive; to a superior, it is insolent.'

Having taken the liberty, this evening, to remark to Dr Johnson that he very often sat quiet silent for a long time, even when in company with only a single friend, which I myself had sometimes sadly experienced, he smiled and said, 'It is true, sir. Tom Tyers' (for so he familiarly called our ingenious friend, who, since his death, has paid a biographical tribute to his memory),[8] 'described me the best. He once said to me, "Sir, you are like a ghost: you never speak till you are spoken to." '

[Skye: Dunvegan, 14 September 1773] M'Leod started the subject of making women do penance in the church for fornication. Johnson: 'It is right, sir. Infamy is attached to the crime, by universal opinion, as soon as it is known. I would not be the man who would discover it, if I alone knew it, for a woman may reform; nor would I commend a parson who divulges a woman's first offence; but being once divulged, it ought to be infamous. Consider, of what importance to society the chastity of women is. Upon that all the property in the world depends. We hang a thief for stealing a sheep; but the unchastity of a woman transfers sheep, and farm and all, from the right owner. I have much more reverence for a common prostitute than for a woman who conceals her guilt. The prostitute is known. She cannot deceive: she cannot bring a strumpet into the arms of an honest man, without his knowledge.' Boswell: 'There is, however, a great difference between the licentiousness of a single woman, and that of a married woman.' Johnson: 'Yes, sir; there is a great difference between stealing a shilling, and stealing a thousand pounds; between simply taking a man's purse, and murdering him first, and then taking it. But when one begins to be vicious, it is easy to go on. Where single women are licentious, you rarely find faithful married women.' Boswell: 'And yet we are told that in some nations in India, the distinction is strictly observed.' Johnson: 'Nay, don't give us India. That puts me in mind of Montesquieu, who is really a fellow of genius too in many respects; whenever he wants to support a strange opinion, he quotes you the practice of Japan or of some other distant country, of which he knows nothing. To support polygamy, he tells you of the island of Formosa, where there are ten women born for one man.[9] He had but to suppose another island, where there are ten men born for one woman, and so make a marriage between them.'

[16 September 1773] Last night much care was taken of Dr Johnson, who was still distressed by his cold. He had hitherto most strangely slept without a night-cap. Miss M'Leod made him a large flannel one, and he was prevailed with to drink a little brandy when he was going to bed. He has great virtue, in not drinking wine or any fermented liquor, because, as he acknowledged to us, he could not do it in moderation. Lady M'Leod would hardly believe him, and said, 'I am sure, sir, you would not carry it too far.' Johnson: 'Nay, madam, it carried me. I took the opportunity of a long illness to leave it off. It was then prescribed to me not to drink wine; and having broken off the habit, I have never returned to it.'

In the argument on Tuesday night, about natural goodness, Dr Johnson denied that any child was better than another, but by difference of instruction; though, in consequence of greater attention being paid to instruction by one child than another, and of a variety of imperceptible causes, such as instruction being counteracted by servants, a notion was conceived, that of two children, equally well educated, one was naturally much worse than another. He owned, this morning, that one might have a greater aptitude to learn than another, and that we inherit dispositions from our parents: 'I inherited a vile melancholy from my father, which has made me mad all my life, at least not sober.' Lady M'Leod wondered he should tell this. 'Madam,' said I, 'he knows that with that madness he is superior to other men.'

I have often been astonished with what exactness and perspicuity he will explain the process of any art. He this morning explained to us all the operation of coining, and, at night, all the operation of brewing, so very clearly, that Mr M'Queen said, when he heard the first, he thought he had been bred in the Mint; when he heard the second, that he had been bred a brewer.

I was elated by the thought of having been able to entice such a man to this remote part of the world. A ludicrous, yet just, image presented itself to my mind, which I expressed to the company. I compared myself to a dog who has got hold of a large piece of meat, and runs away with it to a corner, where he may devour it in peace, without any fear of others taking it from him. 'In London, Reynolds, Beauclerk, and all of them, are contending who shall enjoy Dr Johnson's conversation. We are feasting upon it, undisturbed, at Dunvegan.'

It was still a storm of wind and rain. Dr Johnson however walked out with M'Leod, and saw Rorie More's cascade in full perfection. Colonel M'Leod, instead of being all life and gaiety, as I have seen him, was at present grave, and somewhat depressed by his anxious concern about M'Leod's affairs, and by finding some gentlemen of the clan by no means disposed to act a generous or affectionate part to their Chief in his distress, but bargaining with him as with a stranger. However, he was agreeable and polite, and Dr Johnson said he was a very pleasing man. My fellow-traveller and I talked of going to Sweden; and, while we were settling our plan, I expressed a pleasure in the prospect of seeing the king. Johnson: 'I doubt, sir, if he would speak to us.' Colonel M'Leod said, 'I am sure Mr Boswell would speak to *him*.' But, seeing me a little disconcerted by his remark, he politely added, 'and with great propriety.' Here let me offer a short defence of that propensity in my disposition, to which this gentleman alluded. It has procured me much happiness. I hope it does not deserve so hard a name as either forwardness or impudence. If I know myself, it is nothing more than an eagerness to share the society of men distinguished either by their rank or their talents, and a diligence to attain what I desire. If a man is praised for seeking knowledge, though mountains and seas are in his way, may he not be pardoned, whose ardour, in the pursuit of the same object, leads him to encounter difficulties as great, though of a different kind?

After the ladies were gone from table, we talked of the Highlanders not having sheets; and this led us to consider the advantage of wearing linen. Johnson: 'All animal substances are less cleanly than vegetables. Wool, of which flannel is made, is an animal substance; flannel therefore is not so cleanly as linen. I remember I used to think tar dirty; but when I knew it to be only a preparation of the juice of the pine, I thought so no longer. It is not disagreeable to have the gum that oozes from a plumb-tree upon your fingers, because it is vegetable; but if you have any candle-grease, any tallow upon your fingers, you are uneasy until you rub it off. I have often thought, that, if I kept a seraglio, the ladies should all wear linen gowns, or cotton; I mean stuffs made of vegetable substances. I would have no silk; you cannot tell when it is clean: it will be very nasty before it is perceived to be so. Linen detects its own dirtiness.'

To hear the grave Dr Samuel Johnson, 'that majestic teacher of moral and religious wisdom', while sitting solemn in an armchair in the Isle of Skye, talk, *ex cathedra*, of his keeping a seraglio, and acknowledge that the supposition had *often* been in his thoughts, struck me so forcibly with ludicrous contrast, that I could not but laugh immoderately. He was too proud to submit, even for a moment, to be the object of ridicule, and instantly retaliated with such keen sarcastic wit, and such a variety of degrading images, of every one of which I was the object, that, though I can bear such attacks as well as most men, I yet found myself so much the sport of all the company, that I would gladly expunge from my mind every trace of this severe retort.

Talking of our friend Langton's house in Lincolnshire, he said, 'the old house of the family was burnt. A temporary building was erected in its room; and to this they have been always adding as the family increased. It is like a shirt made for a man when he was a child, and enlarged always as he grows older.'

We talked tonight of Luther's allowing the Landgrave of Hesse two wives, and that it was with the consent of the wife to whom he was first married. Johnson: 'There was no harm in this, so far as she was only concerned, because *volenti non fit injuria*.[10] But it was an offence against the general order of society, and against the law of the Gospel, by which one man and one woman are to be united. No man can have two wives, but by preventing somebody else from having one.'

[20 September 1773] When I awaked, the storm was higher still. It abated about nine, and the sun shone; but it rained again very soon, and it was not a day for travelling. At breakfast, Dr Johnson told us, 'There was once a pretty good tavern in Catharine Street in the Strand, where very good company met in an evening, and each man called for his own half-pint of wine, or gill, if he pleased; they were frugal men, and nobody paid but for what he himself drank. The house furnished no supper; but a woman attended with mutton-pies, which anybody might purchase. I was introduced to this company by Cumming the Quaker, and used to go there sometimes when I drank wine. In the last age, when my mother lived in London, there were two sets of people, those who gave the wall, and those who took it; the peaceable and the quarrelsome. When I returned to Lichfield, after having been in London, my mother asked me whether I was one of those who gave the wall, or those who took it. Now, it is fixed that every man keeps to the right; or, if one is taking the wall, another yields it, and it is never a dispute.' He was very severe on a lady, whose name was mentioned. He said he would have her sent to St Kilda. That she was as bad as negative badness could be, and stood in the way of what was good: that insipid beauty would not go a great way; and that such a woman might be cut out of a cabbage, if there was a skilful artificer.

M'Leod was too late in coming to breakfast. Dr Johnson said, laziness was worse than the tooth-ache. Boswell: 'I cannot agree with you, sir; a bason of cold water, or a horse-whip, will cure laziness.' Johnson: 'No, sir; it will only put off the fit; it will not cure the disease. I have been trying to cure my laziness all my life, and could not do it.' Boswell: 'But if a man does in a shorter time what might be the labour of a life, there is nothing to be said against him.' Johnson (perceiving at once that I alluded to him and his *Dictionary*): 'Suppose that flattery to be true, the consequence would be, that the world would have no right to censure a man; but that will not justify him to himself.'

[Coll, 12 October 1773] He has particularities which it is impossible to explain. He never wears a night-cap, as I have already mentioned; but he puts a handkerchief on his head in the night. The day that we left Talisker, he bade us ride on. He then turned the head of his horse back towards Talisker, stopped for some time; then wheeled round to the same direction with ours, and then came briskly after us. He sets open a window in the coldest day or night, and stands before it. It may do with his constitution; but most people, amongst whom I am one, would say, with the frogs in the fable, 'This may be sport to you; but it is death to us.' It is in vain to try to find a meaning in every one of his particularities, which, I suppose, are mere habits, contracted by chance; of which every man has some that are more or less remarkable. His speaking to himself, or rather repeating, is a common habit with studious men accustomed to deep thinking; and, in consequence of their being thus rapt, they will even laugh by themselves, if the subject which they are musing on is a merry one. Dr Johnson is often uttering pious ejaculations, when he appears to be talking to himself; for sometimes his voice grows stronger, and parts of the Lord's Prayer are heard. I have sat beside him with more than ordinary reverence on such occasions.

In our Tour, I observed that he was disgusted whenever he met with coarse manners. He said to me, 'I know not how it is, but I cannot bear low life: and I find others, who have as good a right as I to be fastidious, bear it better, by having mixed more with different sorts of men. You would think that I have mixed pretty well too.'

NOTES

James Boswell (1740–95), the greatest of Johnson's (and of English) biographers, toured Scotland with him from 14 August to 22 November 1773 and made the most of his unparalleled opportunities for day-to-day contact with and observation of Johnson – he compared himself to 'a dog who has got hold of a large piece of meat, and runs away with it to a corner, where he may devour it in peace, without any fear of others taking it from him'. Boswell kept a journal during (at least) the period 18 August–22 October, and based his later account of the tour on it; the manuscript of the original journal was discovered in 1930 and published in 1936. As Philip Collins points out (*James Boswell* (1956) p. 29), the published work is not a simple transcript of the journal but omits about a quarter of the material. In revising the work for publication, Boswell received considerable assistance from Edmund Malone (1741–1812), critic, who was a member of the Literary Club. The *Journal* was published on 1 October 1785, nine or ten months after Johnson's death. Johnson's own account of the tour had appeared in 1775.

1. The *Town and Country Magazine* for September 1769 provides an earlier version of this *mot*:

> Dr Jn being one evening in company with some of the first-rate *literati* of the age *roundly* asserted in his *rough* way, that 'Swift was a shallow fellow, a very shallow fellow'. The ingenious Mr Sh[erida]n … replied warmly, but modestly, 'Pardon me, Sir, for differing from you, but I always thought the dean a very *clear* writer'. To this modest reply the following *laconic* answer was immediately vociferated: 'All *shallows* are clear.'

2. John Arbuthnot (1667–1735), physician and author, was a friend of Swift; he is commemorated in Pope's *Epistle to Dr Arbuthnot*.
3. 'Unequal to himself.'
4. James Macpherson's alleged translation from the Gaelic poet Ossian, published in the early 1760s, was the subject of intense controversy.
5. Lord Monboddo (1714–99), Scottish judge, published pioneering works in anthropology and was much ridiculed for his suggestion that the orang-outang represented 'the infantine state of our species'.
6. Croation soldier.
7. Hawkins published a *General History of Music* in 1776; Burney's *History of Music* began publication in the same year.
8. On Tyers, see p. 33.
9. The reference seems to be to *L'Esprit des Lois*, xvi, 4, by Montesquieu, French political philosopher.
10. 'Injury cannot be suffered by one who is willing' (legal maxim).

Shrewsbury and Birmingham (1774)*

HESTER LYNCH THRALE

[Shrewsbury, 11 September 1774] Mr Johnson sent for Gwynn the Architect to go with us from place to place; we walked until we were weary, and Mr Johnson snubbed the poor fellow so hard that I half pitied him, though he was so coarse a creature.

* A. M. Broadley, *Doctor Johnson and Mrs Thrale* (1910) pp. 209, 214.

[Birmingham, 20 September] Mr Johnson said how much he had been in love with Mr Hector's sister, the old lady who made breakfast for us in the morning, and when I recollected her figure I thought she had the remains of a beauty.

NOTES

Johnson toured Wales with Mrs Thrale between July and September 1774 and visited Shrewsbury and Birmingham on the way home. Broadley's book reproduces both Mrs Thrale's journal of the tour and the diary that Johnson kept during that period. Of this tour, Boswell drily notes that it 'did not give occasion to such a discursive exercise of his mind as our tour to the Hebrides'.

France I (1775)*

HESTER LYNCH THRALE

[The party set off from London on 15 September 1775 and travelled via Rochester and Canterbury (visiting the cathedrals of both of those cities) to Dover, then crossing to Calais.]

[Calais, 17 September] We had an excellent Dinner which a Capuchin Fryar enlivened by his Company. When it was over we were entertained with a sight of his Convent, Cells, Chapel & Refectory; the Library was locked, & I was not sorry, for Mr Johnson would never have come out of it. . . . We saw a Ship such as might serve for a Model of a Man of War hung up in the Chapel of the Convent. I asked the meaning & the Fryer told me it was a Ship some honest Man had made, & grown more fond of it than it is fit to be of any earthly Thing – so he had piously given it away to the Capuchin Chapel. Johnson observed that I ought to give them Queeney.

[18 September] Dr Johnson's Birthday; we walked early to the great Church. . . .

* *The French Journals of Mrs Thrale and Doctor Johnson*, ed. Moses Tyson and Henry Guppy (Manchester, 1932) pp. 71, 79, 90, 142, 143, 164, 203.

[22 September] Mr Johnson has made a little Distich at every Place we have slept at, for example

A Calais	St Omer	Arras	A Amiens
Trop de frais.	Tout est cher.	Helas!	On n'a rien.

[27 September] [The party meet with an accident on the road in which Mr Thrale is injured.] Dr Johnson's perfect unconcern for the Lives of three People, who would all have felt for his, shocked and amazed me – but that, as Baretti says, is true Philosophy. Mrs Strickland did not give it so kind a Name; I soon saw her indignation towards him prevailing over her Friendship for me.

[29 September[We have made it all up with Johnson who protests it was not unconcern for Mr Thrale but anger at me that [made] him sullenly forbear Enquiry, when he found Me unwilling (as he thought it) to give him a ready or rational Answer.

[27 October] Captain Killpatrick came [to] breakfast. . . . He finds the way to Dr Johnson's heart by abusing the French. . . . [At St Cloud] The Busts in the Gallery, all Antiques, are very valuable. Johnson abuses the French for writing the names of [these] ancient Heroes in their own Language always & not in Greek or Latin.

[28 October] . . . the Men went to the Play – I was not well enough to venture so Mr Johnson sat at home by me, & we criticised & talked & were happy in one another – he in huffing me, & I in being huffed.

[9 November] There was some French Company at the Captain's in the Afternoon to Tea & Cards, who seemed much diverted with the odd Appearance of Johnson's wig . . . and refrained from laughing out with the greatest difficulty. . . . The Road [for the next stage of the journey] is said to be bad but we have been so often frightened with false *formidabilities* that I begin to laugh at them *now* as Mr Johnson has done all this while.

NOTE

On Mrs Thrale (later Mrs Piozzi), see p. 82. Johnson accompanied the Thrales on a tour of France in 1775; the tour lasted 58 days, the party returning to England on 12 November. The manuscript of Mrs Thrale's diary of the tour was discovered in 1931. Boswell quotes Johnson's own diary, which covers only 26 days of the tour. The next extract represents some of her recollections of the tour a decade later.

France II (1775)*

HESTER LYNCH PIOZZI

He delighted no more in music than painting; he was almost as deaf as he was blind: travelling with Dr Johnson was for these reasons tiresome enough. Mr Thrale loved prospects, and was mortified that his friend could not enjoy the sight of those different dispositions of wood and water, hill and valley, that travelling through England and France affords a man. But when he wished to point them out to his companion: 'Never heed such nonsense,' would be the reply: 'a blade of grass is always a blade of grass, whether in one country or another: let us if we *do* talk, talk about something; men and women are my subjects of enquiry; let us see how these differ from those we have left behind.'

When we were at Rouen together, he took a great fancy to the Abbé Roffette, with whom he conversed about the destruction of the order of Jesuits, and condemned it loudly, as a blow to the general power of the church, and likely to be followed with many and dangerous innovations, which might at length become fatal to religion itself, and shake even the foundation of Christianity. The gentleman seemed to wonder and delight in his conversation: the talk was all in Latin, which both spoke fluently, and Mr Johnson pronounced a long eulogium upon Milton with so much ardour, eloquence, and ingenuity, that the Abbé rose from his seat and embraced him. My husband seeing them apparently so charmed with the company of each other, politely invited the Abbé to England, intending to oblige his friend; who, instead of thanking, reprimanded him severely before the man, for such a sudden burst of tenderness towards a person he could know nothing at all of; and thus put a sudden finish to all his own and Mr Thrale's entertainment from the company of the Abbé Roffette.

When at Versailles the people showed us the theatre. As we stood on the stage looking at some machinery for playhouse purposes: Now we are here, what shall we act, Mr Johnson – The Englishman at Paris? 'No, no,' replied he, 'we will try to act Harry the Fifth.' His dislike of the French was well known to both nations, I believe; but he applauded the number of their books and the graces of their style. 'They have few sentiments,' said he, 'but they express them neatly; they have little meat too, but they dress it well.' Johnson's own notions about eating, however,

* *Anecdotes of Dr Johnson*, pp. 66–9.

were nothing less than delicate; a leg of pork boiled until it dropped from the bone, a veal pie with plums and sugar, or the outside cut of a salt buttock of beef, were his favourite dainties: with regard to drink, his liking was for the strongest, as it was not the flavour, but the effect he sought for, and professed to desire; and when I first knew him, he used to pour capillaire into his port wine. For the last twelve years however, he left off all fermented liquors. To make himself some amends indeed, he took his chocolate liberally, pouring in large quantities of cream, or even melted butter; and was so fond of fruit, that though he usually ate seven or eight large peaches of a morning before breakfast began, and treated them with proportionate attention after dinner again, yet I have heard him protest that he never had quite as much as he wished of wall-fruit, except once in his life, and that was when we were all together at Ombersley, the seat of my Lord Sandys. I was saying to a friend one day, that I did not like goose; one smells it so while it is roasting, said I. 'But you, Madam,' replies the Doctor, 'have been at all times a fortunate woman, having always had your hunger so forestalled by indulgence, that you never experienced the delight of smelling your dinner beforehand' Which pleasure, answered I pertly, is to be enjoyed in perfection by such as have the happiness to pass through Porridge-Island of a morning. 'Come, come,' says he gravely, let's have no sneering at what is serious to so many: hundreds of your fellow-creatures, dear Lady, turn another way, that they may not be tempted by the luxuries of Porridge-Island to wish for gratifications they are not able to obtain: you are certainly not better than all of *them*; give God thanks that you are happier.'

Oxford (1782)*

HANNAH MORE

[The first two extracts are dated April 1782; the visit to Oxford belongs to the following June.]

Poor Johnson is in a bad state of health; I fear his constitution is broken up: I am quite grieved at it, he will not leave an abler defender of religion and virtue behind him, and the following little touch of tenderness which I heard of him last night from one of the Turk's Head Club, endears him

---

* *Johnsonian Miscellanies*, ii, 196–9 (excerpted from Roberts's *Memoirs*).

to me exceedingly. There are always a great many candidates ready, when any vacancy happens in that club, and it requires no small interest and reputation to get elected; but upon Garrick's death,[1] when numberless applications were made to succeed him, Johnson was deaf to them all; he said, No, there never could be found any successor worthy of such a man; and he insisted upon it there should be a year's widowhood in the club, before they thought of a new election. In Dr Johnson some contrarieties very harmoniously meet; if he has too little charity for the opinions of others, and too little patience with their faults, he has the greatest tenderness for their persons. He told me the other day, he hated to hear people whine about metaphysical distresses, when there was so much want and hunger in the world. I told him I supposed then he never wept at any tragedy but Jane Shore, who had died for want of a loaf.[2] He called me a saucy girl, but did not deny the inference. . . .

I dined very pleasantly one day last week at the Bishop of Chester's. Johnson was there, and the Bishop was very desirous to draw him out, as he wished to show him off to some of the company who had never seen him. He begged me to sit next him at dinner, and to devote myself to making him talk. To this end, I consented to talk more than became me, and our stratagem succeeded. You would have enjoyed seeing him take me by the hand in the middle of dinner, and repeat with no small enthusiasm, many passages from the 'Fair Penitent',[3] &c. I urged him to take a *little* wine; he replied, 'I can't drink a *little*, child, therefore I never touch it. Abstinence is as easy to me, as *temperance* would be difficult.' He was very good-humoured and gay. One of the company happened to say a word about poetry: 'Hush, hush,' said he, 'it is dangerous to say a word of poetry before her; it is talking of the art of war before Hannibal.' He continued his jokes, and lamented that I had not married Chatterton,[4] that posterity might have seen a propagation of poets. . . .

Who do you think is my principal Cicerone at Oxford? Only Dr Johnson! And we do so gallant it about! You cannot imagine with what delight he showed me every part of his own College (Pembroke), nor how rejoiced Henderson looked, to make one in the party. Dr Adams, the master of Pembroke, had contrived a very pretty piece of gallantry. We spent the day and evening at his house. After dinner Johnson begged to conduct me to see the College, he would let no one show it me but himself – 'This was my room; this Shenstone's.'[5] Then after pointing out all the rooms of the poets who had been of his college, 'In short,' said he, 'we were a nest of singing-birds.' – 'Here we walked, there we played at cricket.' He ran over with pleasure the history of the juvenile days he passed there. When we came into the common room, we spied a fine large print of Johnson, framed and hung up that very morning, with this motto: '*And is not Johnson ours, himself a host.*' Under which stared you in the face, 'From

Miss More's Sensibility.[6] This little incident amused us; but alas! Johnson looks very ill indeed – spiritless and wan. However, he made an effort to be cheerful, and I exerted myself much to make him so.

NOTES

Hannah More (1745–1833), prolific author best known in her later years for her religious writings. Her life spanned a remarkably long period: as a child she had a nurse who had been previously employed by Dryden, and in her old age she befriended the young Macaulay, who described her as his 'second mother'. She came to London in about 1774 and became a friend of Garrick, Burke and Reynolds, by the last of whom she was introduced to Johnson (probably in 1775), as well as a prominent member of the Blue-stocking Circle. Her memoirist describes her first meeting with Johnson in these terms:

> Reynolds . . . prepared her, as he handed her upstairs, for the possibility of [Johnson's] being in one of his moods of sadness and silence.
> She was surprised in his coming to meet her as she entered the room, with good humour in his countenance, and a macaw of Sir Joshua's in his hand; and still more, at his accosting her with a verse from a Morning Hymn which she had written. . . . In the same pleasant humour he continued the whole of the evening.   (Roberts, *Memoirs*, I, 48.)

Her admiration for Johnson seems at times to have been too much of a good thing, and Boswell and others record Johnson's dislike of her excessive flattery: on one occasion, according to Mrs Thrale, he 'bade [her] . . . consider what her flattery was worth before she choked *him* with it'. (Boswell's milder version of his speech runs 'before you bestow it so freely'.) But, as Leslie Stephen points out in the *DNB*, 'the flattery was not all one-sided', and Johnson seems to have enjoyed her company and admired her work (see p. 152 and the accompanying note 2). See M. G. Jones, *Hannah More* (Cambridge, 1952).

1. David Garrick had died on 20 January 1779.
2. Nicholas Rowe's *The Tragedy of Jane Shore* (1714).
3. Another of Rowe's tragedies, produced in 1703.
4. Thomas Chatterton (1752–70), poet and forger.
5. William Shenstone (1714–63), poet, went up to Pembroke College, Oxford, in 1732, three years after Johnson had left.
6. Hannah More's poem *Sensibility* was published in 1782.

Part V

Last Days

'A very melancholy spectacle'*

ANNA SEWARD

[Letter written from Lichfield to Miss Weston, and dated 29 October 1784] I have lately been in the almost daily habit of contemplating a very melancholy spectacle. The great Johnson is here, labouring under the paroxysms of a disease, which must speedily be fatal. He shrinks from the consciousness with the extremest horror. It is by his repeatedly expressed desire that I visit him often: yet I am sure he neither does, nor ever did feel much regard for me; but he would fain escape, for a time, in any society, from the terrible idea of his approaching dissolution. I never would be awed by his sarcasms, or his frowns, into acquiescence with his general injustice to the merits of *other* writers; with his national, or party aversions; but I feel the truest compassion for his present sufferings, and fervently wish I had power to relieve them.

A few days since I was to drink tea with him, by his request, at Mrs Porter's.[1] When I went into the room, he was in deep but agitated slumber, in an armchair. Opening the door with that caution due to the sick, he did not awaken at my entrance. I stood by him several minutes, mournfully contemplating the temporary suspension of those vast intellectual powers, which must so soon, as to *this* world, be eternally quenched.

Upon the servant entering to announce the arrival of a gentleman of the university, introduced by Mr White,[2] he awoke with convulsive starts – but rising, with more alacrity than could have been expected, he said, 'Come, my dear lady, let you and I attend these gentlemen in the study.' He received them with more than usual complacence; but whimsically chose to get astride upon his chair-seat, with his face to its back, keeping a trotting motion as if on horseback; but, in this odd position, he poured forth streams of eloquence, illuminated by frequent flashes of wit and humour, without any tincture of malignity. That amusing part of this conversation, which alluded to the learned Pig,[3] and his demi-rational exhibitions, I shall transmit to you hereafter.

* *Letters of Anna Seward* (Edinburgh, 1811) I, 7–9.

NOTES

Anna Seward (1747–1809), authoress, whose poems earned her the title of 'the Swan of Lichfield', spent most of her life in that city. Boswell obtained from her anecdotes relating to Johnson's early years which she had obtained from her father and grandfather (the latter, John Hunter, had been headmaster of Lichfield Grammar School during Johnson's time there: see p. 6, note 3). She was one of the party whose conversation is reported at length by Boswell under the date 15 April 1778.

    1. Lucy Porter (1715–86), Johnson's step-daughter.

    2. 'Mr Henry White [1761–1836], a young clergyman, with whom [Johnson] now formed an intimacy, so as to talk to him with great freedom' (Boswell, under November 1784). It was to White that Johnson told the moving story of his standing 'bareheaded in the rain' in the market-place at Uttoxeter in order to atone for a proud refusal to accompany his father there many years earlier.

    3. Boswell reports Miss Seward as saying that she had seen 'a wonderful learned pig' exhibited in Nottingham.

'Extremely far from well'*

FANNY BURNEY

[10 January 1783] I made a visit to poor Dr Johnson, to inquire after his health. I found him better, yet extremely far from well. One thing, however, gave me infinite satisfaction. He was so good as to ask me after Charles, and said, 'I shall be glad to see him; pray tell him to call upon me.' I thanked him very much, and said how proud he would be of such a permission.

    'I should be glad,' said he, still more kindly, 'to see him, if he were not your brother; but were he a dog, a cat, a rat, a frog, and belonged to you, I must needs be glad to see him!'

[19 June 1783] We heard today that Dr Johnson had been taken ill, in a way that gave a dreadful shock to himself, and a most anxious alarm to his friends.[1] Mr Seward brought the news here, and my father and I instantly went to his house. He had earnestly desired me, when we lived so much together at Streatham, to see him frequently if he should be ill. He saw my father, but he had medical people with him, and could not admit me upstairs, but he sent me down a most kind message, that he

---

* *Diary and Letters of Madame d'Arblay*, II, 177, 213–14, 270–2.

thanked me for calling, and when he was better should hope to see me often. I had the satisfaction to hear from Mrs Williams that the physicians had pronounced him to be in no danger, and expected a speedy recovery.

The stroke was confined to his tongue. Mrs Williams told me a most striking and touching circumstance that attended the attack. It was at about four o'clock in the morning: he found himself with a paralytic affection; he rose, and composed in his own mind a Latin prayer to the Almighty, 'that whatever were the sufferings for which he must prepare himself, it would please Him, through the grace and mediation of our blessed Saviour, to spare his intellects, and let them all fall upon his body.' When he had composed this, internally, he endeavoured to speak it aloud, but found his voice was gone.

[28 November 1784] Last Thursday, 25 November, my father set me down at Bolt Court, while he went on upon business. I was anxious to again see poor Dr Johnson, who has had terrible health since his return from Lichfield. He let me in, though very ill. He was alone, which I much rejoiced at; for I had a longer and more satisfactory conversation with him than I have had for many months. He was in rather better spirits, too, than I have lately seen him; but he told me he was going to try what sleeping out of town might do for him.

'I remember,' said he, 'that my wife, when she was near her end, poor woman, was also advised to sleep out of town; and when she was carried to the lodgings that had been prepared for her, she complained that the staircase was in very bad condition – for the plaster was beaten off the walls in many places. "Oh," said the man of the house, "that's nothing but by the knocks against it of the coffins of the poor souls that have died in the lodgings!" '

He laughed, though not without apparent secret anguish, in telling me this. I felt extremely shocked, but, willing to confine my words at least to the literal story, I only exclaimed against the unfeeling absurdity of such a confession.

'Such a confession,' cried he, 'to a person then coming to try his lodging for her health, contains, indeed, more absurdity than we can well lay our account for.'

I had seen Miss T[hrale] the day before.

'So,' said he, 'did I.'

I then said, 'Do you ever, sir, hear from her mother?'[2]

'No,' cried he, 'nor write to her. I drive her quite from my mind. If I meet with one of her letters, I burn it instantly. I have burnt all I can find. I never speak of her, and I desire never to hear of her more. I drive her, as I said, wholly from my mind.'

Yet, wholly to change this discourse, I gave him a history of the Bristol milk-woman,[3] and told him the tales I had heard of her writing so wonderfully, though she had read nothing but Young and Milton; 'though those,' I continued, 'could never possibly, I should think, be the first authors with anybody. Would children understand them? And grown people who have not read are children in literature.'

'Doubtless,' said he; 'but there is nothing so little comprehended among mankind as what is genius. They give to it all, when it can be but a part. Genius is nothing more than knowing the use of tools; but there must be tools for it to use: a man who has spent all his life in this room will give a very poor account of what is contained in the next.'

'Certainly, sir; yet there is such a thing as invention? Shakespeare could never have seen a Caliban.'

'No; but he had seen a man, and knew, therefore, how to vary him to a monster. A man who would draw a monstrous cow, must first know what a cow commonly is; or how can he tell that to give her an ass's head or an elephant's tusk will make her monstrous? Suppose you show me a man who is a very expert carpenter; another will say he was born to be a carpenter – but what if he had never seen any wood? Let two men, one with genius, the other with none, look at an overturned wagon: he who has no genius, will think of the wagon only as he sees it, overturned, and walk on; he who has genius, will paint it to himself before it was overturned – standing still, and moving on, and heavy loaded, and empty; but both must see the wagon, to think of it at all.'

How just and true all this, my dear Susy! He then animated, and talked on, upon this milk-woman, upon a once as famous shoemaker,[4] and upon our immortal Shakespeare, with as much fire, spirit, wit, and truth of criticism and judgment, as ever yet I have heard him. How delightfully bright are his faculties, though the poor and infirm machine that contains them seems alarmingly giving way.

Yet, all brilliant as he was, I saw him growing worse, and offered to go, which, for the first time I ever remember, he did not oppose; but, most kindly pressing both my hands, 'Be not,' he said, in a voice of even tenderness, 'be not longer in coming again for my letting you go now.'

I assured him I would be the sooner, and was running off, but he called me back, in a solemn voice, and, in a manner the most energetic, said, 'Remember me in your prayers!'

NOTES

On Fanny Burney, see p. 99. These extracts from her journal relating to the closing stages of Johnson's life may be compared with the fuller account of the same period in her memoirs of her father, written almost fifty years later, and excerpted below.

1. Johnson suffered a stroke on the morning of 17 June 1783. Although

temporarily deprived of the power of speech, he was already showing signs of recovery the next day, and wrote to Mrs Thrale on 19 June, as she records in *Thraliana* (p. 568):

[24 June] A Stroke of the Palsy has robbed Johnson of his Speech I hear, dreadful Event! & I at a Distance – poor Fellow! a Letter from himself in his usual Style convinces me that none other of his Faculties have failed him, & his Physicians say that all present Danger is over.

2. Mrs Thrale wrote to Johnson and her other friends on 30 June 1784, informing them of her intention to marry Piozzi. Johnson, who is said to have burst into tears on receiving the news, replied in an angry note of 2 July, reproaching her for being 'ignominiously married' (though the wedding did not take place for another three weeks). His last letter to her, in which he shows more tenderness and thanks her for her 'kindness which soothed twenty years of a life radically wretched', was written on 8 July. They never met again.

3. Mrs Ann Yearsley (1756–1806), known as 'Lactilla', was patronised by Hannah More and published *Poems on Several Occasions* (1784).

4. James Woodhouse (1735–1820), 'the poetical shoemaker', was patronised by Mrs Montagu and published *Poems on Sundry Occasions* (1764). Boswell reports Dr Maxwell as saying that in 1770 Johnson 'spoke with much contempt of the notice taken of Woodhouse. . . . "They had better (said he) furnish the man with good implements for his trade, than raise subscriptions for his poems. He may make an excellent shoemaker, but can never make a good poet." '

'This great and good man'*

MADAME D'ARBLAY

But all that Dr Burney possessed, either of spirited resistance or acquiescent submission to misfortune, was again to be severely tried in the summer that followed the spring of this unkindly year [1783]; for the health of his venerated Dr Johnson received a blow from which it never wholly recovered; though frequent rays of hope intervened from danger to danger; and though more than a year and a half were still allowed to his honoured existence upon earth.

Mr Seward first brought to Dr Burney the alarming tidings, that this great and good man had been afflicted by a paralytic stroke. The Doctor hastened to Bolt Court, taking with him this memorialist, who had frequently and urgently been desired by Dr Johnson himself, during the

* *Memoirs of Doctor Burney*, pp. 212–14, 218–19, 228–36.

time that they lived so much together at Streatham, to see him often if he should be ill. But he was surrounded by medical people, and could only admit the Doctor. He sent down, nevertheless, the kindest message of thanks to the truly sorrowing daughter, for calling upon him; and a request that, 'when he should be better, she would come to him again and again'.

From Mrs Williams, with whom she remained, she then received the comfort of an assurance that the physicians had pronounced him not to be in danger; and even that they expected the illness would be speedily overcome. The stroke had been confined to the tongue.

Mrs Williams related a very touching circumstance that had attended the attack. It had happened about four o'clock in the morning, when, though she knew not how, he had been sensible to the seizure of a paralytic affection. He arose, and composed, in his mind, a prayer in Latin to the Almighty, That, however acute might be the pains, for which he must befit himself, it would please him, through the grace and mediation of our Saviour, to spare his intellects, and to let all his sufferings fall upon his body.

When he had internally conceived this petition, he endeavoured to pronounce it, according to his pious practice, aloud – but his voice was gone! He was greatly struck, though humbly and resignedly. It was not, however, long, before it returned; but at first with very imperfect articulation.

Dr Burney, with the zeal of true affection, made time unceasingly for inquiring visits: and no sooner was the invalid restored to the power of reinstating himself in his drawing-room, than the memorialist received from him a summons, which she obeyed the following morning.

She was welcomed with the kindest pleasure; though it was with much difficulty that he endeavoured to rise, and to mark, with wide extended arms, his cordial gladness at her sight; and he was forced to lean back against the wainscot as impressively he uttered, 'Ah! – dearest of all dear ladies!'

He soon, however, recovered more strength, and assumed the force to conduct her himself, and with no small ceremony, to his best chair.

'Can you forgive me, sir,' she cried, when she saw that he had not breakfasted, 'for coming so soon!'

'I can less forgive your not coming sooner!' he answered, with a smile.

She asked whether she might make his tea, which she had not done since they had left poor Streatham; where it had been her constant and gratifying business to give him that regale, Miss Thrale being yet too young for the office.

He readily, and with pleasure, consented.

'But, sir,' quoth she, 'I am in the wrong chair.' For it was on his own sick large armchair, which was too heavy for her to move, that he had formally seated her, and it was away from the table.

'It is so difficult,' cried he, with quickness, 'for anything to be wrong that belongs to you, that it can only be I that am in the wrong chair to keep you from the right one!'

This playful good humour was so reviving in showing his recovery, that though Dr Burney could not remain above ten minutes, his daughter, for whom he sent back his carriage, could with difficulty retire at the end of two hours. Dr Johnson endeavoured most earnestly to engage her to stay and dine with him and Mrs Williams; but that was not in her power; though so kindly was his heart opened by her true joy at his re-establishment, that he parted from her with a reluctance that was even, and to both, painful. Warm in its affections was the heart of this great and good man; his temper alone was in fault where it appeared to be otherwise. . . .

Very ill again Dr Johnson grew on the approach of winter; and with equal fear and affection, both father and daughter sought him as often as it was in their power; though by no means as frequently as their zealous attachment, or as his own kind wishes might have prompted. But fulness of affairs, and the distance of his dwelling, impeded such continual intercourse as their mutual regard would otherwise have instigated.

This new failure of health was accompanied by a sorrowing depression of spirits; though unmixed with the smallest deterioration of intellect.

One evening – the last but one of the sad year 1783 – when Dr Burney and the memorialist were with him, and some other not remembered visitors, he took an opportunity during a general discourse in which he did not join, to turn suddenly to the ever-favoured daughter, and, fervently grasping her hand, to say: 'The blister I have tried for my breath has betrayed some very bad tokens! But I will not terrify myself by talking of them. Ah! – *priez Dieu pour moi!*'

Her promise was as solemn as it was sorrowful; but more humble, if possible, than either. That such a man should condescend to make her such a request, amazed, and almost bewildered her: yet, to a mind so devout as that of Dr Johnson, prayer, even from the most lowly, never seemed presumptuous; and even, where he believed in its sincerity, soothed him – for a passing moment – with an idea that it might be propitious.

This was the only instance in which Dr Johnson ever addressed her in French. He did not wish so serious an injunction to reach other ears than her own. . . .

Towards the end of this year, 1784, Dr Johnson began again to nearly monopolise the anxious friendship of Dr Burney.

On 16 November, Dr Johnson, in the carriage, and under the revering care of Mr Windham, returned from Lichfield to the metropolis, after a fruitless attempt to recover his health by breathing again his natal air.

The very next day he wrote the following note to St Martin's Street.

To Dr Burney
'Mr Johnson, who came home last night, sends his respects to dear Dr
Burney; and to all the dear Burneys, little and great.
Bolt Court, 17 Nov. 1784.

Dr Burney hastened to this kind call immediately; but had the grief to
find his honoured friend much weakened, and in great pain; though
cheerful and struggling to revive. All of the Doctor's family who had the
honour of admission, hastened to him also; but chiefly his second
daughter, who chiefly and peculiarly was always demanded.

She was received with his wonted, his never-failing partiality; and, as
well as the Doctor, repeated her visits by every opportunity during the
ensuing short three weeks of his earthly existence.

She will here copy, from the diary she sent to Boulogne, an account of
what, eventually, though unsuspectedly, proved to be her last interview
with this venerated friend.

To Mrs Phillips
25th Nov. 1784 – Our dear father lent me the carriage this morning for Bolt
Court. You will easily conceive how gladly I seized the opportunity for
making a longer visit than usual to my revered Dr Johnson, whose
health, since his return from Lichfield, has been deplorably deteriorated.

He was alone, and I had a more satisfactory and entertaining
conversation with him than I have had for many months past. He was in
better spirits, too, than I have seen him, except upon our first meeting,
since he came back to Bolt Court.

He owned, nevertheless, that his nights were grievously restless and
painful; and told me that he was going, by medical advice, to try what
sleeping out of town might do for him. And then, with a smile – but a
smile of more sadness than mirth! – he added: 'I remember that my wife,
when she was near her end, poor woman! – was also advised to sleep out
of town: and when she was carried to the lodging that had been prepared
for her, she complained that the staircase was in a very bad condition; for
the plaster was beaten off the walls in many places. "O!" said the man of
the house, "that's nothing; its only the knocks against it of the coffins of
the poor souls that have died in the lodging." '

He forced a faint laugh at the man's brutal honesty; but it was a laugh
of ill-disguised, though checked, secret anguish.

I felt inexpressibly shocked, both by the perspective and retrospective
view of this relation: but, desirous to confine my words to the literal
story, I only exclaimed against the man's unfeeling *absurdity* in making so
unnecessary a confession.

'True!' he cried; 'such a confession, to a person then mounting his stairs for the recovery of her health, or, rather for the preservation of her life, contains, indeed, more absurdity than we can well pay our account to.'

We talked then of poor Mrs Thrale – but only for a moment – for I saw him so greatly moved, and with such severity of displeasure, that I hastened to start another subject; and he solemnly enjoined me to mention that no more!

I gave him concisely the history of the Bristol milk-woman, who is at present zealously patronised by the benevolent Hannah More. I expressed my surprise at the reports generally in circulation, that the first authors that the milk-woman read, if not the only ones, were Milton and Young. 'I find it difficult,' I added, 'to conceive how Milton and Young could be the first authors with any reader. Could a child understand them? And grown persons, who have never read, are, in literature, children still.'

'Doubtless,' he answered. 'But there is nothing so little comprehended as what is genius. They give it to all, when it can be but a part. The milk-woman had surely begun with some ballad – Chevy Chace or the Children in the Wood. Genius is, in fact, *knowing the use of tools*. But there must be tools, or how use them? A man who has spent all his life in this room, will give a very poor account of what is contained in the next.'

'Certainly, sir; and yet there is such a thing as invention? Shakespeare could never have seen a Caliban?'

'No, but he had seen a man, and knew how to vary him to a monster. A person who would draw a monstrous cow, must know first what a cow is commonly; or how can he tell that to give her an ass's head, or an elephant's tusk, will make her monstrous? Suppose you show me a man, who is a very expert carpenter, and that an admiring stander-by, looking at some of his works, exclaims: "O! He was born a carpenter!" What would have become of that birth-right, if he had never seen any wood?'

Presently, dwelling on this idea, he went on. 'Let two men, one with genius, the other with none, look together at an overturned wagon; he who has no genius will think of the wagon only as he then sees it; that is to say, overturned, and walk on: he who has genius will give it a glance of examination, that will paint it to his imagination such as it was previously to its being overturned; and when it was standing still; and when it was in motion; and when it was heavy loaded; and when it was empty; but both alike must see the wagon to think of it at all.'

The pleasure with which I listened to his illustration now animated him on; and he talked upon this milk-woman, and upon a once as famous shoemaker; and then mounted his spirits and his subject to our immortal Shakespeare; flowing and glowing on, with as much wit and truth of criticism and judgment, as ever yet I have heard him display; but, alack-a-day, my Susan, I have no power to give you the participation so justly your due. My paper is filling; and I have no francs for doubling letters across the channel! But delightfully bright are his faculties, though the poor, infirm, shaken machine that contains them seems alarmingly giving way! And soon, exhilarated as he became by the pleasure of bestowing pleasure, I saw a palpable increase of suffering in the midst of his sallies; I offered, therefore, to go into the next room, there to wait for the carriage; an offer which (for the first time!) he did not oppose; but taking, and most affectionately pressing, both my hands, 'Be not,' he said, in a voice of even melting kindness and concern, 'be not longer in coming again for my letting you go now!'

I eagerly assured him that I would come the sooner, and was running off; but he called me back, and in a solemn voice, and a manner the most energetic, said: 'Remember me in your prayers!'

How affecting, my dearest Susanna, such an injunction from Dr Johnson! It almost – as once before – made me tremble, from surprise and emotion – surprise he could so honour me, and emotion that he should think himself so ill. I longed to ask him so to remember *me*! But he was too serious for any parleying, and I knew him too well for offering any disqualifying speeches: I merely, in a low voice, and I am sure a troubled accent, uttered an instant, and heart-felt assurance of obedience; and then, very heavily, indeed, in spirits, I left him. Great, good and surpassing that he is, how short a time will he be our boast! I see he is going. This winter will never glide him on to a more genial season here. Elsewhere, who may hope a fairer? I now wish I had asked for *his* prayers! And perhaps, so encouraged, I ought: but I had not the presence of mind.

Melancholy was the rest of this year to Dr Burney; and truly mournful to his daughter, who, from this last recorded meeting, felt redoubled anxiety for both the health and the sight of this illustrious invalid. But all accounts thenceforward discouraged her return to him, his pains daily becoming greater, and his weakness more oppressive: added to which obstacles, he was now, she was informed, almost constantly attended by a group of male friends.

Dr Burney, however, resorted to Bolt Court every moment that he could tear from the imperious calls of his profession; and was instantly admitted; unless held back by insuperable impediments belonging to the malady. He might, indeed, from the kind regard of the sufferer, have seen him every day, by watching like some other assiduous friends, particularly Messrs Langton, Strahan, the Hooles, and Sastres, whole hours in the house to catch a favourable minute; but that, for Dr Burney, was utterly impossible. His affectionate devoirs could only be received when he arrived at some interval of ease, and then the kind invalid constantly, and with tender pleasure, gave him welcome.

The memorialist was soon afterwards engaged on a visit to Norbury

Park; but immediately on her return to town, presented herself, according to her willing promise, at Bolt Court.

Frank Barber, the faithful negro, told her, with great sorrow, that his master was very bad indeed, though he did not keep his bed. The poor man would have shown her upstairs. This she declined, desiring only that he would let the Doctor know that she had called to pay her respects to him, but would by no means disturb him, if he were not well enough to see her without inconvenience.

Mr Strahan, the clergyman, was with him, Frank said, alone; and Mr Strahan, in a few minutes, descended.

Dr Johnson, he told her, was very ill indeed, but very much obliged to her for coming to him; and he had sent Mr Strahan to thank her in his name, but to say that he was so very bad, and very weak, that he hoped she would excuse his not seeing her.

She was greatly disappointed; but, leaving a message of the most affectionate respect, acquiesced, and drove away; painfully certain how extremely ill, or how sorrowfully low he must be, to decline the sight of one whom so constantly, so partially, he had pressed, nay, adjured, 'to come to him again and again'.

Fast, however, was approaching the time when he could so adjure her no more!

From her firm conviction of his almost boundless kindness to her, she was fearful now to importune or distress him, and forebore, for the moment, repeating her visits; leaving in Dr Burney's hands all propositions for their renewal. But Dr Burney himself, not arriving at the propitious interval, unfortunately lost sight of the sufferer for nearly a week, though he sought it almost daily.

On Friday 10 December, Mr Seward brought to Dr Burney the alarming intelligence from Frank Barber, that Dr Warren had seen his master, and told him that he might take what opium he pleased for the alleviation of his pains.

Dr Johnson instantly understood, and impressively thanked him, and then gravely took a last leave of him: after which, with the utmost kindness, as well as composure, he formally bid adieu to all his physicians.

Dr Burney, in much affliction, hurried to Bolt Court; but the invalid seemed to be sleeping, and could not be spoken to until he should open his eyes. Mr Strahan, the clergyman, gave however the welcome information, that the terror of death had now passed away; and that this excellent man no longer looked forward with dismay to his quick approaching end; but, on the contrary, with what he himself called the irradiation of hope.

This was, indeed, the greatest of consolations, at so awful a crisis, to his grieving friend; nevertheless, Dr Burney was deeply depressed at the heavy and irreparable loss he was so soon to sustain; but he determined to make, at least, one more effort for a parting sight of his so long honoured friend. And, on Saturday, 11 December, to his unspeakable comfort, he arrived at Bolt Court just as the poor invalid was able to be visible; and he was immediately admitted.

Dr Burney found him seated on a great chair, propped up by pillows, and perfectly tranquil. He affectionately took the Doctor's hand, and kindly inquired after his health, and that of his family; and then, as evermore Dr Johnson was wont to do, he separately and very particularly named and dwelt upon the Doctor's second daughter; gently adding, 'I hope Fanny did not take it amiss, that I did not see her that morning! I was very bad indeed!'

Dr Burney answered, that the word *amiss* could never be *à propos* to her; and least of all now, when he was so ill.

The Doctor ventured to stay about half an hour, which was partly spent in quiet discourse, partly in calm silence; the invalid always perfectly placid in looks and manner.

When the Doctor was retiring, Dr Johnson again took his hand and encouraged him to call yet another time; and afterwards, when again he was departing, Dr Johnson impressively said, though in a low voice, 'Tell Fanny – to pray for me!' And then, still holding, or rather grasping, his hand, he made a prayer for himself, the most pious, humble, eloquent, and touching, Dr Burney said, that mortal man could compose and utter. He concluded it with an amen! in which Dr Burney fervently joined, and which was spontaneously echoed by all who were present.

This over, he brightened up, as if with revived spirits, and opened cheerfully into some general conversation; and when Dr Burney, yet a third time, was taking his reluctant leave, something of his old arch look played upon his countenance as, smilingly, he said, 'Tell Fanny – I think I shall yet throw the ball at her again!'

A kindness so lively, following an injunction so penetrating, reanimated a hope of admission in the memorialist; and, after church, on the ensuing morning, Sunday 12 December, with the fullest approbation of Dr Burney, she repaired once more to Bolt Court.

But grievously was she overset on hearing, at the door, that the Doctor again was worse, and could receive no one.

She summoned Frank Barber, and told him she had understood, from her father, that Dr Johnson had meant to see her. Frank then, but in silence, conducted her to the parlour. She begged him merely to mention to the Doctor, that she had called with most earnest inquiries; but not to hint at any expectation of seeing him until he should be better.

Frank went upstairs; but did not return. A full hour was consumed in anxious waiting. She then saw Mr Langton pass the parlour door, which she watchfully kept open, and ascend the stairs. She had not courage to stop or speak to him, and another hour lingered on in the same suspense.

But, at about four o'clock, Mr Langton made his appearance in the parlour.

She took it for granted he came accidentally, but observed that, though he bowed, he forbore to speak, or even to look at her, and seemed in much disturbance.

Extremely alarmed, she durst not venture at any question; but Mrs Davis, who was there, uneasily asked, 'How is Dr Johnson now, sir?'

'Going on to death very fast!' was the mournful reply.

The memorialist, grievously shocked and overset by so hopeless a sentence, after an invitation so sprightly of only the preceding evening from the dying man himself, turned to the window to recover from so painful a disappointment.

'Has he taken anything, sir?' said Mrs Davis.

'Nothing at all! We carried him some bread and milk; he refused it, and said, "The less the better!" '

Mrs Davis then asked sundry other questions, from the answers to which it fully appeared that his faculties were perfect, and that his mind was quite composed.

This conversation lasted about a quarter of an hour, before the memorialist had any suspicion that Mr Langton had entered the parlour purposely to speak to her, and with a message from Dr Johnson.

But as soon as she could summon sufficient firmness to turn round, Mr Langton solemnly said, 'This poor man, I understand, ma'am, from Frank, desired yesterday to see you.'

'My understanding, or hoping that, sir, brought me hither today.'

'Poor man! 'Tis a pity he did not know himself better; and that you should not have been spared this trouble.'

'Trouble?' she repeated: 'I would come a hundred times to see Dr Johnson the hundreth and first!'

'He begged me, ma'am, to tell you that he hopes you will excuse him. He is very sorry, indeed, not to see you. But he desired me to come and speak to you for him myself, and to tell you that he hopes you will excuse him; for he feels himself too weak for such an interview.'

Struck and touched to the very heart by so kind, though sorrowful a message, at a moment that seemed so awful, the memorialist hastily expressed something like thanks to Mr Langton, who was visibly affected, and, leaving her most affectionate respects, with every warmly kind wish she could half utter, she hurried back to her father's coach.

The very next day, Monday 13 December, Dr Johnson expired – and without a groan. Expired, it is thought, in his sleep.

'A prey to melancholy'*

HANNAH MORE

[Letter to her sister dated April 1784] Did I tell you I went to see Dr Johnson? Miss Monckton[1] carried me, and we paid him a very long visit. He received me with the greatest kindness and affection, and as to the *Bas Bleu*,[2] all the flattery I ever received from everybody together would not make up the sum. He said – but I seriously insist you do not tell anybody, for I am ashamed of writing it even to you – he said there was no name in poetry that might not be glad to own it. You cannot imagine how I stared: all this from Johnson, that parsimonious praiser! I told him I was delighted at his approbation; he answered quite characteristically, 'And so you may, for I give you the opinion of a man who does not rate his judgment in these things very low, I can tell you.'

[Letter to Mrs Boscawen, referring to Johnson's visit to Oxford in November 1784] My appointment at Oxford was to flirt with Dr Johnson, but he was a recreant knight, and had deserted. He had been for a fortnight at the house of my friend Dr Adams, the head of Pembroke, with Mr Boswell; but the latter being obliged to go to town, Johnson was not thought well enough to remain behind, and afterwards to travel by himself; so that he left my friend's house the very day I got thither, though they told me he did me the honour to be very angry and out of humour, that I did not come so soon as I had promised. I am grieved to find that his mind is still a prey to melancholy, and that the fear of death operates on him to the destruction of his peace. It is grievous – it is unaccountable! He who has the Christian hope upon the best foundation; whose faith is strong, whose morals are irreproachable! But I am willing to ascribe it to bad nerves, and bodily disease.

[Letter of December 1784] Poor dear Johnson! He is past all hope. The dropsy has brought him to the point of death; his legs are scarified; but nothing will do. I have, however, the comfort to hear that his dread of dying is in a great measure subdued; and now he says 'the bitterness of death is past'.

---

* William Roberts, *Memoirs of the Life and Correspondence of Mrs Hannah More* (2nd edn, 1834) I, pp. 319–20, 330, 376–80.

[In another letter to a friend, Hannah More recounts 'a conversation which I had with the late Revd Mr Storry, of Colchester . . .'.] We were riding together near Colchester, when I asked Mr Storry whether he had ever heard that Dr Johnson expressed great dissatisfaction with himself on the approach of death, and that in reply to friends, who, in order to comfort him spoke of his writings in defence of virtue and religion, he had said, 'admitting all you urge to be true, how can I tell when I have done enough'.

Mr S. assured me that what I had just mentioned was perfectly correct; and then added the following interesting particulars.

Dr Johnson, said he, did feel as you describe, and was not to be comforted by the ordinary topics of consolation which were addressed to him. In consequence he desired to see a clergyman, and particularly described the views and character of the person whom he wished to consult. After some consideration a Mr Winstanley was named, and the Doctor requested Sir John Hawkins to write a note in his name, requesting Mr W.'s attendance as a minister.

Mr W., who was in a very weak state of health, was quite overpowered on receiving the note, and felt appalled by the very thought of encountering the talents and learning of Dr Johnson. In his embarrassment he went to his friend Colonel Pownall, and told him what had happened, asking, at the ame time for his advice how to act. The Colonel, who was a pious man, urged him immediately to follow what appeared to be a remarkable leading of providence, and for the time argued his friend out of his nervous apprehension: but after he had left Colonel Pownall, Mr W.'s fears returned in so great a degree as to prevail upon him to abandon the thought of a personal interview with the Doctor. He determined in consequence to write him a letter: that letter I think Mr Storry said he had seen, at least a copy of it, and part of it he repeated to me as follows.

Sir – I beg to acknowledge the honour of your note, and am very sorry that the state of my health prevents my compliance with your request: but my nerves are so shattered that I feel as if I should be quite confounded by your presence, and instead of promoting, should only injure the cause in which you desire my aid. Permit me therefore to write what I should wish to say were I present. I can easily conceive what would be the subjects of your inquiry. I can conceive that the views of yourself have changed with your condition, and that on the near approach of death, what you once considered mere peccadillos have risen into mountains of guilt, while your best actions have dwindled into nothing. On whichever side you look, you see only positive transgressions or defective obedience; and hence, in self-despair, are eagerly inquiring, 'What shall I do to be saved?' I say to you, in the language of the Baptist, 'Behold the Lamb of God!' &c. &c.

When Sir John Hawkins came to this part of Mr W.'s letter, the

Doctor interrupted him, anxiously asking, '*Does he say so?* Read it again! Sir John.' Sir John complied: upon which the Doctor said, 'I must see that man; write again to him.' A second note was accordingly sent: but even this repeated solicitation could not prevail over Mr Winstanley's fears. He was led, however, by it to write again to the Doctor, renewing and enlarging upon the subject of his first letter; and these communications, together with the conversation of the late Mr Latrobe, who was a particular friend of Dr Johnson, appear to have been blessed by God in bringing this great man to the renunciation of self, and a simple reliance on Jesus as his Saviour, thus also communicating to him that peace which he had found the world could not give, and which, when the world was fading from his view, was sufficient to fill the void, and dissipate the gloom, even of the valley of the shadow of death.

NOTES

On Hannah More, see p. 136.
    1. The Hon. Mary Monckton, another member of the Blue-stocking Circle, and later Countess of Cork.
    2. Hannah More's *Bas Bleu*, a poem describing the 'blue-stocking clubs', was circulated in manuscript in 1784 and published in 1786.

The Final Weeks I*

JOHN HOOLE

Saturday 20 Nov. 1784 – This evening, about eight o'clock, I paid a visit to my dear friend Dr Johnson, whom I found very ill and in great dejection of spirits. We had a most affecting conversation on the subject of religion, in which he exhorted me, with the greatest warmth of kindness, to attend closely to every religious duty, and particularly enforced the obligation of private prayer and receiving the Sacrament. He desired me to stay that night and join in prayer with him; adding, that he always went to prayer every night with his man Francis [Barber]. He conjured me to read and meditate upon the Bible, and not to throw it aside for a play or a novel. He said he had himself lived in great

* *European Magazine* (September 1799); reprinted in *Johnsonian Miscellanies*, II, 146–60 (where the date of original publication is given incorrectly as 1779).

negligence of religion and worship for forty years; that he had neglected to read his Bible, and had often reflected what he could hereafter say when he should be asked why he had not read it. He begged me repeatedly to let his present situation have due effect upon me; and advised me, when I got home, to note down in writing what had passed between us, adding, that what a man writes in that manner dwells upon his mind. His said many things that I cannot now recollect, but all delivered with the utmost fervour of religious zeal and personal affection. Between nine and ten o'clock his servant Francis came upstairs: he then said we would all go to prayers, and, desiring me to kneel down by his bedside, he repeated several prayers with great devotion. I then took my leave. He then pressed me to think of all he had said, and to commit it to writing. I assured him I would. He seized my hand with much warmth, and repeated, 'Promise me you will do it', on which we parted, and I engaged to see him the next day.

Sunday 21 Nov. – About noon I again visited him; found him rather better and easier, his spirits more raised and his conversation more disposed to general subjects. When I came in, he asked if I had done what he desired (meaning the noting down what passed the night before); and upon my saying that I had, he pressed my hand and said earnestly, 'Thank you.' Our discourse then grew more cheerful. He told me, with apparent pleasure, that he heard the Empress of Russia had ordered *The Rambler* to be translated into the Russian language, and that a copy would be sent him.

Before we parted, he put into my hands a little book, by Fleetwood, on the Sacrament,[1] which he told me he had been the means of introducing to the University of Oxford by recommending to it a young student there.

Monday 22 Nov. – Visited the Doctor: found him seemingly better of his complaints, but extremely low and dejected. I sat by him until he fell asleep, and soon after left him, as he seemed little disposed to talk; and, on my going away, he said, emphatically, 'I am very poorly indeed!'

Tuesday 23 Nov. – Called about eleven: the Doctor not up: Mrs Gardiner in the dining-room: the Doctor soon came to us, and seemed more cheerful than the day before. He spoke of his design to invite a Mrs Hall to be with him, and to offer her Mrs Williams's room. Called again about three: found him quite oppressed with company that morning, therefore left him directly.

Wednesday 24 Nov. – Called about seven in the evening: found him very ill and very low indeed. He said a thought had struck him that his rapid decline of health and strength might be partly owing to the town air, and spoke of getting a lodging at Islington. I sat with him until past nine, and then took my leave.

Thursday 25 Nov. – About three in the afternoon was told that he desired that day to see no company. In the evening, about eight, called with Mr Nicol,[2] and, to our great surprise, we found him then setting out for Islington, to the Revd Mr Strahan's.[3] He could scarce speak. We went with him down the court to the coach. He was accompanied by his servant Frank and Mr Lowe the painter.[4] I offered myself to go with him but he declined it.

Friday 26 Nov. – Called at his house about eleven: heard he was much better, and had a better night than he had known a great while, and was expected home that day. Called again in the afternoon – not so well as he was, nor expected home that night.

Saturday 27 Nov. – Called again about noon: heard he was much worse: went immediately to Islington, where I found him extremely bad, and scarce able to speak, with the asthma. Sir John Hawkins, the Revd Mr Strahan, and Mrs Strahan, were with him. Observing that we said little, he desired that we would not constrain ourselves, though he was not able to talk with us. Soon after he said he had something to say to Sir John Hawkins, on which we immediately went down into the parlour. Sir John soon followed us, and said he had been speaking about his will.[5] Sir John started the idea of proposing to him to make it on the spot; that Sir John should dictate it, and that I should write it. He went up to propose it, and soon came down with the Doctor's acceptance. The will was then begun; but before we proceeded far, it being necessary, on account of some alteration, to begin again, Sir John asked the Doctor whether he would choose to make any introductory declaration respecting his faith. The Doctor said he would. Sir John further asked if he would make any declaration of his being of the Church of England: to which the Doctor said '*No!*' But, taking a pen, he wrote on a paper the following words, which he delivered to Sir John, desiring him to keep it: 'I commit to the infinite mercies of Almighty God my soul, polluted with many sins; but purified, I trust, with repentance and the death of Jesus Christ.' While he was at Mr Strahan's, Dr Brocklesby[6] came in, and Dr Johnson put the question to him, whether he thought he could live six weeks? To which Dr Brocklesby returned a very doubtful answer, and soon left us. After dinner the will was finished, and about six we came to town in Sir John Hawkins's carriage; Sir John, Dr Johnson, Mr Ryland[7] (who came in after dinner), and myself. The Doctor appeared much better on the way home, and talked pretty cheerfully. Sir John took leave of us at the end of Bolt Court, and Mr Ryland and myself went to his house with the Doctor, who began to grow very ill again. Mr Ryland soon left us, and I remained with the Doctor until Mr Sastres[8] came in. We stayed with him about an hour, when we left him on his saying he had some business to do. Mr Sastres and myself went together homewards, discoursing on the dangerous state of our friend, when it was resolved that Mr Sastres should write to Heberden;[9] but going to his house that night, he fortunately found him at home, and he promised to be with Dr Johnson next morning.

Sunday 28 Nov. – Went to Dr Johnson's about two o'clock: met Mrs Hoole coming from thence, as he was asleep: took her back with me: found Sir John Hawkins with him. The Doctor's conversation tolerably cheerful. Sir John reminded him that he had expressed a desire to leave some small memorials to his friends, particularly a Polyglot Bible to Mr Langton; and asked if they should add the codicil then. The Doctor replied he 'had forty things to add, but could not do it at that time'. Sir John then took his leave. Mr Sastres came next into the dining-room, where I was with Mrs Hoole. Dr Johnson hearing that Mrs Hoole was in the next room, desired to see her. He received her with great affection, took her by the hand, and said nearly these words: 'I feel great tenderness for you: think of the situation in which you see me, profit by it, and God Almighty keep you for Jesus Christ's sake, Amen.' He then asked if we would both stay and dine with him. Mrs Hoole said she could not; but I agreed to stay. Upon my saying to the Doctor that Dr Heberden would be with him that morning, his answer was, 'God has called me, and Dr Heberden comes too late.' Soon after this Dr Heberden came. . . .

After Dr Heberden was gone, Mr Sastres and I returned into the chamber. Dr Johnson complained that sleep this day had powerful dominion over him, that he waked with great difficulty, and that probably he should go off in one of these paroxysms. Afterwards he said that he hoped his sleep was the effect of opium taken some days before, which might not be worked off. We dined together – the Doctor, Mr Sastres, Mrs Davies, and myself. He ate a pretty good dinner with seeming appetite, but appearing rather impatient; and being asked unnecessary and frivolous questions, he said he often thought of Macbeth – 'Question enrages him.'[10] He retired immediately after dinner, and we soon went, at his desire (Mr Sastres and myself), and sat with him till tea. He said little, but dozed at times. At six he ordered tea for us, and we went out to drink it with Mrs Davies; but the Doctor drank none. The Revd Dr Taylor, of Ashbourne, came soon after; and Dr Johnson desired our attendance at prayers, which were read by Dr Taylor. Mr Ryland came and sat some time with him: he thought him much better. Mr Sastres and I continued with him the remainder of the evening, when he exhorted Mr Sastres in nearly these words: 'There is noone who has shown me more attention than you have done, and it is now right you should claim some attention from me. You are a young man, and are to struggle through life: you are in a profession that I dare say you will exercise with great fidelity and innocence; but let me exhort you always to think of my situation, which must one day be yours: always remember that life is short, and that eternity never ends! I say nothing of your religion; for if you conscientiously keep to it, I have little doubt but you may be saved: if you read the controversy, I think we have the right on our side; but if you do not read it, be not persuaded, from any worldly consideration, to alter the religion in which you were educated: change not, but from conviction of reason.' He then most strongly enforced the motives of virtue and piety from the consideration of a future state of reward and punishment and concluded with 'Remember all this, and God bless you! Write down what I have said – I think you are the third person I have bid do this.' At ten o'clock he dismissed us, thanking us for a visit which he said could not have been very pleasant to us.

Monday 29 Nov. – Called with my son[11] about eleven: saw the Doctor, who said, 'You must not now stay.' But, as we were going away, he said, 'I will get Mr Hoole to come next Wednesday and read the Litany to me, and do you and Mrs Hoole come with him.' He appeared very ill. Returning from the city I called again to inquire, and heard that Dr Butter was with him. In the evening, about eight, called again and just saw him; but did not stay, as Mr Langton was with him on business. I met Sir Joshua Reynolds going away.

Tuesday 30 Nov. – Called twice this morning, but did not see him: he was much the same. In the evening, between six and seven, went to his house: found there Mr Langton, Mr Sastres and Mr Ryland: the Doctor being asleep in the chamber, we went all to tea and coffee; when the Doctor came in to us rather cheerful, and entering said, 'Dear gentlemen, how do you do?' He drank coffee, and, in the course of the conversation, said that he recollected a poem of his, made some years ago on a young gentleman coming of age. He repeated the whole with great spirit: it consisted of about fifteen or sixteen stanzas of four lines, in alternate rhyme. He said he had repeated it only once since he composed it, and that he never gave but one copy. He said several excellent things that evening, and among the rest, that 'scruples made many men miserable, but few men good'. He spoke of the affectation that men had to accuse themselves of petty faults or weaknesses, in order to exalt themselves into notice for any extraordinary talents which they might possess; and instanced Waller,[12] which he said he would record if he lived to revise his life. Waller was accustomed to say that his memory was so bad he would sometimes forget to repeat his grace at table, or the Lord's Prayer, perhaps that people might wonder at what he did else of great moment; for the Doctor observed that no man takes upon himself small blemishes without supposing that great abilities are attributed to him; and that, in short, this affectation of candour or modesty was but another kind of indirect self-praise, and had its foundation in vanity. Frank bringing him a note, as he opened it he said an odd thought struck him, that 'one should receive no letters in the grave'. His talk was in general very serious and devout, though occasionally cheerful: he said, 'You are all serious men, and I will tell you something. About two years since I feared that I had neglected God, and that then I had not a *mind* to give him: on which I set about to read Thomas à Kempis[13] in Low Dutch, which I accomplished, and thence I judged that my mind was not impaired, Low Dutch having no affinity with any of the languages which I knew.' With respect to his recovery, he seemed to think it hopeless. There was to be a consultation of physicians next day: he wished to have his legs scarified to let out the water; but this his medical friends opposed, and he submitted to their opinion, though he said he was not satisfied. At half-past eight he dismissed us all but Mr Langton. I first asked him if my son should attend him next day, to read the Litany, as he had desired; but he declined it on account of the expected consultation. We went away, leaving Mr Langton and Mr Desmoulins,[14] a young man who was employed in copying his Latin epigrams.

Wednesday 1 Dec. – At his house in the evening: drank tea and coffee with Mr Sastres, Mr Desmoulins, and Mr Hall: went into the Doctor's chamber after tea, when he gave me an epitaph to copy, written by him for his father, mother and brother. He continued much the same.

Thursday 2 Dec. – Called in the morning, and left the epitaph: with him in the evening about seven; found Mr Langton and Mr Desmoulins; did not see the Doctor; he was in his chamber, and afterwards engaged with Dr Scott.[15]

Friday 3 Dec. – Called; but he wished not to see anybody. Consultations of physicians to be held that day: called again in the evening; found Mr Langton with him; Mr Sastres and I went together into his chamber; he was extremely low. 'I am very bad indeed, dear gentlemen,' he said; 'very bad, very low, very cold, and I think I find my life to fail.' In about a quarter of an hour he dismissed Mr Sastres and me; but called me back again, and said that next Sunday, if he lived, he designed to take the sacrament, and wished me, my wife, and son to be there. We left Mr Langton with him.

Saturday 4 Dec. – Called on him about three: he was much the same; did not see him, he had much company that day. Called in the evening with Mr Sastres about eight; found he was not disposed for company; Mr Langton with him; did not see him.

Sunday 5 Dec. – Went to Bolt Court with Mrs Hoole after eleven; found there Sir John Hawkins, Revd Mr Strahan, Mrs Gardiner, and Mr Desmoulins, in the dining-room. After some time the Doctor came to us from the chamber, and saluted us all, thanking us all for this visit to him. He said he found himself very bad, but hoped he should go well through the duty which he was about to do. The sacrament was then administered to all present, Frank being of the number. The Doctor repeatedly desired Mr Strahan to speak louder; seeming very anxious not to lose any part of the service, in which he joined in very great fervour of devotion. The service over, he again thanked us all for attending him on the occasion; he said he had taken some opium to enable him to support the fatigue: he seemed quite spent, and lay in his chair some time in a kind of doze: he then got up and retired into his chamber. Mr Ryland then called on him. I was with them: he said to Mr Ryland, 'I have taken my viaticum: I hope I shall arrive safe at the end of my journey, and be accepted at last.' He spoke very despondingly several times: Mr Ryland comforted him, observing that 'we had great hopes given us'. 'Yes,' he replied, 'we have hopes given us; but they are conditional, and I know not how far I have fulfilled those conditions.' He afterwards said 'However, I think that I have now corrected all bad and vicious habits.' Sir Joshua Reynolds called on him: we left them together. Sir Joshua being gone, he called Mr Ryland and me again to him: he continued talking very seriously, and repeated a prayer or collect with great fervour, when Mr Ryland took his leave. My son came to us from his church: we were at dinner – Dr Johnson, Mrs Gardiner, myself, Mrs Hoole, my son, and Mr Desmoulins. He ate a tolerable dinner, but retired directly after dinner. He had looked out a sermon of Dr Clarke's,[16] 'On the Shortness of Life', for me to read to him after dinner, but he was too ill to hear it. After six o'clock he called us all into his room, when he dismissed us for that night with a prayer, delivered as he sat in his great chair in the most fervent and affecting manner, his mind appearing wholly employed with the thoughts of another life. He told Mr Ryland that he wished not to come to God with opium, but that he hoped he had been properly attentive. He said before us all, that when he recovered the last spring, he had only called it a *reprieve*, but that he did think it was for a longer time; however he hoped the time that had been prolonged to him might be the means of bringing forth fruit meet for repentance.

Monday 6 Dec. – Sent in the morning to make inquiry after him; he was much the same; called in the evening; found Mr Cruikshanks the surgeon with him; he said he had been that day quarrelling with all his physicians; he appeared in tolerable spirits.

Tuesday 7 Dec. – Called at dinner time; saw him eat a very good dinner: he seemed rather better, and in spirits.

Wednesday 8 Dec. – Went with Mrs Hoole and my son, by appointment: found him very poorly and low, after a very bad night. Mr Nichols the printer was there. My son read the Litany, the Doctor several times urging him to speak louder. After prayers Mr Langton came in: much serious discourse: he warned us all to profit by his situation; and, applying to me, who stood next him, exhorted me to lead a better life than he had done. 'A better life than you, my dear Sir!' I repeated. He replied warmly, 'Don't compliment now.' He told Mr Langton that he had the night before enforced on —— a powerful argument to a powerful objection against Christianity.

He had often thought it might seem strange that the Jews, who refused belief to the doctrine supported by the miracles of our Saviour, should after his death raise a numerous church; but he said that they expected fully a temporal prince, and with this idea the multitude was actuated when they strewed his way with palm-branches on his entry into

Jerusalem; but finding their expectations afterwards disappointed, rejected him, till in process of time, comparing all the circumstances and prophecies of the Old Testament, confirmed in the New, many were converted; that the Apostles themselves once believed him to be a temporal prince. He said that he had always been struck with the resemblance of the Jewish passover and the Christian doctrine of redemption. He thanked us all for our attendance, and we left him with Mr Langton.

Thursday 9 Dec. – Called in the evening; did not see him, as he was engaged.

Friday 10 Dec. – Called about eleven in the morning; saw Mr La Trobe there: neither of us saw the Doctor, as we understood he wished not to be visited that day. In the evening I sent him a letter, recommending Dr Dalloway (an irregular physician) as an extraordinary person for curing the dropsy. He returned me a verbal answer that he was obliged to me, but that it was too late. My son read prayers with him this day.

Saturday 11 Dec. – Went to Bolt Court about twelve; met there Dr Burney, Dr Taylor, Sir John Hawkins, Mr Sastres, Mr Paradise, Count Zenobia and Mr Langton. Mrs Hoole called for me there: we both went to him; he received us very kindly; told me he had my letter, but 'it was too late for doctors, *regular* or *irregular*'. His physicians had been with him that day, but prescribed nothing. Mr Cruikshanks came; the Doctor was rather cheerful with him; he said, 'Come, give me your hand,' and shook him by the hand, adding, 'You shall make no other use of it now,' meaning he should not examine his legs. Mr Cruikshanks wished to do it, but the Doctor would not let him. Mr Cruikshanks said he would call in the evening.

Sunday 12 Dec. – Was not at Bolt Court in the forenoon; at St Sepulchre's school in the evening with Mrs Hoole, where we saw Mrs Gardiner and Lady Rothes; heard that Dr Johnson was very bad, and had been something delirious. Went to Bolt Court about nine, and found there Mr Windham and the Revd Mr Strahan. The Doctor was then very bad in bed, which I think he had only taken to that day: he had now refused to take any more medicine or food. Mr Cruikshanks came about eleven: he endeavoured to persuade him to take some nourishment, but in vain. Mr Windham then went again to him, and, by the advice of Mr Cruikshanks, put it upon this footing – that by persisting to refuse all sustenance he might probably defeat his own purpose *to preserve his mind clear*, as his weakness might bring on paralytic complaints that might affect his mental powers. The Doctor, Mr Windham said, heard him patiently; but when he had heard all, he desired to be troubled no more. He then took a most affectionate leave of Mr Windham, who reported to us the issue of the conversation, for only Mr Desmoulins was with them in the chamber. I did not see the Doctor that day, being fearful of disturbing him, and never conversed with him again. I came away about half-past eleven with Mr Windham.

Monday 13 Dec. – Went to Bolt Court at eleven o'clock in the morning; met a young lady coming downstairs from the Doctor, whom, upon inquiry, I found to be Miss Morris (a sister to Miss Morris, formerly on the stage). Mrs Desmoulins told me that she had seen the Doctor; that by her desire he had been told she came to ask his blessing, and that he said, 'God bless you!' I then went up into his chamber, and found him lying very composed in a kind of doze: he spoke to nobody. Sir John Hawkins, Mr Langton, Mrs Gardiner, Revd Mr Strahan and Mrs Strahan, Doctors Brocklesby and Butter, Mr Steevens, and Mr Nichols the printer, came; but noone chose to disturb him by speaking to him, and he seemed to take no notice of any person. While Mrs Gardiner and I were there, before the rest came, he took a little warm milk in a cup, when he said something upon its not being properly given into his hand: he breathed very regular, though short, and appeared to be mostly in a calm sleep or dozing. I left him in this state, and never more saw him alive. In the evening I supped with Mrs Hoole and my son at Mr Braithwaite's, and at night my servant brought me word that my dearest friend died that evening about seven o'clock: and next morning I went to the house, where I met Mr Seward; we went together into the chamber, and there saw the most awful sight of Dr Johnson laid out in his bed, without life!

NOTES

John Hoole (1727–1803), translator of Tasso and Ariosto, was a member of the Essex Head Club. Boswell mentions several occasions on which he was in Johnson's company from the mid-1770s onwards. He kept a diary of his visits to Johnson during his last illness, originally published under the title 'Narrative of what passed in the visits paid by J. Hoole to Dr Johnson in his last illness'.

1. *The Reasonable Communicant* (1704) by William Fleetwood (1656–1723).

2. Presumably John Nichols (1745–1826), printer, author and editor, who was a member of the Essex Head Club.

3. The Revd George Strahan (1744–1824), Vicar of Islington, published Johnson's *Prayers and Meditations* in 1785.

4. Mauritius Lowe (1746–93), artist, was befriended by Johnson, who stood godfather to his son and daughter and left them a legacy of £100 each.

5. For Hawkins's account of this episode, see pp. 163–4.

6. Dr Richard Brocklesby (1722–97), physician, a member of the Essex Head Club.

7. John Ryland (?1717–98), West India merchant and a member of the Essex Head and other clubs.

8. Francesco Sastres, teacher of Italian, mentioned in Johnson's will, where he receives 'the sum of five pounds, to be laid out in books of piety for his own use'.

9. Dr William Heberden (1710–1801), eminent physician (he was the first to describe *angina pectoris*), attended Johnson when he suffered a stroke in June 1783.

10. *Macbeth*, III, iv, 118.

11. 'The Reverend Mr Hoole', son of John Hoole, is mentioned in Johnson's will, father and son each receiving a book of their own choice from Johnson's library.

12. Edmund Waller (1606–87), the subject of one of Johnson's *Lives of the Poets*.

13. Thomas à Kempis (1380–1471), author of *The Imitation of Christ*.

14. John Desmoulins, son of Johnson's long-time protégée, received £200 in Johnson's will.

15. Dr William Scott, later Baron Stowell (1745–1836), lawyer and politician, was, with Hawkins and Reynolds, one of Johnson's executors.

16. Dr Samuel Clarke (1675–1729); Boswell reports Johnson as saying on 7 April 1778, 'I should recommend Dr *Clarke's* sermons, were he orthodox'.

The Final Weeks II*

SIR JOHN HAWKINS

His complaints still increasing, I continued pressing him to make a will, but he still procrastinated that business. On 27 November [1784], in the morning, I went to his house, with a purpose still farther to urge him not to give occasion, by dying intestate, for litigation among his relations; but finding that he was gone to pass the day with the Revd Mr Strahan, at Islington, I followed him thither, and found there our old friend Mr Ryland, and Mr Hoole. Upon my sitting down, he said that the prospect of the change he was about to undergo, and the thought of meeting his Saviour, troubled him, but that he had hope that he would not reject him. I then began to discourse with him about his will, and the provision for Frank [Barber], until he grew angry. He told me that he had signed and sealed the paper I left him. But that, said I, had blanks in it, which, as it seems, you have not filled up with the names of the executors. 'You should have filled them up yourself,' answered he. I replied that such an act would have looked as if I meant to prevent his choice of a fitter person. 'Sir,' said he, 'these minor virtues are not to be exercised in matters of such importance as this.' At length, he said that on his return home, he would send for a clerk, and dictate a will to him. You will then,

* *Life of Samuel Johnson, LL.D.*, pp. 580–94.

said I, be *inops consilii*;[1] rather do it now. With Mr Strahan's permission, I will be his guest at dinner; and, if Mr Hoole will please to hold the pen, I will, in a few words, make such a disposition of your estate as you shall direct. To this he assented; but such a paroxysm of the asthma seized him, as prevented our going on. As the fire burned up, he found himself relieved, and grew cheerful. 'The fit,' said he, 'was very sharp; but I am now easy.' After I had dictated a few lines, I told him that he being a man of eminence for learning and parts, it would afford an illustrious example, and well become him, to make such an explicit declaration of his belief, as might obviate all suspicions that he was any other than a Christian. He thanked me for the hint, and, calling for paper, wrote on a slip, that I had in my hand and gave him, the following words: 'I humbly commit to the infinite and eternal goodness of Almighty God, my soul polluted with many sins; but, as I hope, purified by repentance, and redeemed, as I trust, by the death of Jesus Christ,' and, returning it to me, said, 'This I commit to your custody.'

Upon my calling on him for directions to proceed, he told me, that his father, in the course of his trade as a bookseller, had become bankrupt, and that Mr William Innys had assisted him with money or credit to continue his business. 'This,' said he, 'I consider as an obligation on me to be grateful to his descendants, and I therefore mean to give £200 to his representative.' He then meditated a devise of his house at Lichfield to the corporation of that city for a charitable use; but, it being freehold, he said, 'I cannot live a twelve-month, and the last statute of mortmain stands in the way: I must, therefore, think of some other disposition of it.' His next consideration was a provision for Frank, concerning the amount whereof I found he had been consulting Dr Brocklesby, to whom he had put this question: 'What would be a proper annuity to bequeath to a favourite servant?' The doctor answered that the circumstances of the master were the truest measure, and that, in the case of a nobleman £50 a year was deemed an adequate reward for many years' faithful service. 'Then shall I,' said Johnson, 'be *nobilissimus*; for I mean to leave Frank £70 a year, and I desire you to tell him so.' And now, at the making of the will, a devise, equivalent to such a provision, was therein inserted. The residue of his estate and effects, which took in, though he intended it not, the house at Lichfield, he bequeathed to his executors, in trust for a religious association, which it is needless to describe.

Having executed the will with the necessary formalities, he would have come home, but being pressed by Mr and Mrs Strahan to stay, he consented, and we all dined together. Towards the evening, he grew cheerful, and I having promised to take him in my coach, Mr Strahan and Mr Ryland would accompany him to Bolt Court. On the way thither he appeared much at ease, and told stories. At eight I sat him down, and Mr Strahan and Mr Ryland betook themselves to their respective homes.

Sunday 28th. I saw him about noon; he was dozing; but waking, he found himself in a circle of his friends. Upon opening his eyes, he said that the prospect of his dissolution was very terrible to him, and addressed himself to us all, in nearly these wrods: 'You see the state in which I am; conflicting with bodily pain and mental distraction: while you are in health and strength, labour to do good, and avoid evil, if ever you hope to escape the distress that now oppresses me.' A little while after, 'I had, very early in my life, the seeds of goodness in me: I had a love of virtue, and a reverence for religion; and these, I trust, have brought forth in me fruits meet for repentance; and, if I have repented as I ought, I am forgiven. I have, at times, entertained a loathing of sin and of myself, particularly at the beginning of this year, when I had the prospect of death before me; and this has not abated when my fears of death have been less; and, at these times, I have had such rays of hope shot into my soul, as have almost persuaded me that I am in a state of reconciliation with God.'

29th. Mr Langton, who had spent the evening with him, reported that his hopes were increased, and that he was much cheered upon being reminded of the general tendency of his writings, and of his example.

30th. I saw him in the evening, and found him cheerful. Was informed, that he had, for his dinner, eaten heartily of a French duck pie and a pheasant.

1 Dec. He was busied in destroying papers. Gave to Mr Langton and another person, to fair copy, some translations of the Greek epigrams, which he had made in the preceding nights, and transcribed the next morning, and they began to work on them.

3rd. Finding his legs continue to swell, he signified to his physicians a strong desire to have them scarified, but they, unwilling to put him to pain, and fearing a mortification, declined advising it. He afterwards consulted his surgeon, and he performed the operation on one leg.

4th. I visited him: the scarification, made yesterday in his leg, appeared to have had little effect. He said to me that he was easier in his mind, and as fit to die at that instant, as he could be a year hence. He requested me to receive the sacrament with him on Sunday, the next day. Complained of great weakness, and of phantoms that haunted his imagination.

5th. Being Sunday, I communicated with him and Mr Langton, and other of his friends, as many as nearly filled the room. Mr Strahan, who was constant in his attendance on him throughout his illness, performed the office. Previous to reading the exhortation, Johnson knelt, and with a degree of fervour that I had never been witness to before, uttered the following most eloquent and energetic prayer: . . .

Upon rising from his knees, after the office was concluded, he said that he dreaded to meet God in a state of idiocy, or with opium in his head; and that having now communicated with the effects of a dose upon him, he doubted if his exertions were the genuine operations of his mind, and repeated from Bishop Taylor this sentiment, 'That little, that has been omitted in health, can be done to any purpose in sickness.'

He very much admired, and often in the course of his illness recited, from the conclusion of old Isaac Walton's life of Bishop Sanderson, the following pathetic request:

> Thus this pattern of meekness and primitive innocence changed this for a better life: 'tis now too late to wish, that mine may be like his; for I am in the eighty-fifth year of my age, and God knows it hath not; but, I most humbly beseech Almighty God, that my death may; and I do as earnestly beg, that, if any reader shall receive any satisfaction from this very plain, and, as true relation, he will be so charitable as to say, Amen.

While he was dressing and preparing for this solemnity, an accident happened which went very near to disarrange his mind. He had mislaid, and was very anxious to find, a paper that contained private instructions to his executors; and myself, Mr Strahan, Mr Langton, Mr Hoole, Frank, and I believe some others that were about him, went into his bed-chamber to seek it. In our search, I laid my hands on a parchment-covered book, into which I imagined it might have been slipped. Upon opening the book, I found it to be meditations and reflections, in Johnson's own handwriting; and having been told a day or two before by Frank that a person formerly intimately connected with his master, a joint proprietor of a newspaper, well known among the booksellers, and of whom Mrs Williams once told me she had often cautioned him to beware; I say, having been told that this person had lately been very importunate to get access to him, indeed to such a degree as that, when he was told that the Doctor was not to be seen, he would push his way upstairs; and having stronger reasons than I need here mention, to suspect that this man might find and make an ill use of the book, I put it, and a less of the same kind, into my pocket; at the same time telling those around me, and particularly Mr Langton and Mr Strahan, that I had got both, with my reasons for thus securing them. After the ceremony was over, Johnson took me aside, and told me that I had a book of his in my pocket; I answered that I had two, and that to prevent their falling into the hands of a person who had attempted to force his way into the house, I had done as I conceived a friendly act, but not without telling his friends of it, and also my reasons. He then asked me what ground I had for my suspicion of the man I mentioned: I told him his great importunity to get admittance; and farther, that immediately after a visit which he made me, in the year 1775, I missed a paper of a public nature, and of great importance; and that a day or two after, and before it could be put to its intended use, I saw it in the newspapers.

At the mention of this circumstance Johnson paused; but recovering himself, said, 'You should not have laid hands on the book; for had I missed it, and not known you had it, I should have roared for my book, as Othello did for his handkerchief, and probably have run mad.'

I gave him time, until the next day, to compose himself, and then wrote him a letter, apologising, and assigning at large the reasons for my conduct; and received a verbal answer by Mr Langton, which, were I to repeat it, would render me suspected of inexcusable vanity; it concluded with these words, 'If I was not satisfied with this, I must be a savage.'[2]

7th. I again visited him. Before my departure, Dr Brocklesby came in, and, taking him by the wrist, Johnson gave him a look of great contempt, and ridiculed the judging of his disorder by the pulse. He complained, that the sarcocele[3] had again made its appearance, and asked if a puncture would not relieve him, as it had done the year before: the doctor answered, that it might, but that his surgeon was the best judge of the effect of such an operation. Johnson, upon this, said, 'How many men in a year die through the timidity of those whom they consult for health! I want length of life, and you fear giving me pain, which I care not for.'

8th. I visited him with Mr Langton, and found him dictating to Mr Strahan another will, the former being, as he had said at the time of making it, a temporary one. On our entering the room, he said, 'God bless you both.' I arrived just time enough to direct the execution, and also the attestation of it. After he had published it, he desired Mr Strahan to say the Lord's Prayer, which he did, all of us joining. Johnson, after it, uttered, extempore, a few pious ejaculations.

9th. I saw him in the evening, and found him dictating, to Mr Strahan, a codicil to the will he had made the evening before. I assisted them in it, and received from the testator a direction, to insert a devise to his executors of the house at Lichfield, to be sold for the benefit of certain of his relations, a bequest of sundry pecuniary and specific legacies, a provision for the annuity of £70 for Francis, and, after all, a devise of all the rest, residue, and remainder of his estate and effects, to his executors, in trust for the said Francis Barber, his executors and administrators; and, having dictated accordingly, Johnson executed and published it as a codicil to his will.

He was now so weak as to be unable to kneel, and lamented that he must pray sitting, but, with an effort, he placed himself on his knees, while Mr Strahan repeated the Lord's Prayer. During the whole of the evening, he was much composed and resigned. Being become very weak and helpless, it was thought necessary that a man should watch with him all night; and one was found in the neighbourhood, who, for half-a-crown a night, undertook to sit up with, and assist him. When the man had left the room, he, in the presence and hearing of Mr Strahan and Mr Langton, asked me where I meant to bury him. I answered, doubtless, in Westminster Abbey: 'If,' said he, 'my executors think it proper to mark the spot of my interment by a stone, let it be so placed as to protect my body from injury.' I assured him it should be done. Before my departure, he desired Mr Langton to put into my hands, money to the amount of upwards of £100 with a direction to keep it until called for.

10th. This day at noon I saw him again. He said to me that the male nurse to whose care I had committed him, was unfit for the office. 'He is,' said he, 'an idiot, as awkward as a turnspit just put into the wheel, and as sleepy as a dormouse.' Mr Cruikshank came into the room, and, looking at his scarified leg, saw no sign of a mortification.

11th. At noon, I found him dozing, and would not disturb him.

12th. Saw him again; found him very weak, and, as he said, unable to pray.

13th. At noon, I called at the house, but went not into his room, being told that he was dozing. I was further informed, by the servants, that his appetite was totally gone, and that he could take no sustenance. At eight in the evening of the same day, word was brought me by Mr Sastres, to whom, in his last moments, he uttered these words '*Jam moriturus*',[4] that, at a quarter past seven, he had, without a groan, or the least sign of pain or uneasiness, yielded his last breath.

At eleven the same evening, Mr Langton came to me, and, in an agony of mind, gave me to understand, that our friend had wounded himself in several parts of the body. I was shocked at the news; but, upon being told that he had not touched any vital part, was easily able to account for an action, which would else have given us the deepest concern. The fact was, that conceiving himself to be full of water, he had done that which he had often solicited his medical assistants to do, made two or three incisions in his lower limbs, vainly hoping for some relief from the flux that might follow.

Early the next morning, Frank came to me; and, being desirous of knowing all the particulars of this transaction, I interrogated him very strictly concerning it, and received from him answers to the following effect.

That, at eight in the morning of the preceding day, upon going into the bedchamber, his master, being in bed, ordered him to open a cabinet, and give him a drawer in it; that he did so, and that out of it his master took a case of lancets, and choosing one of them, would have conveyed it into the bed, which Frank, a young man that sat up with him, seeing, they seized his hand, and intreated him not to do a rash action: he said he would not; but drawing his hand under the bed-clothes, they saw his arm move. Upon this they turned down the clothes, and saw a great effusion of blood, which soon stopped. That soon after, he got a pair of scissors that lay in a drawer by him, and plunged them deep in the calf of each leg. That immediately they sent for Mr Cruikshanks, and the apothecary, and they, or one of them, dressed the wounds. That he then fell into that dozing which carried him off. That it was conjectured he lost eight or ten ounces of blood; and that this effusion brought on the dozing, though his pulse continued firm until three o'clock.

That this act was not done to hasten his end, but to discharge the water that he conceived to be in him, I have not the least doubt. A dropsy was his disease; he looked upon himself as a bloated carcase; and, to attain the power of easy respiration, would have undergone any degree of temporary pain. He dreaded neither punctures nor incisions, and, indeed, defied the trochar[5] and the lancet; he had often reproached his physicians and surgeon with cowardice; and, when Mr Cruikshanks scarified his leg, he cried out 'Deeper, deeper; I will abide the consequence: you are afraid of your reputation, but that is nothing to me.' To those about him, he said, 'You all pretend to love me, but you do not love me so well as I myself do.'

I have been thus minute in recording the particulars of his last moments, because I wished to attract attention to the conduct of this great man, under the most trying circumstances human nature is subject to. Many persons have appeared possessed of more serenity of mind in this awful scene: some have remained unmoved at the dissolution of the vital union; and, it may be deemed a discouragement from the severe practice of religion, that Dr Johnson, whose whole life was a preparation for his death, and a conflict with natural infirmity, was disturbed with terror at the prospect of the grave. Let not this relax the circumspection of any one. It is true that natural firmness of spirit, or the confidence of hope, may buoy up the mind to the last; but, however heroic an undaunted death may appear, it is not what we should pray for. As Johnson lived the life of the righteous, his end was that of a Christian: he strictly fulfilled the injunction of the apostle, to work out his salvation with fear and trembling;[6] and, though his doubts and scruples were certainly very distressing to himself, they give his friends a pious hope, that he, who added to almost all the virtues of Christianity that religious humility which its great Teacher inculcated, will, in the fullness of time, receive the reward promised to a patient continuance in well-doing.

A few days after his departure, Dr Brocklesby and Mr Cruikshanks, who, with great assiduity and humanity (and I must add, generosity, for neither they, nor Dr Heberden, Dr Warren, or Dr Butter, would accept any fees) had attended him, signified a wish, that his body might be opened. This was done, and the report made was to this effect.

Two of the valves of the aorta ossified.

The air-cells of the lungs unusually distended.

One of the kidneys destroyed by the pressure of the water.

The liver schirrous.

A stone in the gall-bladder, of the size of a common gooseberry.

On Monday 20 December, his funeral was celebrated and honoured by a numerous attendance of his friends, and among them, by particular invitation, of as many of the literary club as were then in town, and not prevented by engagements. The dean of Westminster, upon my application, would gladly have performed the ceremony of his interment, but, at the time, was much indisposed in his health; the office, therefore, devolved upon the senior prebendary, Dr Taylor, who performed it with becoming gravity and seriousness. All the prebendaries, except such as were absent in the country, attended in their surplices and hoods: they met the corpse at the west door of their church, and performed, in the most respectful manner, all the honours due to the memory of so great a man.[7]

His body, enclosed in a leaden coffin, is deposited in the south transept of the abbey, near the foot of Shakespeare's monument, and close to the coffin of his friend Garrick. Agreeable to his request, a stone of black marble covers his grave, thus inscribed:

Samuel Johnson, LL.D.
Obiit xiii die Decembris,
Anno Domini
M DCC LXXXIV,
Ætatis suæ LXXV.

The truth of the matter is that his whole life was a conflict with his passions and humours, and that few persons bore reprehension with more patience than himself. After his decease, I found among his papers an anonymous letter, that seemed to have been written by a person who had long had his eye on him, and remarked the offensive particulars in his behaviour, his propensity to contradiction, his want of deference to the opinions of others, his contention for victory over those with whom he disputed, his local prejudices and aversions, and other his evil habits in conversation, which made his acquaintance shunned by many, who, as a man of genius and worth, highly esteemed him. It was written with great temper, in a spirit of charity, and with a due acknowledgment of those great talents with which he was endowed, but contained in it several home truths. In short, it was such a letter as many a one, on the receipt of it, would have destroyed. On the contrary, Johnson preserved it, and placed it in his bureau, in a situation so obvious, that, whenever he opened that repository of his papers, it might look him in the face; and I have not the least doubt, that he frequently perused and reflected on its contents, and endeavoured to correct his behaviour by an address which he could not but consider as a friendly admonition.

NOTES

Sir John Hawkins (1719–89), man of letters, musicologist, lawyer and magistrate, was a friend of Johnson from the 1740s and a member of the King's Head and other clubs (though Johnson once described him as 'a most unclubable man'). He drew up Johnson's will and became one of his executors, thus gaining access to his papers. His biography – somewhat unfairly dismissed by Leslie Stephen in the *DNB* as 'pompous and feeble' – held pride of place in a crowded field until supplanted by Boswell's. Elizabeth Carter, who knew Johnson, observed more generously that '[Hawkins's] character of Dr Johnson is impartially, and very decently and candidly, represented'. Predictably, Boswell has little that is favourable to say about either Hawkins or his 'bulky tome', 'compiled for the booksellers of London': he even refers to Hawkins as 'a man, whom, during my long intimacy with Dr Johnson, I never saw in his company, I think but once, and I am sure not above twice'. The fact is that Hawkins was one of the earliest friends of Johnson's London years, and had known him much longer than Boswell; and, though he could not be described as an intimate friend, he was loyal to the end. As well as writing his life, Hawkins produced an edition (1787–9) of Johnson's collected works.

    1. Incapable of acting.

    2. Boswell's somewhat caustic comment on this passage includes some details not given by Hawkins:

> One of these volumes, Sir John Hawkins informs us, he put into his pocket; for which the excuse he states is, that he meant to preserve it from falling into the hands of a person whom he describes so as to make it sufficiently clear who is meant; 'having strong reasons (said he) to suspect that this man might find and make an ill use of the book'. Why Sir John should suppose that the gentleman alluded to would act in this manner, he has not thought fit to explain. But what he did was not approved of by Johnson; who, upon being acquainted of it without delay by a friend, expressed great indignation, and warmly insisted on the book being delivered up; and, afterwards, in the supposition of his missing it, without knowing by whom it had been taken, he said, 'Sir, I should have gone out of the world distrusting half mankind.'

It is as well to remember that, unlike Hawkins, Boswell was not present at the time. The 'gentleman alluded to' was identified by Miss Hawkins as George Steevens.

    3. 'Hard fleshy enlargement of the testicle' (*OED*). Johnson had used the word in a letter to Mrs Thrale on 22 September 1783.

    4. 'Now I am about to die' (Latin).

    5. Defined in Johnson's *Dictionary* as 'a chirurgical instrument'.

    6. Philippians, ii, 12.

    7. For a different view of the matter, to which Hawkins's claim reads like a retort, see Dr Burney's letter on p. 172.

172 LAST DAYS

Last Requests to Reynolds*

WILLIAM SHAW

A few days before his decease he sent for Sir Joshua Reynolds, and told
him that he had three favours to ask of him. Sir Joshua, confiding in the
Doctor's good sense and discretion, frankly promised an implicit
compliance with his request. The first was, that though he owed Sir
Joshua thirty pounds, he was not to expect to be repaid. This was readily
granted. The second demand was that Sir Joshua should not paint on
Sundays. To this a small degree of hesitation appeared, but, however, no
positive objection was made. He desired as his third and last request that
he would regularly every day read more or less of the scriptures; Sir
Joshua boggled most at this, but the Doctor assuming much earnestness,
told him how much he had it at heart, and hoped Sir Joshua's pledging
himself to a dying friend might insure the literal and punctual performance of a duty, which would for certain be attended with the best
effects, promised to comply.

* *Memoirs of the Life and Writings of the Late Dr Samuel Johnson*, pp. 181–2.

'Genius, learning and piety'*

CHARLES BURNEY

[Letter to the Revd Thomas Twining, dated 25 December 1784] . . .
Poor Johnson is gone! I truly reverenced his genius, learning and piety,
without being blind to his prejudices. I think I know and could name
them all. We often differed in matters of taste, and in our judgments of
individuals. My respect for what I thought excellent in him never
operated on my reason sufficiently to incline me to subscribe to his
decisions when I thought them erroneous. The knight, Sir John
[Hawkins], and I met two or three times during his sickness and at his

* Robina Napier, *Johnsoniana*, pp. 303–5.

funeral. He steps forth as one of poor Johnson's six or eight biographers, with as little taste or powers of writing worthy of such an occupation as for musical history. The Dean and Chapter of Westminster Abbey lay all the blame on him for suffering Johnson to be so unworthily interred. The knight's first inquiring at the Abbey, in giving orders, as the most acting executor, was 'What would be the difference in the expense between a public and a private funeral?' and was told only a few pounds to the prebendaries, and about ninety pairs of gloves to the choir and attendants; and he then determined that, 'as Dr Johnson had no music in him he should choose the cheapest manner of interment'. And for this reason there was no organ heard, or burial service sung, for which he suffers the Dean and Chapter to be abused in all the newspapers, and joins in their abuse when the subject is mentioned in conversation. Dr Bell has stated the case, in a letter to my friend Dr Warren, just as I tell it to you. Again, I was told by a lady 'that she found Dr Johnson had not always been so pious and good a Christian as in the latter part of his life'. 'How do you know, madam?' 'Why, Sir John Cullum was told so by Sir John Hawkins, who says that when Dr Johnson came up to London first, he lived a very profligate life with Savage and others, and was an infidel, and that he [Hawkins] first converted him to Christianity!' This astonished me so much that I could not help mentioning the story and my authority to Johnson's oldest and most intimate friends, with whom I dined after attending the funeral to Westminster Abbey, and asked them if they ever heard of Johnson having been a profligate and an infidel in his younger days, and they one and all cried out with astonishment and indignation, 'No!' Dr Scott, one of the three executors, said that he had found among his papers a great number of prayers penned with great force, elegance and devotion, some of them as high up as the year 1738, which would be a sufficient answer to such a charge; and I hear today that Dr Scott, without mentioning names, has said to the knight that such a report had got about. 'Oh!' says Sir John, 'I can best confute such a rumour, who have so long known him, and ever found him a man of the most exemplary life, and a most steady believer of the doctrines of the Christian religion.' This strange story, for the honour of Johnson and true piety, as well as the clearing up the point which now lies between the reverend and the irreverend knight, I hope and trust will be sifted to the bottom.

Index

The symbol *n* indicates an entry in the notes.